DISAGREEMENT AND DISSENT in Judicial Decision-making

DISAGREEMENT AND DISSENT in Judicial Decision-making

Frederic Reynold

WS &H

Wildy, Simmonds & Hill Publishing

ISBN: 9780854901272

British Library Cataloguing in Publication Data

A catalogue record for this book is available from the British Library

First published in 2013 by

Wildy, Simmonds & Hill Publishing
58 Carey Street
London WC2A 2JF
England
www.wildy.com

Typeset by Cornubia Press Ltd, Bristol.
Printed and bound by CPI Group (UK) Ltd, Croydon, CR0 4YY

MIX
Paper from responsible sources
FSC® C013604

For Sandra, who, having noted that my (one) previous book
was published more than forty years ago, told me in no
uncertain terms that the time was now ripe to publish another

Contents

ACKNOWLEDGEMENTS

I am immensely grateful to Professor Cheryl Thomas, co-director of UCL's Judicial Institute, for her help and encouragement, and for enabling me to make use of the Institute's database. Likewise, I owe a huge debt of gratitude to Sarah Docherty, whose research into disagreement in both the UK and US Supreme Courts has been invaluable.

I would like to acknowledge the practical help provided by my friends Nigel Pleming QC and Edwin Glasgow QC, in pointing me in a direction that led to converting what was simply an idea into a reality. A number of other friends and colleagues, many of them occupying senior judicial positions, have from time to time made helpful and occasionally mischievous suggestions: I would not wish to cause embarrassment by naming them.

It would be churlish not to mention Andrew Riddoch, who, in his capacity of commissioning editor, displayed a patience, understanding and flexibility which were frankly quite exemplary.

Finally, I would like to thank Old Square Chambers for providing me with such a congenial and supportive working environment, and specifically with colleagues who uncomplainingly rescued me from one computer-related crisis after another.

Frederic Reynold QC

PREFACE

This book has been written in the hope that it may appeal to both lawyers and non-lawyers alike who have an interest in the dynamics of judicial decision-making in our highest court. Essentially, it is an attempt to explain why the Law Lords, and (since 2009) the Justices of the Supreme Court, have quite frequently disagreed with each other, and what they have tended to disagree about. The book does not discuss the *merits* of the competing arguments and points of view: it is about why and how disagreements occur, and what this may mean in the general scheme of things. Inevitably, it has been written from the perspective of someone who has spent the entirety of his professional life as an advocate, and not as an academic.

Finding the right authorial tone has proved a tricky business. On the one hand it seemed appropriate to avoid the customary impersonal style associated with the writing of legal text books or works of legal scholarship; and on the other, it seemed equally appropriate to avoid what may be described as a somewhat journalistic approach with the occasional lapse into the first person. As in this case much of the comment and analysis reflect what is essentially the writer's personal point of view, the latter, in particular, has not proved easy to achieve.

Finally, three editorial decisions should be mentioned. First, to avoid causing unnecessary confusion to non-lawyers, names of cases and citations do not appear in the body of the main text but have been consigned to the footnotes. Second, whilst the aim has been to reproduce in a way which is readily intelligible the essence of the particular judgment under discussion, this has had to be balanced against the need to capture the flavour both of the judgment and the debate: it is hoped that this has been achieved by a liberal use of direct quotation. And third, those Law Lords who have customarily been referred to in the law reports by their full title (i.e. Lord X of Y) are referred to here by their surnames only, although regrettably this means that the reader will be denied the pleasure of savouring the whimsical charm of some of the titles which adorn the law reports (such as Lord Brown of Eaton-under-Heywood and Lord Clarke of Stone-cum-Ebony) without consulting the Appendix.

Frederic Reynold QC
London, July 2013

INTRODUCTION

It is nearly four years since the Supreme Court of the United Kingdom replaced the obscurely located Appellate Committee of the House of Lords, and since the Lords of Appeal in Ordinary – the "Law Lords" – were transformed into Justices of the Supreme Court. There has been much discussion about what difference, if any, this change has brought about: in particular, whether disagreement occurs more frequently than was formerly the case. In fact the statistics show that up to May 2013, 26 per cent of Supreme Court decisions have been majority decisions, which happens to be a figure broadly in line with the decisions of the House of Lords Appellate Committee over the last 50 years of its existence. There is, however, an unmistakably sharper edge to the disagreement – horns are locked and arguments are met head on – previously it had frequently been the case that no reference was made at all to the judgments of one's colleagues, let alone to their arguments.

The right to express dissent in the deciding of appeals at the highest level is taken for granted in common law countries, but even so it has attracted much high-blown academic theorising: the need for the judiciary to function democratically and transparently, and to reflect differing societal and democratic values, are the arguments most commonly advanced. (It has not been without its critics, however. Sir Rupert Cross, the late Vinerian Professor of English Law at Oxford, was one. He took the view that it created uncertainty and tended to undermine the authority of the decision in question.[1]) Most appeal judges would probably agree with the view of the retired Law Lord, Lord Nicholls of Birkenhead:

> Dissenting judgments do more than attract passing interest. They are an important aspect of judicial freedom. They have no legal effect on the cases in which they are given, but they can have a practical effect. At best a dissenting

---

1 R. Cross, 'The Ratio Decidendi and a Plurality of Speeches in the House of Lords' (1977) 93 Law Quarterly Review 378.

> judgment may be so obviously right that the courts or Parliament soon steer the law along a better path.[2]

As far as the general public is concerned, they are surely a reassuring indication of an independent mind at work.

Whatever the pros and cons, it is historically the case that disagreement and dissent has always been a feature of the British appellate system: legal historians point to the first decade of the twentieth century as being arguably the only possible exception, when there was evidence of a deliberate policy in the House of Lords to encourage the delivery of single judgments.[3] There was something of a precedent for this. In the early days of the US Supreme Court there was an unsuccessful attempt (by Chief Justice Marshall) to impose unanimity in its decisions. Thomas Jefferson, the US President at the time, would have none of it. "[T]he practice [would be] certainly convenient for the lazy, the modest and incompetent", he famously wrote to a private correspondent. Apart from the very occasional case where feelings had clearly run high, or where there was an evident clash of personalities,[4] disagreement appears not to have had any adverse impact on the collegiality of either the Appellate Committee or its successor, the Supreme Court. Other common law countries have not fared so well. It is part of the fabric of US history that its Supreme Court has endured many periods when divided opinion and absence of collegiality have gone hand in hand. And so great was the mutual hostility displayed by members of the High Court of Australia during the presidency of Chief Justice Statham in the 1940s, that the practice of "case conferencing" was suspended: Mr Justice Starke and Mr Justice Evatt, in particular, were barely on speaking terms, and even declined to exchange draft judgments.[5]

That a quarter of the appeals to our highest court have provoked disagreement amongst its members – often reflected in the slenderest of majorities – is surely a statistic of some significance. The occasional case of technical complexity and difficult analysis and interpretation, for example,

---

2 Foreword to N. Geach and C. Monaghan, (2012) *Dissenting Judgments in the Law*, Wildy, Simmonds and Hill.

3 L. Blom-Cooper *et al.* (eds), (2009) *The Judicial House of Lords 1876–2009*, Oxford University Press.

4 Lord Simonds and Lord Denning in the late 1950s provide a well-known example of such a clash.

5 A. Lynch, 'Judicial Disagreement in the High Court of Australia' (2003) 27 Melbourne University Law Review 724.

will obviously be likely to attract differing views;[6] but what explains the overall frequency of disagreement, given the absence of the kind of ideological/political divide which has traditionally characterised the US Supreme Court? The purpose of this book is to explore and explain what are the root causes of disagreement in some of the more notable cases decided over the last 25 years or so, and to consider the light which they throw on the nature of judicial decision-making at House of Lords/Supreme Court level. For example, is there really a distinction (as conventional wisdom has it) between legal policy (recognised as the legitimate concern of the judges) and public policy, which, with certain recognised exceptions, is not? Does a distinction emerge between conservative and so-called "black letter" lawyers on the one hand, and those who are liberal and "merit-orientated" on the other – even when there is no agreement as to where the merits actually lie?[7] And what light, if any, does all this throw on the present composition of our Supreme Court and the much talked of need to achieve a "balance"? The cases discussed have themes in common, and are grouped accordingly. Those themes are: the differing notions of what is fair and just; the impossibility of interpreting the language of Parliament "objectively"; the clash of principles and competing moral judgments; and differing responses to constitutional and human rights issues. This book is written in the firm belief that non-lawyers are in as good a position as lawyers to make their own assessment of the strength of the arguments which feature in these cases; and where the use of technical expressions is unavoidable, an explanatory footnote will be provided.

---

6 However, even in such cases subjective value judgments play a role, as in this example: a Ms T and Ms M purchased a house from funds generated by a business which they ran jointly. The house was purchased in the name of Ms M alone to enable Ms T to perpetrate a benefit fraud, which was later admitted and the money repaid. In due course the two fell out. Ms M sought a court order for the sole possession of the property and Ms T counterclaimed for a declaration that she was entitled to an equal share. The Law Lords divided 3:2 on the issue of whether there was any applicable exception to the principle that the courts will not assist a claimant who has been guilty of fraudulent or illegal conduct connected with the transaction. The minority concluded there was not, and were unwilling to create one in this case because in their view the principle served as a deterrent and it would be "difficult to distinguish between degrees of iniquity". Of the majority, one Law Lord was highly sceptical whether the principle actually had any deterrent value, and the remaining Law Lords did not even think the point worthy of discussion: *Tinsley v Milligan* [1993] UKHL 3, [1994] 1 AC 340.

7 There are different labels which mean much the same thing: the former Law Lord, Lord Steyn, in a Presidential lecture to the Bentham Club, drew a distinction between formalists and liberals. David Robertson, in his well-known work *Judicial Discretion in the House of Lords* (Clarendon Press, 1998), drew a distinction between restrictivist and expansionist lawyers.

PART ONE

WHAT EXACTLY IS FAIR AND JUST?

(1) "THE IMPULSE TO DO PRACTICAL JUSTICE"

The development of the law of negligence in recent years has been dominated by attempts, some more successful than others, to confine liability to what practising lawyers and judges regard as acceptable limits; and that has particularly been the case where what was in issue was financial or "economic" loss. There was a recurring pattern: judges (usually the Law Lords) would produce what they thought was an effective formula to solve a particular problem, but one which by its very nature happened to store up further trouble for the future. Following a number of decisions in the House of Lords, the position had eventually been reached that a person would be liable for causing financial loss to another through his negligence if the loss was foreseeable; the relationship between the parties was one of "proximity"; and it was fair, just and reasonable to impose a duty of care upon that person for the benefit of the other. This was certainly a pragmatic and flexible position, but whatever the concept of what is "fair, just and reasonable" gained in flexibility, it certainly lacked in precision. (What had become clear, however, was that for the imposition of a duty of care to be judged as fair, just and reasonable, it was necessary that the claimant had relied upon the defendant and that the defendant had "assumed responsibility".) Then along came a case[1] which resurrected a problem which had arisen in a case decided in the High Court some 14 years previously, and which now revealed a surprising lack of consensus as to what the limits of accountability of a professional person should be. It posed the question: can a solicitor be liable to a person other than his client in failing to exercise reasonable care in performing the services which he contracted to perform?

---

1 *White v Jones* [1995] UKHL 5, [1995] 2 AC 207.

The facts could be said to be typical of everyday life, but the legal problem which they posed has been referred to as "a legal philosopher's dream." After a family row following the death of his wife, a father cut his two married daughters out of his will. Some six months later they became reconciled, and he therefore instructed his solicitors to change his will so as to provide legacies for both daughters. Both daughters were aware of this development. The matter was entrusted to a legal executive in a firm who, despite reminders, delayed taking any steps to prepare a new will or revise the old one, with the result that that the father died before his instructions were implemented and the will executed. Both daughters sued the firm of solicitors for negligence. The judge at first instance rejected the claim on the basis that the solicitors did not owe the claimants any duty of care: the firm had entered into a contract with the father to provide professional services for the father alone, and for his benefit. The only duty they owed was to him as their professional client. The Court of Appeal reversed the decision, their reasoning being that the loss suffered by the claimants from the failure to prepare the new will was foreseeable; that although the duty owed by a solicitor to his client was paramount, the acceptance of instructions by the firm to make the changes to the will, or prepare a new one, created a special relationship with the intended beneficiaries; and that in those circumstances it would be fair, just and reasonable to impose on a solicitor a duty of care to the claimants as otherwise there would be no sanction on the solicitor for his failure to exercise professional care and skill in carrying out his instructions. As mentioned, they approved a decision of the High Court some 14 years previously in a case in which the claimant had likewise lost the expectation of a legacy as a result of a solicitor's negligence, the judge holding that it would be unfair and unjust to deny her a remedy against the solicitor when his carelessness had deprived her of a share of the estate, and when she had no other remedy.

The stark fact which had impressed itself both on the High Court judge some 14 years previously, and on the Court of Appeal, was that if the position was that the solicitor did not owe a duty of care to persons other then the client, the party entitled to a remedy (i.e. the estate of the testator) would not in fact have suffered any loss, and the parties who suffered the loss (i.e. the claimants) would have no remedy. There were, however, strong arguments pointing in the other direction. Can it be a fair and just solution for a solicitor to owe a professional duty of care to persons other than to the client who is paying for his services and who gives him his instructions, simply because they have an expectation of benefitting from those services when they have been performed? Can it, for example, be fair and just for the solicitor to be exposed to such open-ended liability in the case of a proposed gift when the intended beneficiary may not have even been aware of the testator's intentions at the time? Furthermore, would not such liability, arising as it did where there was no mutual relationship of any kind between the parties, undermine, or circumvent the need for, the contract between the solicitor and the client? Unsurprisingly, the Law Society became concerned as to the possible implications of the decision on behalf of its members, and in due course the case arrived in the House of Lords. Over 11 months elapsed between the hearing and the handing down of the judgments, and in the event the panel divided three to two in favour of the beneficiaries and upholding the decision of the Court of Appeal.

Of the majority, the leading judgment was delivered by Lord Goff, who in his years as a practising barrister had been a distinguished commercial lawyer. He acknowledged frankly both the extent to which his conclusion was influenced by his view of the merits of the particular case, and the formidable nature of the difficulties (in the form of existing precedents) which confronted him in reaching that conclusion. Yes, the general rule was that a solicitor acting on behalf of a client owes a duty of care only to the client, and the scope of those duties will be determined by the terms of the contract of retainer between them. Yes, where the claim for negligence was in respect of financial loss, liability depends upon there having been an assumption of responsibility and the fact that the party suffering the loss had relied on the other party. Yes, unlike in cases of breach of contract, damages are not recoverable in tort[2] for mere loss of an expectation. And, yes, it would not seem logical to limit the right to recover damages only to those intended beneficiaries who were disappointed: i.e. those who had been aware of the testator's intentions; and therefore there could be a difficulty in drawing a meaningful distinction between those beneficiaries entitled to be compensated, and those who were not.

But at the heart of the matter for Lord Goff was:

> the extraordinary fact that, if such a duty [of care] is not recognised, the only persons who might have a valid claim (i.e. the testator and his estate) have suffered no loss, and the only person who has suffered a loss (i.e. the disappointed beneficiary) has no claim ... It can therefore be said that if the solicitor owes no duty to the intended beneficiaries, there is a lacuna in the law which needs to be filled. *This I regard as being a point of cardinal importance in the present case.* (emphasis added)

---

2 Essentially, this is a civil wrong other than a breach of contract, such as negligence, nuisance or libel.

Lord Goff went on to point out that the "injustice of denying such a remedy is reinforced if one considers the importance of legacies in a society [such as ours]" and the fact that the negligent solicitor escapes any form of sanction. For Lord Goff the crucial question was whether "it is possible to give effect in law to the strong impulse for practical justice."

Having looked at a number of possible solutions, many of which had been advanced by counsel in the course of lengthy and scholarly argument – including the concept of "transferred loss" borrowed from German law – and found them all wanting, Lord Goff alighted on a solution nearer home: in other words, within the framework of the existing law of negligence. His solution was that the solicitor's assumption of responsibility towards his client should be deemed in law to extend to the intended beneficiary who, as could be foreseen by the solicitor, would be deprived of her legacy by the solicitor's non-compliance with his instructions in circumstances in which neither the testator nor his estate would have a remedy. This solution commended itself to his colleague, Lord Browne-Wilkinson: in his view the relationship between the solicitor and the intended beneficiary was a special relationship – even though it lacked "mutuality" – by virtue of the solicitor accepting instructions to prepare or revise the will; and that his assumption of responsibility to the client should be extended accordingly. He viewed the merits of the claimants' case in the same way as Lord Goff. Likewise, Lord Nolan concluded that the conceptual difficulties in establishing liability "should not stand in the way of the simple justice of the ... claim." In Lord Nolan's view the acceptance by the solicitor of the instructions to prepare the will necessarily involved the extension of his assumption of responsibility to those affected by his client's instructions.

The perspective of the minority, however, could not have been more different. Neither Lord Keith nor Lord Mustill, whose lengthy and closely reasoned judgment was widely regarded in professional circles as something of a *tour de force,* experienced the impulse, strong or otherwise, to achieve "practical justice" in the terms advocated by the majority. Indeed, as far as Lord Keith was concerned, there was simply no moral dimension to the discussion whatsoever, let alone any reason for sympathy for the claimants. His introductory paragraph set the tone:

> I am unable to reconcile the allowance of the [claimants'] claim with principle, or to accept that to do so would represent an appropriate advance on an incremental basis from decided cases. The position is that the defendant, Mr Jones, contracted with the testator ... to perform a particular service for him, namely to take appropriate steps [to give effect to the change in his

> instructions]. He ... failed to take these steps with due expedition with the result that upon [the testator's] death the claimants did not become entitled to the [benefit of the changed instructions] which but for that failure they would have taken.

He went on to point out that there was no relationship between the claimants and Mr Jones; Mr Jones did not say or do anything which caused the claimants to act to their prejudice; and that to allow their claim "would in substance ... be to give them the benefit of a contract to which they were not parties." And that, as far as Lord Keith was concerned, was that. One suspects that, unlike his colleagues, Lord Keith did not spend any significant amount of time in the intervening 11 months grappling with the issues to which this case had given rise.

It is to the judgment of Lord Mustill, like Lord Goff a distinguished commercial lawyer in his years as a practising barrister, that one must look for the precise reason for the divergence of views. At the very outset he was at pains to explain why he:

> ... felt it difficult to join company with those who, judges and commentators alike, have almost unanimously found it too plain to need elaboration that the ... claims ought to succeed, if only an intellectually sustainable means can be found; and that ... the proper route to such a conclusion passes through the law of tort.

He then proceeded to challenge the correctness of both these assumptions, but of course it is the first of these which is primarily of interest for present purposes. He pointed out that the assumption that:

> there must be something wrong with the law if the claimants do not succeed ... itself embodies two distinct propositions – that the [claimants'] disappointment should be relieved by an award of money, and that the money should, if the law permits, come from the solicitor. *I am sceptical on both points.* (emphasis added).

Even under the most benign of legal regimes, Lord Mustill pointed out, "there must be many situations in which the well-founded expectations of a potential beneficiary are defeated by an untoward turn of events, and yet he or she is left without [a remedy]." He rejected the suggestion that what takes this case out of the ordinary is the additional ingredient of "fault": or more precisely – disappointment – resulting (foreseeably) from "fault". Assume, he argued, the solicitor prepared the will in good time but the testator was killed in a road accident through the negligence of a motorist en route to the solicitor's office to sign the will. The fault for the non-execution of the will was that of the motorist, but it could not be linked to the right of the disappointed beneficiary to obtain any compensation. A "legal fault cannot exist in a vacuum" and likewise nothing linked the culpable delay of the solicitor to a free-standing right of the potential beneficiary to compensation. Lord Mustill argued:

> In the present instance, it is tempting to say that the solicitor failed to do his job properly; and that it was all his fault that the [claimants] are less well off than they should have been; and the law ought to do something about it. This temptation ... should be resisted. The assertion of fault is either tautologous or inaccurate, and the analysis is safer without it.

For good measure, Lord Mustill did not accept it was a significant feature of the case that were the claim to fail, no sanction would have been imposed on the solicitor for a breach of what was his professional duty. The purpose of the courts in awarding damages for actionable breaches of duty, he pointed out, was to compensate, not to punish.

In Lord Mustill's view, the real cause of the problem to which the case had given rise was the strict rule of probate law that a disposal of property, designed only to take effect after death, is ineffectual unless contained in a valid will. As far as the claimants were concerned, the position would have been just the same if the solicitor had been prompt and diligent but the testator happened to have died sooner than he did, and before the will could be executed. As with Lord Keith, he could see no justification for tinkering with existing principles in order to accommodate the particular facts.

The dynamics of the decision-making in this case were striking. The majority were propelled by "a strong impulse" to achieve what they regarded as "practical justice." The position established by the existing case law, against which backcloth the appeal had been argued, was that liability for negligently causing financial loss required proof of explicit (or necessarily implicit) assumption of responsibility on the part of the defendant and explicit or necessarily implicit reliance on the defendant by the claimant. The majority dealt with this difficulty by introducing the notion of a deemed assumption of responsibility by the solicitor and deemed reliance on the solicitor by the claimants arising as a matter of legal principle in the light of the solicitor's acceptance of the instructions in question. Without what they regarded as a moral imperative, it is improbable that the majority would have contemplated this solution. On the other hand, Lord Keith and Lord Mustill were wholly unpersuaded by the view that the rejection of the claim would be tantamount to an injustice: for them the search for a solution to overcome the conceptual difficulties recognised by all five Law Lords was far from being a moral imperative. The main "protagonists" in this appeal, Lord Goff and Lord Mustill, both happened to come from a commercial law and university teaching background, yet no amount of analytical discussion could really have reconciled these contrasting positions and resolved the point at issue. The discussion could just as profitably have taken place in a seminar composed of social scientists and experts in professional indemnity insurance.

(2) "IT IS UNREALISTIC TO SAY THERE IS ONLY ONE RIGHT ANSWER"

It can be said that the division of opinion amongst the Law Lords as to what was fair and just in relation to a solicitor's liability for negligently failing to comply with a client's changed instructions in the preparation of a will could be regarded as one of distinctly marginal significance in terms of everyday life. The same could certainly not be said, however, of the division of opinion amongst the Law Lords as to what was fair and just in relation to the issue of liability for the birth of unwanted children to disabled mothers – and specifically, the birth of an unwanted child to a partially sighted mother resulting from negligently performed surgery. The issue was considered in an appeal heard by a panel of seven Law Lords instead of the customary five.[3] The facts were that the claimant, a single woman then in her late twenties, underwent a sterilisation operation: she had severely impaired vision, and did not want in those circumstances to risk the responsibility of bringing up a child with the additional financial burden which that would entail. The operation was negligently performed, and she subsequently gave birth to a daughter. She sued the hospital for damages in respect of the additional cost she would incur attributable to her disability in bringing up the unwanted, although otherwise healthy, child. The Court of Appeal, reversing the trial judge, had decided by a majority in her favour.

It is important to appreciate the legal background to the hearing of the appeal. Four years previously the House of Lords had unanimously ruled in a case where the parents had been negligently advised as to the effect of a vasectomy, that damages were not recoverable in respect of the cost of

---

3 *Rees v Darlington Memorial Hospital NHS Trust* [2003] UKHL 52, [2004] 1 AC 309.

bringing up an unwanted child who was completely healthy and normal.[4] Subsequently the Court of Appeal ruled that this did not apply where the unwanted child was born with a disability and the damages reflected the additional cost to the parents attributable to that disability. The rationale common to all the judgments in the previous House of Lords case had been that whereas the inconvenience, pain and discomfort of an unwanted pregnancy, as well as any financial loss flowing from that condition, could properly be compensated by the award of damages, the birth and upbringing up of a healthy and normal child brings pleasure and joy as well as cost, and that it would not be fair, just and reasonable to make the negligent doctor or his employer responsible for the cost incurred in bringing up that child until he or she was self-supporting. The benefits, which were incalculable, would surely outweigh the cost. One Law Lord commented that "it is morally offensive to regard a normal healthy baby as more trouble and expense than it is worth"; and another surmised that the overwhelming response of commuters on the London Underground, if confronted with the question whether the parents should be entitled to recover the cost of bringing up the unwanted but healthy child until that child reached adulthood, would have been an "emphatic 'No'" In the present case the majority in the Court of Appeal, in reaching its decision in favour of the disabled mother, regarded the case as "a legitimate extension" of the earlier decision of the Court of Appeal in respect of the disabled child.

There were two issues which required a decision by the panel of seven Law Lords. The first was whether in fact the principle that damages were not recoverable in respect of a healthy child was good law and should be reaffirmed. (In exceptional cases the House of Lords was free to "depart" from its previous decisions, and when this was a possibility, seven Law Lords would sit instead of five.) In fact the panel unanimously approved the earlier House of Lords decision, acknowledging that the "no damages for a healthy child" principle amounted to an exception to the usual rules governing compensation for negligence. All members of the panel recognised that the decision had been based on policy rather than legal logic, and ultimately on individual moral judgments, but they did not consider that this detracted from its force and merit: sometimes the need for the courts to make policy decisions was inescapable. Lord Bingham, the senior Law Lord, wryly pointed out that if in fact the House of Lords had instead opted for

---

4 *Macfarlane and Another v Tayside Health Board (Scotland)* [1999] UKHL 50, [2000] 2 AC 59.

holding the doctor and/or the employing health authority liable for the cost of bringing up the healthy child:

> it is hard to think ... that its decision would have long survived the first award to well-to-do parents of the estimated cost of providing private education, presents, clothing and foreign holidays for an unwanted child ... against a National Health Service found to be responsible by its negligence for the birth of the child.[5]

It was on the second issue – namely whether the "no damages for a healthy child" principle should apply in the case of a disabled mother – that the real battle was joined: the Law Lords divided four to three, the majority deciding in favour of rejecting the mother's claim and reversing the decision of the Court of Appeal. With hindsight, it could be said that the novelty of the specific issue and the fact that the competing arguments were so finely balanced, made disagreement virtually inevitable.

Lord Bingham[6] was firmly of the view that no exception should be made to the principle either in the case of a disabled child or a disabled mother. Firstly, he regarded it as anomalous and unsatisfactory that a doctor's or surgeon's liability in regard to the cost of bringing up an unwanted child should be determined by a factor for which he was not responsible (i.e. the disability) and not by the unwanted birth, for which, through his negligence, he clearly was. Secondly, and agreeing with the dissenting judge in the

---

5 That the problem was ultimately one that could only be resolved by policy rather than purely legal analysis is demonstrated by the experience of other jurisdictions where the issue has been litigated. The High Court of Australia, by a bare majority of four to three, rejected the "no damages for a healthy child" solution, holding that damages were recoverable in principle in respect of the cost of raising an unwanted but healthy child. In Germany, the Federal Constitutional Court has ruled that such a claim was unconstitutional because it was detrimental to the dignity of the child, but subsequently the Federal Court of Appeal rejected this line of reasoning and ruled in favour of the parents. The courts in the US have varied from state to state in responding to the problem. Some have adopted the same uncompromising approach of the House of Lords; some adopted a solution which involved the bizarre exercise (dismissed as absurd in both House of Lords cases) of calculating the likely cost of raising the child and then deducting an appropriate sum reflecting the joy and the benefits derived from its birth; and others have adopted the same approach as the High Court of Australia and the Federal Appeal Court of Germany.

6 The so-called "Senior Law Lord" at the time, having achieved the impossible by having previously been successively appointed Master of the Rolls and Lord Chief Justice.

Court of Appeal, the creation of an exception in the case of a disabled mother produces other unsatisfactory anomalies. Thus, a mother without a disability who already had three children, and for whom the birth of yet another child would create a crisis in terms of her health unless help in caring for that child was available, would be unable to recover the costs of such help, although her need to avoid a breakdown in health was no different from that of someone with a disability. And what if that mother was poor, and a mother entitled to recover the costs of such help by virtue of her disability was rich? And what if a disabled mother gives birth to a healthy child and, contrary to her anxieties, finds that in the event she can cope with the help of her family and friends? Further, in Lord Bingham's view it was "undesirable that parents, in order to recover compensation, should be encouraged to portray either their children or themselves as disabled". And finally he doubted whether it was actually possible to make a realistic calculation as to the additional cost of bringing up the child which was properly attributable to the mother's disability.

Lord Nicholls, like Lord Bingham, saw no reason to differentiate between a disabled mother and a disabled child. In his view neither should be treated as an exception to the "no damages for a healthy child" principle: to do so would be productive of undesirable anomalies such as those referred to by the dissenting judge in the Court of Appeal.

Lord Millett, who was a party to the earlier House of Lords decision affirming the principle, considered that the Court of Appeal's decision to create an exception in the case of a disabled parent was not a legitimate extension of the earlier "disabled child" decision (as to the correctness of which he had an open mind) but in fact an illegitimate gloss on the healthy child principle. The rule was that the costs of bringing up a child, even though reasonably incurred, were not recoverable. "Such costs are infinitely variable. They will differ from one family to another. They may be greater in the case of a single parent and less when there are grandparents or siblings ... [and] they may be greater when the mother chooses or has to go out to work." But, points out Lord Millett, none of these costs are recoverable in the case of a healthy child. "*In principle the same must be true of the disabled parent* [emphasis added]. To the extent that her disability has any effect, it increases the amount of the costs which she reasonably incurs in bringing up the child, costs which are nevertheless not recoverable."

Like Lord Bingham, Lord Millett makes the point that in reality an award of the additional costs attributable to the parent's disability is an award for disability, not for the negligent treatment. Disability, he observes, was a misfortune for which the state assumes responsibility in providing financial assistance properly funded by general taxation, but it "is not the responsibility of the private citizen whose conduct has neither caused nor contributed to the disability."

Like Lord Bingham, he noted the troublesome anomalies identified by the dissenting judge in the Court of Appeal, and summarised his criticism of the court's majority decision in the following robust terms: "The decision of the majority ... is destructive of the concept of distributive justice. It renders the law incoherent and is bound to lead to artificial and indefensible distinctions being drawn as the courts struggle to draw a principled line between costs which are recoverable and those which are not."

The four-strong majority was completed by Lord Scott. He saw no basis for creating an exception because of the claimant's visual disability: her baby was healthy and well-loved; she chose to keep it, and there could be no doubt that it added value to her life, "and that value is not capable of assessment in monetary terms. A balance sheet of detriment and benefit ... cannot be drawn up." So far as a case of a disabled child was concerned, he was inclined to think that a distinction might be meaningfully drawn between a case where the avoidance of the risk of a birth of a child with a particular disability was the specific reason for the parent seeking treatment or advice, and cases where the treatment was sought simply to avoid conception.

All four Law Lords, however, were of the view that the claimant was entitled to an award of damages, albeit modest, reflecting the fact that she had been the victim of what was indisputably negligent clinical treatment, as a result of which she had been denied the opportunity to live her life in the way she had wished and planned: in other words, she should be compensated for the interference with her personal autonomy in respect of lifestyle choices. They agreed that the sum of £15,000 as a "conventional award" would be appropriate.

Two of the three Law Lords forming the minority, Lord Steyn and Lord Hope, had been parties to the original House of Lords "healthy child" decision. In Lord Steyn's view the legal policy underlying that decision was "critically dependent on the birth of a healthy and normal child." He therefore concluded that in the case of a *disabled* child "normal principles of corrective justice permit recovery of compensation for the costs of providing for the child's needs and care relating to his disability." He found the case of a disabled mother, on the other hand, a difficult one. He recognised the anomalies which could arise by creating an exception to the rule, but equally, in his view it was important to recognise that the law should give special consideration to the serious disability of a mother who had wanted to avoid having a child because of her disability by opting for a sterilisation operation. "This is a truly hard case", he acknowledged, and it was "unrealistic to say that there is only one right answer." At the end of the day he was persuaded that "the injustice of denying to such a seriously disabled mother the limited remedy of the extra costs caused by her disability outweighs the considerations [which influenced the dissenting judge in the Court of Appeal.]"

Lord Hope, like Lord Steyn, found the issue a difficult one, and "on balance" concluded that:

> the fact that the child's parent is a seriously disabled person does provide a ground for [not applying the healthy child principle] and that it would be fair, just and reasonable to hold that such extra costs as ... can be attributed to the disability are within the scope of [wrongdoer's] duty of care and are recoverable.

He thought there were good grounds for distinguishing disabled parents from other kinds of disadvantaged parents: circumstances affecting the non-disabled but disadvantaged may change, but disability remains a constant factor:

> It is the inescapable fact that the seriously disabled parent cannot, however hard she tries do all the things that a normal, healthy parent can do when carrying out the ordinary tasks in a child's upbringing ... By allowing the seriously disabled parent to recover the extra costs of child-rearing which are due to her disability the law will best to enable her to perform this task on equal terms with those who are not affected by [such] impairment.

The third of the minority Law Lords, Lord Hutton, considered the "disabled child" decision of the Court of Appeal to have been correct, and likewise the reasoning of the majority of the Court of Appeal in the present case. In his view the decision of the House of Lords had been "grounded on the principle that it is not fair, just or reasonable to award damages to healthy parents for bringing up a healthy baby; the House did not consider the position where the mother was disabled." In his opinion it was not unjust, unfair or unreasonable to award damages for the extra costs of bringing up the child. In his view there was a clear distinction between a disabled mother and a mother in normal health; and the fact that "hard cases can be pointed to very close to the line which divides recovery from non-recovery", should not stop the courts from giving effect to this distinction.

Both Lord Steyn and Lord Hope were sharply critical of the inclination on the part of the majority, notwithstanding its rejection of the claim for additional costs attributable to her disability, to award the claimant a "conventional sum" of £15,000 by way of damages. Both clearly felt it undermined the logic of the majority's position as to the recoverability of the additional costs relating to the claimant's disability. "The splitting up of a claim for damages into these two parts", observed Lord Hope, "in order to allow recovery of one part and deny recovery of the other part is a novel concept and seems to me, with respect, contrary to principle." He did not think that Lord Bingham had answered this objection by stating that the basis of the award was simply recognition of the wrong done, and was not intended to be compensatory: the governing principle in the assessment of damages, he pointed out, was that any award *should be* compensatory and not punitive.

Leaving aside the point made by both Lord Bingham and Lord Millett that allowing the disability of a parent to determine liability for the cost of bringing up an unwanted child would introduce an element of randomness, the reason why most of the Law Lords found the issue a difficult one, and for the striking divergence in approach, was because the outcome depended on seven personal responses to the question: what significance, if any, should attach to the disability of a parent compared to other kinds of disadvantage from which a parent may suffer? For most of the Law Lords, in fact, the key question seems to have been even more narrow and specific than that: namely, was there a material distinction between a parent who sought to avoid the risk of conception because of her disability, and a healthy parent who sought to avoid the risk of conception because of some other *involuntary* disadvantage, whether economic, personal or family related? The majority saw no reason to distinguish between them: the minority did. Both sides of the argument thought their respective conclusions were consistent with distributive justice, and met the criterion of being fair, just and reasonable. Clearly this was not a question that was ever capable of being resolved by legal analysis.

(3) SUCCUMBING TO THE ATTRACTION OF A WHOLLY ILLOGICAL ARGUMENT?

Just as the debate in the case of the beneficiaries deprived of their legacies had centred on whether, in relation to the law of negligence, the conventional rules then in play should be relaxed in order to accommodate a particular misfortune or, as the majority preferred to see it, a perceived injustice, some eight years later exactly the same kind of debate took place in the House of Lords in relation to another aspect of the law of negligence. To establish liability, a claimant not only has to prove there was negligence, but that the negligent act or omission caused the damage complained of. In certain circumstances this can be very tricky. A doctor or surgeon who advises a patient to undergo a particular treatment or surgical procedure is under a duty to warn that patient of any risks attached to such course of action, so as to enable him or her to make an informed decision: in the absence of such warning the patient is not in a position to give his or her "informed consent." But what if the doctor or surgeon (negligently) fails to warn the patient of the risk and the risk eventuates, but the patient is unable to say truthfully one way or another whether, had he or she been appropriately warned, he or she would not have consented to undergo the treatment or the surgery in question. This is precisely the set of circumstances which confronted the House of Lords.[7]

The claimant suffered from repeated low back pain and consulted a neurosurgeon. He advised her to undergo a surgical procedure on her spine, to which she reluctantly agreed. However, when advising her he had negligently failed to warn her of a small (2 per cent) risk of partial paralysis through nerve damage. She underwent the procedure three days later, and sustained nerve damage resulting in partial paralysis. The operation itself had nonetheless been performed with due skill and care. The claimant sued the surgeon for damages in respect of her injury, and at the trial of the action she was unable to say that, on the balance of probabilities, had she been warned of the risk she would not have consented to the surgery. What she could say was that had she been warned, she would have taken time to consult friends and/or obtain a second opinion, and that the procedure would not have been carried out when it was, i.e. three days after the consultation.

---

7 *Chester v Afshar* [2004] UKHL 41, [2005] 1 AC 134.

Both the High Court judge who tried the case, and the Court of Appeal, held that she was entitled to recover damages in respect of her condition, despite her inability to prove on the balance of probabilities that she would not have undergone the procedure had she been warned of the risk. It was sufficient for her to prove that she would not have agreed to have the operation performed on the day and at the time when in fact it was performed.

The Court of Appeal was strongly influenced by a majority (three to two) decision of the High Court of Australia in a case where the issue was identical.[8] (The claimant had undergone a throat operation and developed an infection, the slight risk of which she had not, but should have, been warned. At some point surgery would have been necessary in any event.) The decision in the Australian case had in fact received warm support from many eminent academic lawyers, including Professor Honoré, the co-author of the leading English work on causation in the law, to which the Law Lords were referred by counsel for the claimant. In an article on the Australian case, Professor Honoré had commented that justice had been done to the claimant despite the absence of proof of a causal connection between the disastrous outcome of the surgery and the surgeon's failure to warn. He argued that the duty to warn minimised the risk of harm to a patient and was intended to enable the patient to make an informed choice as to the recommended treatment, and by whom and when that treatment should be carried out. The surgeon had:

> ... violated [the claimant's] right to choose for herself, even if he did not increase the risk to her ... Morally he was responsible for the outcome of what he did ... All the High Court [of Australia] has therefore done is to give a legal sanction to an underlying moral responsibility for causing injury of the very sort against the risk of which [the surgeon] should have warned her.[9]

It was against this background that the appeal was heard by the House of Lords. By a majority of three to two they decided in favour of the claimant and of upholding the decision of the Court of Appeal. The views expressed were sharply polarised. The minority (Lord Bingham and Lord Hoffmann) saw no reason to relax the "conventional" approach to causation in relation to negligence, and their respective judgments explaining why this was the case were clear and succinct.

---

8 *Chappell v Hart* (1998) 195 CLR 232.

9 T. Honoré, "Medical non-disclosure, causation and risk" (1999) 7 Torts Law Journal 1.

For Lord Bingham both the issue and the analysis were perfectly simple and straightforward. The indisputable evidence was that the risk was liable to occur at random, and would remain the same whenever and by whom the operation was performed. Since the claimant was unable to say that had she been warned of the risk she would not have consented to the operation, she was unable to establish the causal link between the breach of duty (i.e. the failure to warn) and the injury which she suffered: that she could show that she would not have consented to the operation being performed on the day in question was irrelevant. What the majority proposed, and the Court of Appeal had decided, was in Lord Bingham's view "a substantial and unjustified departure from sound and established principle." A claimant was entitled to be compensated for the damage which the negligence of another had caused, and a defendant was bound to compensate a claimant for the damage which his or her negligence had caused the claimant; but, argued Lord Bingham, "the corollaries are also true: a claimant is not entitled to be compensated, and a defendant is not bound to compensate a claimant, for damage not caused by the negligence complained of." Whilst he recognised that a patient's right to be appropriately warned was an important right, he did not think that "the law should seek to reinforce that right by providing for the payment of potentially very large damages by a defendant whose violation of that right is not shown to have worsened the physical condition of the claimant."

Lord Bingham concluded his judgment by expressing his agreement with the analysis of one of the dissenting judges in the Australian case, Mr Justice McHugh: as a matter of principle the law should not require the surgeon to pay damages if the negligent act or omission "has done no more than expose the patient to a class of risk to which he or she would have been exposed irrespective of [that] omission"; that there had to be in terms of common sense a causal connection between the negligent act or omission and the harm which the claimant has suffered; and "if the evidence suggests that the omission of the [surgeon to warn the claimant] would have made no difference to the [claimant's] course of action, the [surgeon] has not caused the harm which the [claimant] has suffered."

For Lord Hoffmann the issue was equally straightforward and simple – indeed to the extent that he found it unnecessary to refer to the judgments in the Australian case. "[The] purpose of a duty to warn someone against the risk involved in what he proposes to do, or to allow to be done to him," he observed, "is to give him the opportunity to avoid or reduce that risk. If he would have been unable or unwilling to take that opportunity, and the risk eventuates, the failure to warn has not caused the damage. It would have happened anyway." In the context of the present case the claimant had not proved that she would have taken the opportunity and not had the operation. Lord Hoffmann described the argument (as will be seen, endorsed by the majority) that it was sufficient for the claimant simply to prove that she would not have had the operation at that particular time or necessarily by the same surgeon:

> as about as logical as saying that if one had been told, on entering a casino, that the odds on the number 7 coming up at roulette were only 1 in 37, one would have gone away and come back next week or gone to a different casino. The question is whether one would have taken the opportunity to avoid or reduce the risk, not whether one would have changed the scenario in some irrelevant detail.

In the present case, he pointed out, it had been found as a fact that the risk would have been precisely the same whether the operation had been carried out at another time or by another surgeon.

Lord Hoffmann concluded his judgment by rejecting the view of Professor Honoré that morally the doctor or surgeon who fails to warn the patient of the relevant risk, thereby depriving the patient of the right to choose, is responsible for the ensuing damage, and that therefore it is right that he should be held liable. He observed:

> That argument seems to me to prove both too much and too little. Too much, because it is an argument for making a doctor the insurer of any damage which he causes, whether the patient knew of the risk or not. Too little, because it would excuse the doctor in a case in which he had a duty to warn but the actual operation was perfectly properly performed by someone else, for example, by his registrar.

All three Law Lords who formed the majority, Lord Steyn, Lord Hope and Lord Walker, accepted that the adoption of the conventional approach to causation would mean that the claimant would fail. Did considerations of legal policy and "corrective justice" point to a relaxation of the rules? For Lord Steyn, the patient's right to an appropriate warning and the requirement of "informed consent" were of central importance, and had to be given "effective protection whenever possible." He agreed with the view of Professor Honoré that "policy and corrective justice pull powerfully in favour of vindicating the patient's right to know." He identified as a distinctive feature of the case that "but for the surgeon's negligent failure to warn the claimant of the small risk of serious injury the actual injury would not have occurred when it did and the chance of it occurring on a subsequent occasion was very small." He concluded that the claimant:

> cannot be said to have given informed consent to the surgery in the full legal sense [and that] her right of autonomy and dignity can and ought to be vindicated by a narrow and modest departure from traditional causation principles.

Lord Hope, like Lord Steyn, acknowledged that for him the issue was one of legal policy: "whether in the unusual circumstances of this case justice require[d] the normal approach to causation to be modified." Again, like Lord Steyn, he regarded the patient's right to choose and to give informed consent as being of central importance:

> The function of the law is to protect the patient's right to choose. If it is to fulfil that function it must ensure that the duty to inform is respected by the doctor. It will fail to do this if an appropriate remedy cannot be given if the duty is breached, and the very risk that the patient should have been told about occurs and she suffers injury.

Lord Hope pointed out that for many patients the choice, when warned of the risk, may not be an easy one, and as was the case with the claimant, would be unable to have given the doctor a clear answer one way or the other:

> To leave the patient who would find the decision difficult without a remedy, as the normal approach to causation would indicate, would render the duty useless in the cases where it is needed most. This would discriminate against those who cannot honestly say that they would have declined the operation once and for all if they had been warned.[10] I would find that result unacceptable.

---

10 Surprisingly, this point appears neither to have been argued nor discussed during the hearing of the appeal. Yet the difficulty in this case arose precisely because of the claimant's honesty in admitting her inability to state one way or another whether it was likely that she would have undergone the operation if warned of the risk.

Adopting the language of Professor Honoré, he declared that "the function of the law is to enable rights to be vindicated and to provide remedies when duties have been breached. Unless this is done the duty is a hollow one ...". He therefore concluded that "on policy grounds" the test of causation was satisfied in the present case, the injury being intimately involved with the duty to warn. He would hold that the injury had been caused in the legal sense by the breach of that duty.

Lord Walker agreed with both the approach and conclusions of Lord Steyn and Lord Hope. He emphasised the danger mentioned by Lord Hope, "of an honest claimant finding herself without a remedy in circumstances where the surgeon has failed in his professional duty, and the claimant has suffered injury directly within the scope and focus of that duty." For good measure, Lord Walker was not impressed with Lord Hoffmann's "roulette" analogy, and for his part would not accept that on that basis there was an absence of a causal connection between the breach of duty and the injury. He pointed out that:

> ... the 1 in 37 chance of a particular number coming up ... is a matter of simple and precise calculation. By contrast the chance of nerve damage occurring (without negligence) during lumbar surgery can be calculated only with hindsight ... by compiling and analysing statistics as to the outcome of that type of surgery.

A number of factors and variables would come into play, so changing the time or date of an operation could not be regarded on the strength of the roulette analogy as "changing the scenario in some irrelevant detail."

The majority and the minority approached the central issue in this case from entirely different perspectives: a halfway house solution was simply not possible. For Lord Bingham and Lord Hoffmann it was wrong in principle and simply unfair to place the doctor or surgeon in the position of an insurer when no causal connection between the failure to warn and the disastrous outcome could be shown, and it could not be shown that the doctor's (albeit culpable) omission had in any way exposed the patient to any greater risk than had the warning been given. Consequently there was no case for relaxing the conventional rules on causation.

For the majority, on the other hand, the plight of someone in the claimant's position was the focus of their concern. She had consented to an operation without having been warned of the particular risk; the risk eventuated, and she suffered a disabling injury. Crucially, and quite understandably – since the risk was a small one – she was unable to say whether, had she been told of the risk, she would have agreed to undergo the operation. For the majority, corrective justice required that the duty to warn should in such circumstances be reinforced by an effective legal remedy.

(4) JUSTICE FOR CONTRACT BREAKERS AS WELL AS FOR THE INJURED PARTIES

Even in appeals concerned with arcane disputes in the world of commercial contracts, the outcome may revolve around differing perceptions as to what exactly is just and fair. Contrary to popular belief, judges have never been slow to resort to moral principle in resolving difficult issues in commercial litigation.[11] A striking illustration of this arose in a case concerning a dispute between the owners and charterers of a ship which had its seeds in the outbreak of the recent Iraqi war.[12] A tanker had been chartered (i.e. leased) for a term of seven years, the charter being cancellable at the option of either the owners or the charterers in the event of a war or hostilities breaking out between, *inter alia*, the US/UK and Iraq. After only three years the charter was terminated by the charterers in circumstances amounting to a breach of contract.[13] The ship owners started legal proceedings, and some 14 months later (whilst the legal proceedings were still pending) the Iraqi war broke out: had the charter still been in existence, the charterers would have been entitled to exercise their right to cancel, and would certainly have exercised that right. The issue at all stages in the litigation concerned the level of damages for which the charterers were liable to the owners. More specifically, the issue was whether the normal rule in assessing damages for breach of contract should apply – namely, that they should be assessed in the

11 Famously, in a case in the early 1960s involving litigation between charterers of a ship and shipbuilders and repairers, Viscount Simonds (Lord Chancellor at the time, and a man much prone to the use of pompous rhetoric) stated that his conclusion that a wrongdoer should only be liable for damage that was reasonably foreseeable and not simply the direct consequence of the wrongful act, reflected "the common conscience of mankind."

12 *Golden Strait Corporation v Nippon Yusen Kubishka Kaisha* [2007] UKHL 12, [2007] 2 AC 353.

13 The breach was held to have been "repudiatory" in character: where there is a repudiation of a contract, the injured party can either still seek to keep the contract alive or treat the contract as having come to an end and, if he wishes, sue for damages. In this case the ship owners "accepted" the repudiation and treated the contract as having come to an end.

light of the circumstances prevailing at the time of the breach: there was a finding of fact in the light of expert evidence that at the time of the breach the outbreak of war between the US and Iraq was simply a mere possibility and not a likely event. Thus if the normal rule applied, the owners would be entitled to recover damages on the basis that the charter at the time of the breach had four years still to run, and, subject to mitigating their loss, would have been entitled to be compensated accordingly.

The Court of Appeal concluded that the normal rule should *not* apply and that the assessment of damages should take into account the fact that some 14 months after the wrongful termination of the charter, war between the US/UK and Iraq did indeed break out. They did so essentially on the ground that considerations of certainty and finality had in this case to give way to the greater importance of achieving an accurate assessment of the damages based on the ship owners' actual loss. Although a number of cases had been cited in argument and referred to in the leading judgment, none were so directly in point as to amount to a precedent. However, the Court derived support from a late-nineteenth-century decision of the House of Lords, strongly relied on by counsel for the charterers, in a case concerned with the assessment of statutory compensation payable to a colliery by a water utility company for interference with the workings of the colliery over a two-year period, during which time the price of coal had risen: the issue was whether the calculation should reflect the position as at the time the statutory notice had been served on the colliery (i.e. at the beginning of the two-year period) or at the end. It was decided that it should be the latter, on the basis that it was quite unnecessary to guess or speculate when the true position was actually known: "Why ... should [the arbitrator] guess when he can calculate? With the light before him, why should he shut his eyes and grope in the dark?"

The House of Lords divided three to two on the issue, the majority approving the decision of the Court of Appeal. It is convenient to consider the minority judgments first. Whilst acknowledging the importance of the so-called compensatory principle (the damages recoverable by the injured party should be such sum as will put him in the same financial position as if the contract had been performed), Lord Bingham roundly declared that in his view the decision of the Court of Appeal "undermine[d] the quality of certainty which is a traditional strength and major selling point of English commercial law, and involves an unfortunate departure from principle." He cited cases where the normal "assessment at date of breach" rule had been beneficially applied, and dismissed as irrelevant those cases in which the event (or in one case a non-event) triggering a subsequent termination of the contract was inevitable at the time of the breach. Crucially, he regarded the colliery case (again heavily relied upon by counsel for the charterers in argument) as having no bearing on the issue: it was concerned with statutory compensation, and not with "a repudiation of a commercial contract where there was an available market".[14]

For Lord Bingham it was of paramount importance that the parties knew where they stood at the time the contract, in this instance the charter, was repudiated. He was not impressed by the argument implicit in the Court of Appeal's decision, and explicit in the submissions of counsel, that the ship owners "would be unfairly over-compensated if they were to recover as damages sums which, with the benefit of hindsight, it is now known they would not have received had there been no repudiation by the charterers." There were, in his view, several answers to this:

> The first is that contracts are made to be performed, not broken. It may prove disadvantageous to break a contract instead of performing it. The second is that if, on their repudiation being accepted, the charterers had promptly honoured ... their obligation to pay damages, the transaction would have been settled well before the second Gulf War became a reality. The third is that the owners were entitled to be compensated for the value of what they had lost on the date it was lost ... and what the owners lost at that date was a [charter] with slightly less than four years to run.

The arbitrator had found that the charter was marketable on that basis. This did not cease to be the case because, fortuitously, later events affected its marketability and depressed its value: the owners would have been fairly compensated.

Finally, Lord Bingham was not impressed by the point that there was in any event an inherent uncertainty as to whether the charter would run its full course in view of the inclusion of the war cancellation clause. In his view commercial contracts must proceed on the basis of certainty and predictability: "The importance of certainty and predictability in commercial transactions has been a constant theme of English commercial law since [the late eighteenth century]".

---

[14] Where there is an available market at the date of the breach, the normal measure of damages will be the difference between the contract rate and the market rate for the chartering of a substitute vessel for the rest of the charter period.

Lord Walker strongly endorsed Lord Bingham's approach and reasoning, and drew attention to the fact that the hindsight issue in assessing damages only arose in this case because of excessive delays at every stage in the progressing of this litigation.

Lords Scott, Carswell and Brown comprised the majority. For Lord Scott, the compensatory principle was paramount: namely, the damages which the injured party is entitled to recover should reflect the loss of his contractual bargain, no more and no less; in the words of a famous mid-nineteenth-century judgment, "where a party sustains a loss by reason of a breach of contract, he is, so far as money can do it, to be placed in the same situation, with respect as to damages, as if the contract had been performed." It was common ground that had the charter still been an ongoing concern when the hostilities broke out, the charterers would have exercised their right to cancel. If, argued Lord Scott, the contract is for performance over a period of time, "the assessment of damages for breach must proceed on the same principle, namely the victim of the breach should be placed so far as damages can do it, in the position he would have been in had the contract been performed."

The contention that in this case the post-breach events should be disregarded, in Lord Scott's view, attributed to the assessment at date of breach rule an inflexibility which was inconsistent with principle and case law. The application of that rule even to sale of goods transactions may not be appropriate. Assume, he argued, a three-year contract for the supply of goods and a repudiatory breach at the end of the first year, which is accepted; before the assessment of damages takes place an event occurs, which would have had the effect of automatically terminating the contract had it still been ongoing, for example, legislation prohibiting the sale of the goods in question; the contractual benefit of which the injured party had been deprived would not have extended beyond the terminating event.

Lord Scott concluded that the application of the normal rule in the instant case would offend the compensatory principle. The owners were seeking compensation exceeding the value of the contractual benefits of which they were deprived. "The argued justification ... is that priority should be given to the so-called principle of certainty ... There is no such principle. Certainty is a desideratum and a very important one. But it is not a principle and must give way to principle. Otherwise incoherence of principle is the result." In his view the same approach should be adopted in this case as was adopted by the House of Lords in the colliery case.

Lord Carswell recognised the importance of certainty in regard to commercial transactions, but like Lord Scott and the Court of Appeal he concluded that the desirability of certainty should give way to principle, and "yield to the greater importance of achieving an accurate assessment of the damages based on the loss actually incurred." Like Lord Scott, he thought the approach of the House of Lords in the colliery case was directly in point.

Lord Brown focused on what he regarded as a central feature of the case: that the contract was subject to a condition which, if activated, could automatically trigger its termination – namely, the war cancellation clause – which provided that the contract was terminable at the option of the charterers in the event of war breaking out in the Middle East. There was therefore an inherent uncertainty as to whether the charter would run its full seven-year course. How, he asked would the interests of certainty be served by requiring an assessment of the degree of likelihood of the charterers being entitled to operate the war clause, and the likely time, to be made as at the date of the breach? "Must the judge really shut his eyes to the known facts and speculate how matters might have looked at some earlier date? Again, not without compelling reason and none appears to me." The colliery case approach, in his view, was the correct one:

> It is one thing to say that the injured party, mitigating his loss as the breach date rule requires him to do, thereby takes any future market movement out of the equation and to that extent crystallises the measure of his loss; it is quite another to say, as the owners do here, that it requires the arbitrator or judge when finally determining the damages to ignore subsequent events ...

There was no justification for not adhering to the compensatory principle in this case.

What has happened here is that the Law Lords disagreed on the question as to which of two competing scenarios most reflected what was fair, just and reasonable. The first scenario, favoured by the minority, was this. The parties should know where they stood in terms of the consequences as at the time of the repudiation: the charterers should know in terms of likely cost the consequence of their repudiation of the charter; the owners would be able to make an informed decision as to whether to accept the repudiation. Both parties would be in a position to negotiate a prompt settlement. The measure of damages should not be at the mercy of post-breach events outside the control of the parties. Not to apply the normal assessment at the date of breach rule in situations as disclosed by the present case would encourage procrastination and delay on the part of the contract breaker. The alternative scenario, favoured by the majority, was that applying the normal assessment at the date of breach rule would involve the ship owners being compensated by an amount substantially in excess of the true value of their loss, and offends the principle that the damages awarded to the injured party should so far as is possible put him in the same position financially as if the contract had been performed. Furthermore, there was an inherent uncertainty about whether the contract could be performed over the specified seven-year period, and the interest of justice would not be served by relying purely on an, albeit expert, assessment of the likelihood or otherwise of an outbreak of a war as at the date of the repudiation, when the actual position was in fact known by the time the question of damages came to be determined.[15]

[15] Oddly enough, this particular area of the law of contract had caused a similarly striking divergence of views in the House of Lords some 25 years earlier. Developers had purchased land under a contract which provided for completion of the sale in five years time. Whilst the sale was still pending, they served a notice on the vendors purporting to terminate the contract, erroneously believing (on legal advice) that under its terms they were entitled to do so. The House of Lords decided by a majority of three to two that this did not amount to a repudiation. The majority thought it would be wrong and "not in accordance with ordinary concepts of justice" to treat the developers' conduct as repudiatory of the contract when in fact what they thought they were doing was in accordance with its terms. The minority took the view that the developers' subjective belief did not matter. "I do not understand", commented one Law Lord, "how [the developers'] honest belief in a bad point of law can avail them". And his fellow dissenter said he was unable to see how "a total renunciation of all future obligations to perform ... the contract can by any circumstances be watered down or deprived of its repudiatory character.": *Woodar Investment Development Ltd v Wimpey Construction UK Ltd* [1980] UKHL 11, [1980] 1 WLR 277.

PART TWO

CLASHES OF PRINCIPLE AND COMPETING MORAL JUDGMENTS

In the early 1960s much interest centred on the so-called Hart-Devlin debate arising from the publication of Lord Devlin's book, *The Enforcement of Morals* and Professor Herbert Hart's celebrated work, *The Concept of Law.* The background to, and to some extent the pretext for, that debate was a clutch of cases heard by the Law Lords which were concerned with criminality, sex and marital behaviour, all of which provoked strong disagreement within their ranks. For example, one such case (the so-called *Ladies Directory* case[1]) raised the issue whether there was such an offence as a conspiracy to corrupt public morals. Following the introduction of the Street Offences Act 1959 (intended to deter soliciting by prostitutes), a booklet was published entitled *The Ladies Directory* which consisted of advertisements inserted and paid for by prostitutes, disclosing their names and addresses and relevant details. Its publisher was charged, *inter alia*, with conspiring with persons unknown to corrupt public morals. It was common ground that the charge was a novel one. The majority view was encapsulated in the quaint, high-flown rhetoric of Lord Simonds. Having prayed in support the statement of the eighteenth-century Chief Justice Lord Mansfield that the courts have the power to "superintend offences which are prejudicial to public welfare", Lord Simonds went on:

> Let it be supposed that at some future date homosexual practices between adult consenting males are no longer a crime. Would it not be an offence if ... such practices were publically advocated and encouraged by pamphlet and advertisement. Or must we wait until Parliament finds time to deal with such conduct? I say, my Lords, that if the Common Law is powerless in such an event, then we should no longer do her reverence. But I say that her hand is still powerful and that it is for Her Majesty's judges to play the part which Lord Mansfield pointed out to them.

---

1 *Shaw v Director of Public Prosecutions* [1961] UKHL 1, [1962] AC 220.

This attracted a sharp retort from Lord Reid, one of the most outstanding of post-war Law Lords:

> Parliament is the proper place ... the only proper place to settle [the question whether and in what circumstances the law should punish immorality]. When there is sufficient support from public opinion, Parliament does not hesitate to intervene. Where Parliament fears to tread it is not for the courts to rush in ...

Another such case (strictly speaking, two cases but heard together in the House of Lords[2]) involving an equally sharp divergence of views on an issue with social implications, was concerned with cruelty as a ground for divorce: at the time the divorce laws revolved around the concept of the matrimonial offence. The issue was whether to constitute cruelty the conduct relied on had to be intentionally "aimed at" the other spouse. In the one case the conduct relied on was extreme laziness and financial irresponsibility on the part of a husband, causing the wife continual anxiety and distress; and in the other, persistent and unjustified accusations of adulterous liaisons by a husband who was suffering from a diagnosed condition of paranoid schizophrenia. The majority were strongly of the view that intention was wholly irrelevant: what mattered was whether, seen objectively, the conduct was such that no reasonable person could be expected to put up with it. Why should the wife be condemned to a life of misery and, if she decided to leave in such circumstances, why should she be guilty of desertion? For the minority, intention was at the heart of the matter. A finding of cruelty implied a degree of moral turpitude. Cruelty was a matrimonial offence: it had serious implications and consequences. In neither case did the husband have the intention of harming the wife.

These cases heard in the 1960s involved clashes of principle and competing moral judgments. Such clashes have continued to characterise the disagreements of succeeding generations of Law Lords in cases which raise moral issues or which involve questions as to the role and powers of the courts. For present purposes, five cases illustrate this very well.

(1) IS THIS REALLY CRIMINAL CONDUCT?

Remarkably, the question raised in the *Ladies Directory* case – namely, whether or when it was open to the courts to hold a particular course of conduct to be criminal – re-emerged in a case heard by the House of Lords

---

2 *Gollins v Gollins* [1964] AC 644; *Williams v Williams* [1964] AC 698.

some 30 years later.[3] To describe the case as unusual is perhaps to understate the position. In the course of conducting an unrelated investigation, the police came across video evidence of a group of men engaged in homosexual sadomasochistic practises which involved the inflicting of wounds on the genital areas and other areas of the body of the consenting victims. Charges were brought under the Offences against the Person Act 1861, of assault occasioning actual bodily harm, resulting in the conviction of those concerned. The Court of Appeal (Criminal Division) upheld the convictions. In the House of Lords, as in the lower courts, the central question was whether consent was a defence to the charges brought.

By a majority of three to two the Law Lords dismissed the appeals. All the Law Lords recognised that none of the precedents referred to in the judgments of the lower courts and cited in the course of argument were directly in point, and that consent could be a defence to a charge of common assault where the "harm" inflicted was trivial or slight and intended to be such. In the absence of helpful precedents, it was inevitable that the willingness or otherwise to invoke public policy and the public interest would play a critical role in determining the outcome. The majority comprised Lords Templeman, Jauncey and Lowry.

In Lord Templeman's view, the existing case law, which mostly concerned cases involving prize fighting and street fighting, suggested that consent could be a defence to the infliction of bodily harm in the course of some lawful activity, but not otherwise. For Lord Templeman it was clear what the proper approach should be: "The question whether the defence of consent should be extended to the consequences of sadomasochistic encounters can only be decided by considerations of policy and public interest."; and that whilst Parliament could call on the advice of doctors, psychiatrists, criminologists, sociologists and other experts and also take into account public opinion, if it were to consider legislation on the matter, the question had to be decided here and now by the House of Lords in its judicial capacity.

His response to the argument that consent was a defence "because every person has a right to deal to deal with his body as he pleases ...", was that he considered this to be simply a slogan which did not really help as to the policy decision which now had to be made. He was also not impressed by the argument that the sexual appetites of sadists and masochists could only be satisfied by the infliction of bodily harm, and that the law should not

---

3 *R v Brown* [1992] UKHL 7, [1994] 1 AC 212.

punish the "consensual achievement of sexual satisfaction." In his view sadomasochism was not just concerned with sex: it was also concerned with violence. The practises revealed by the evidence in the present case "were unpredictably dangerous and degrading to body and mind" and involved the use of drink and drugs to obtain consent and increase enthusiasm. In principle, so Lord Templeman argued, there is a difference between violence which is incidental and violence which is inflicted "for the indulgence of cruelty." He was not prepared "to invent a defence for sadomasochistic encounters which breed and glorify cruelty" and which attract serious charges under the Offences against the Person Act 1861. In his view "Society is entitled and bound to protect itself against a cult of violence. Pleasure derived from the infliction of pain is an evil thing. Cruelty is uncivilised."

Lord Jauncey concluded that the case law indicated "the infliction of actual or more serious bodily harm is an unlawful activity to which consent is no answer"; and that a line had properly to be drawn between assault at common law and actual and grievous bodily harm cases brought under the Offences against the Person Act 1861. Consent could be a defence to the former but not to the latter. Furthermore, in his view:

> it would not be in the public interest that deliberate infliction of actual bodily harm during the course of homosexual sadomasochistic activities should be held to be lawful ... If it is to be decided that such activities as the nailing by A of B's foreskin or scrotum to a board ... are injurious neither to B, C and D nor to the public interest, then it is for Parliament with its accumulated wisdom and sources of information to declare them to be lawful.

Lord Lowry agreed with Lords Templeman and Jauncey that in principle consent cannot be a defence to a statutory charge of causing actual bodily harm. For him the critical question was whether an exception should be made in the case of consensual sadomasochistic practises. His answer was an emphatic: No. The case advanced on behalf of the appellants, he pointed out, entailed the proposition that "the deliberate and painful infliction of physical injury should be exempted from the operation of [the Offences against the Person Act 1861], the object of which was to prevent or punish that very thing," on the ground that "both those who inflict, and those who will suffer, the injury wish to satisfy a perverted and depraved sexual desire." Sadomasochistic homosexual activity could not be regarded as "conducive to the enhancement or enjoyment of family life ... or to the welfare of society" and a relaxation of the Act's provisions could only encourage this practice with its accompanying cruelty. Furthermore there was a real risk of serious injury resulting from such practice.

Lord Lowry poured scorn on the argument that to place a restriction on the practice of sadomasochism was an unjustified interference with the private life and activities of those concerned, who were doing no harm to anyone except possibly themselves. He pointed out that this argument rested on the fallacy that what was involved was the restraint of a lawful activity, whereas what was involved was the refusal to relax the relevant statutory provisions so that what was unlawful could now be made lawful. In his view the position was simple, "there [was] no legal right to cause actual bodily harm in the course of sadomasochistic activity."

Except for sharing their distaste for the sadomasochistic practises in question, the minority fundamentally disagreed with both the approach and the reasoning of the majority. Lord Mustill[4] started his lengthy and closely reasoned judgment on a note which signalled very clearly the direction in which he proposed to travel: "My Lords, this is a case about the criminal law of violence. In my opinion it should be a case about the criminal law of private sexual relations, if about anything at all." In his view the involvement of the Offences Against the Person Act 1861, under which the charges had been brought, was "adventitious": the clue surely was in the title "Offences *Against* the Person"; the conduct which the Act was intended to catch "[t]ypically ... involves brutality, aggression and violence of a kind far removed from the appellant's behaviour which, however worthy of censure, involved no animosity, no aggression, no personal rancour on the part of the person inflicting the hurt ... " He thought the words of an eminent Victorian judge in a case in which charges of assault causing actual or grievous bodily harm were brought under the Offences against the Person Act 1861, particularly apt. (A husband had infected his wife with gonorrhoea in the course of consensual sexual relations, knowing that he suffered from the disease.) The judge had reflected:

> [S]uch considerations [i.e. the absence of any assault] lead one to pause on the threshold, and inquire whether the enactment ... could really have been intended to apply to circumstances so far removed from those which are usually understood when assault is spoken of [,]or ... matters involving ... the sexual act.

---

4 The reader will recall the clinical detachment shown by Lord Mustill in the case of the disappointed beneficiaries in Part 1 (10) (see pp. 5–6).

He, Lord Mustill, too was led "to pause at the threshold."

Having examined the case law in some detail, Lord Mustill concluded that the cases cited in argument and referred to in the judgments in the lower courts did nothing "to found a general theory of violence and consent", and certainly did nothing to help in resolving the issue in this particular case. He therefore concluded (as indeed had his colleagues) that the Law Lords were free to consider with entirely fresh eyes whether the public interest required that the conduct of the appellants fell within the ambit of section 47 (assault occasioning actual bodily harm) of the Offences against the Person Act 1861, and specifically where the harm was inflicted in private and took place "not only with the consent of the recipient but with his willing and glad co-operation", and solely for the purpose of mutual sexual gratification.

This he duly did. He emphasised that the issue was not whether the conduct in question was morally acceptable, but whether the appellants had been rightly charged under the Offences Against the Person Act 1861; and that in concluding (as he was about to do) that they had *not* been rightly charged, he was not pronouncing in favour of any libertarian doctrine or on the validity of ethical judgments. Crucially, one was here essentially concerned with private morality: "the standards by which they [fell] to be judged [were] not those of the criminal law." In Lord Mustill's view one proceeded from the premise that the state should interfere with the rights of an individual to live his or her life as he or she may choose "no more than [was] necessary to ensure a proper balance between the special interests of the individual and the general interests" of society at large. He concluded that there was no good reason to impress upon section 47 of the Offences Against the Person Act 1861 an interpretation "which penalises the relevant level of harm irrespective of consent", such as to include sadomasochistic activities among the special category of acts such as street brawling and prize fighting "which the law says shall not be done." It therefore followed, in his view, that "these consensual private acts [were not] offences against the existing law of violence."

Lord Slynn, the other dissentient, was keen to make the same point as Lord Mustill: "The determination of the appeal does not depend on bewilderment or revulsion or whether the right approach ... ought to be liberal or otherwise." He found nothing helpful in the existing case law other than an indication that consent was not a defence to the infliction of serious harm. In his view a clear, workable distinction could be drawn between actual and really serious bodily harm: consent could be a defence to the former and not to the latter. As the law stood, so concluded Lord Slynn, "adults can consent to acts done in private which do not result in serious bodily harm, so that [homosexual sadomasochistic practises] do not constitute criminal assaults for the purposes of the Act of 1861." He agreed with the written submission of the then Director of Public Prosecutions that at the end of the day it was a matter of policy, but only in the limited sense that it was a matter for Parliament to decide whether to legislate to make consensual sadomasochistic practises involving the infliction of actual bodily harm a criminal offence, and thus to declare it unlawful.

In truth it is quite apparent that the decision in this case was a policy decision with a vengeance. For the majority, these sadomasochistic activities involved not only violence and cruelty but the risk of serious injury: it was therefore not in the public interest to treat them as lawful. For the minority it was not the business of the criminal law to deal with homosexual sadomasochistic activities conducted in private and between consenting adults. A clear line had to be drawn. Thus in no sense was this remarkable case decided on purely legal principles. Its oddity can be gauged by the fact both the majority and the minority contemplated the possibility that Parliament might one day set aside time to pass legislation either (in the case of the majority) excluding sadomasochistic practises from the operation of the Offences Against the Person Act 1861, or (in the case of the minority) including them within the operation of the Act.[5]

(2) UPHOLDING A PRINCIPLE OR PRAGMATICALLY TURNING A BLIND EYE

For those interested in the recent controversy about the efficacy of super-injunctions and the like, the *Spycatcher* case,[6] although not concerned with salacious disclosures about celebrities, will certainly have some resonance. For present purposes it serves as a notable example of a spectacular clash of principles on an issue about which feelings clearly ran high. The factual background is a little complex.

---

5 This majority decision still represents the law. However, it is interesting to note that *The Times*, 23 January 2013, reported that a man who had whipped his girlfriend in the course of consensual sadomasochistic activity "inspired" by the erotic novel *Fifty Shades of Grey*, and who had been charged with assault occasioning actual bodily harm, was acquitted by a jury in the Ipswich Crown Court after only 15 minutes of deliberation.

6 *Attorney General v Guardian Newspapers Ltd (No. 1)* [1987] UKHL 13, [1987] 1 WLR 1248.

A former member of MI5, Peter Wright, retired to live in Tasmania, where he intended to write a book under the title *Spycatcher* which chronicled his experiences in the intelligence services and the alleged unlawful activities of some of his former colleagues. It could not of course have been published in the UK: the Official Secrets Act and the terms of Mr Wright's contract of employment would have made this impossible. However, Mr Wright succeeded in entering into an agreement with an Australian publisher for publication of the book in Australia. This galvanised the British Government into bringing an action for breach of confidence in the courts of New South Wales to stop its future publication. Prior to the start of the actual hearing two British newspapers published an outline of the allegations which they understood would be made by Mr Wright in those proceedings. The Government, in the shape of the Attorney-General, thereupon obtained an interim injunction[7] preventing those newspapers from publishing any further information which derived either directly or indirectly from that obtained by Mr Wright in his former capacity of a member of the security service. In the judge's view the public interest in protecting the proper functioning of the security services trumped the public interest in permitting the media to expose alleged wrongdoing within the ranks of those services.

Meanwhile, whilst all this was happening, arrangements were made for the publication and distribution of the book in the US, where its publication and sale could not be prevented. The book subsequently enjoyed large sales throughout the US, and received considerable publicity. Inevitably, copies were brought from the US into the UK. On the basis that there had been a significant change in circumstances since the interim injunction was originally granted, the two newspapers – joined by others with plans to publish the *Spycatcher* revelations – applied to the Vice-Chancellor for the injunction to be discharged. They argued that the relevant information was now in the public domain and therefore there was no longer any confidentiality worth protecting. The Government argued against its discharge mainly on two grounds. Firstly, there was an "arguable case"[8] that where information has been "impressed" with a duty of confidentiality, and someone acquired that information knowing this to be so, then such person himself would come under a duty not to further disclose it. Secondly, it was

7 i.e. pending a final hearing to determine whether the Government was entitled to a permanent injunction and/or other remedies.

8 To obtain an interim injunction it was essential for a party to show that it had an arguable case – i.e. a case which might succeed at the trial of the action.

in the public interest that persons in Mr Wright's position – i.e. those formerly employed in the security services but who have now retired or are contemplating retirement – should be deterred from following in his footsteps, and for whom the UK market would be by far the largest and most profitable market.

The application was heard by the Vice-Chancellor (Sir Nicholas Browne-Wilkinson, later Lord Browne-Wilkinson), who decided to discharge the injunction. Although he was impressed by the Government's "deterrence" argument, what was critical for the Vice-Chancellor was that it was in the public interest that the legal system and courts commanded public respect; and, in his view there was a limit to what could be achieved by orders of the court: " ... if the courts were to make orders manifestly incapable of achieving their avowed purpose, such as to prevent the dissemination of information which [has] already [been] disseminated, the law would be ... indeed an ass." The Government appealed. The Court of Appeal decided to reinstate the injunction, with the proviso that it should not prevent the publication of a summary in general terms of Mr Wright's allegations. The Court of Appeal was impressed with the arguments concerning potential damage to the morale and reputation of the security services, and the need to limit the extent to which Mr Wright could exploit his flagrant breach of trust for financial gain.

The newspapers duly appealed to the House of Lords. On their behalf it was argued first, that even assuming it was the case (as the Government maintained) that a party who acquired confidential information knowing that it had been communicated in breach of a duty to maintain confidentiality and secrecy, was under the same duty not to further disclose that information, then once the information became public knowledge that duty lapsed and ceased to be binding. Secondly, it was argued that the continuation of the injunction was futile because, as a result of *Spycatcher*'s publication in the US, the damage to the security services had already been done. In the event the Law Lords decided by a majority of three to two to continue the injunction.

The majority comprised Lords Brandon, Templeman and Ackner. Lord Brandon's analysis of the issue lacked nothing in coherence and conciseness. There was a clear public interest in maintaining the secrecy and effective functioning of the security services, to which the public interest in allowing the press the freedom to report allegations of wrongdoing must yield: this was indeed evident from the words of Article 10(2) of the

European Convention of Human Rights (the Convention).[9] Although damage had indeed already been done by the publication of *Spycatcher* in the US, there was a strongly arguable case that the confidence in the British security service placed by friendly foreign countries would be seriously impaired were the injunction lifted; that the prevention of Mr Wright from exploiting the UK market in terms of sales and publication rights would have a significant deterrent effect; and that the continuing of the injunction would mitigate any adverse impact on the morale and reputation of the security services. The proposition underpinning the Government's case that the newspapers were under the same duty not to disclose the information as was the case with Mr Wright, was, in Lord Brandon's view, a strongly arguable one; and since the present injunction was only temporary, and intended simply to hold the ring until the trial itself took place, the injustice to the Government would be greater to the Government were the injunction discharged than to that suffered by the newspapers were the injunction continued. (The reasoning and analysis of Lord Ackner was in substance identical.)

By contrast, Lord Templeman expressed himself in rather less temperate terms. He described Mr Wright's conduct as "treachery". It was indisputably the position that Mr Wright could not publish his memoirs as a former employee of the security services "without committing flagrant breaches of the duty of secrecy and confidentiality which he owed to the public in the national interest." He noted that both Mr Wright and the press maintained that his memoirs would be helpful in achieving much needed amendments to the Official Secrets Act and the enactment of freedom of information legislation, "[b]ut", he continued, "these objects [were] unlikely to be attained so long as the British press [was] prepared to publish confidential information without investigation or corroboration, and in disregard of orders of the court designed to preserve the Security Service from harm." There were existing channels through which Mr Wright could have raised any serious concerns about possible wrongdoing whilst he was still employed. Like Lord Brandon, and citing Article 10(2) of the Convention, he had no doubt that the public's "right to know" yielded to the public interest in preserving the secrecy and efficiency of the security services.

---

9 "The exercise of [the freedom of expression], since it carries duties and responsibilities, may be subject to such ... restrictions ... as are prescribed by law and are necessary ... in the interests of national security ... ".

Warming to his theme, Lord Templeman observed that so long as there were only odd copies of *Spycatcher* circulating in the UK:

> members of the Security Service [were] substantially free from harassment. But once mass circulation [took] place in newspapers, and particularly once *The Sunday Times* publishe[d] *Spycatcher* in serial form, then members of the Security Service will be liable to be harassed with accusations to which they [could] not respond.

In his view publication would:

> cause grievous harm to individuals and deal a blow to the morale of the Security Service. The British public will lose confidence. ... Our friends will be dismayed and our enemies will rejoice at the failure of the British to protect the Security Service from calumny reported in the British press.

Lord Templeman went on to reject the suggestion that the law would appear to be ridiculous if it imposed a restriction on mass circulation when any individual member of the public could obtain a copy of the book from abroad. "The court cannot exceed its territorial jurisdiction but the court can prevent the harm which will result from mass circulation within its own jurisdiction and can prevent Mr Wright and British newspapers profiting from [Mr Wright's] unlawful conduct." He went on to state that whilst it was true that the Attorney-General could obtain an order from the court requiring Mr Wright and the newspapers to account to him for any profits they may make from *Spycatcher*, the public interest did not lie in making profits "but in preventing profits being made in this country from treachery to this country." Unsurprisingly, Lord Templeman concluded that the continuance of the injunction was "necessary" in the public interest and within the meaning of Article 10(2) of the Convention.

The minority comprised Lords Bridge and Oliver. Lord Bridge made little effort to disguise the fact that he regarded the majority's reasoning, and much of Lord Templeman's rhetoric in particular, as complete nonsense. For him, the publication of *Spycatcher* in the US, and the Government's announcement that it would not attempt to prevent the book's importation into the UK was "the watershed" in the whole sorry saga. In his view "these two vital facts set the scene for the present controversy." He pointed out that it was conceded by the Government that if no case for a permanent injunction could be made out now, then it was pointless to keep in force the interim injunction: the case could not grow in strength between now and the trial. Once information was freely available to the public, "it [was] nonsensical to talk about preventing its 'disclosure'." He went on:

> The fact is that the intelligence and security services of any country in the world can buy the book … and read what is in it. The fact is that any citizen of this country can buy the book in America and bring it home with him, or order the book from America and receive a copy by post. Some enterprising small traders have apparently found it worth their while to import copies of the book and sell them by the roadside.

It was manifestly too late for the present injunction to serve the purpose of protecting the information in question. He continued, "[i]f the confidence of friendly countries in the ability of [the UK] to protect its secrets has been undermined by the publication of [the book] in the United States", the maintaining of the injunction would "do nothing to restore that confidence."

The key question, in Lord Bridge's view, was whether there was any remaining interest of national security which the injunction was capable of protecting, and if so what weight should be attached to it to justify the "massive encroachment on freedom of speech which the continuance of the ... injunction … necessarily involved." The only interest to which the Government could point was the importance of deterring other members of the intelligence and security services from following Mr Wright's example. Lord Bridge regarded the notion that a future Mr Wright, contemplating retirement or self-exile in the US with the intention of publishing his memoirs, would be deterred by the prospect of being prevented from access to the UK market as "wholly fanciful". The remedy for Mr Wright's breach of confidence lay in an action for an account of profits and not in "a futile injunction." The maintenance of the ban, as more and more copies of *Spycatcher* circulated throughout the country, would "seem more and more ridiculous." He regarded the attempt to "insulate the public in this country from information … freely available elsewhere" as a "significant step down [a] dangerous road", and predicted that if the Government persisted in maintaining the ban, it would face "inevitable condemnation and humiliation" by the European Court of Human Rights.

Lord Bridge's fellow dissenter, Lord Oliver, gently pointed to the absurdity of the situation were the injunction to remain in force, suggesting that a visitor to this country "carrying perhaps copies of *Spycatcher* and the *Washington Post* in his hand" would probably be surprised by what he saw. Whereas outside this country (including Scotland, Ireland and the Channel Islands) he and every other member of the public could read newspaper reports or comments on Mr Wright's memoirs, and hear and see such reports and comments on radio and television, "*ad nauseam*" if he so desired, yet in this country effectively the entire English press and other news media were prevented from reproducing or commenting on such material.

Like Lord Bridge, Lord Oliver was unimpressed by the deterrence argument. He thought that even if there was any substance in it, it was a misuse of the injunction as a remedy in the court's armoury to grant it on what he called the Admiral Byng principle – "*pour encourager les autres*" – in other words, "to impose an injunction on A in order to punish B and so as to provide an example to C." In his view it could not be right to:

> continue [an injunction] against parties in no way concerned with flouting the court's order … , and to interfere with their legitimate business of publishing and commenting upon matters already in the public domain for the purpose not of preventing that which can no longer be prevented, but of punishing Mr Wright and providing an example to others.

In Lord Oliver's view there could not "in practical terms" be any prospect of the Government ultimately succeeding in obtaining a permanent injunction, intended to prevent the use of information "which every other newspaper and the news media generally throughout the western hemisphere were free [to use and/or comment on]". Efforts to create "a sort of judicial *cordon sanitaire* against the infection from abroad of public discussion and comment" would not only prove ineffective, but would be a dangerous precedent.

It is quite apparent that the disagreement in this case (most clearly demonstrated in the respective judgments of Lord Bridge and Lord Templeman)[10] did not for a single moment have anything to do with complex points of law: it was common ground that there was an arguable case for treating the newspapers as being under the same duty of confidence as Mr Wright despite the publication of the book in the US – though, as far as Lords Bridge and Oliver were concerned, a barely arguable one; and likewise it was common ground that the newspapers could be liable to account for any profits. It had everything to do with differing perceptions of how best to deal with a bizarre and troublesome situation: Mr Wright had behaved badly, but the cat was long since out of the bag. The majority felt that nevertheless the Government should be given the opportunity to make its point and make things as difficult as possible for someone in Mr Wright's

---

10 The tendency of Lord Templeman to occupy the high moral ground was perhaps most noticeable in his well-known and ill-concealed hatred of tax avoidance schemes.

position, whereas the minority took the view that in doing so the Government would only succeed in making both it and the English legal system look ridiculous, as well as jeopardising our reputation for freedom of expression. The majority were unwilling to turn, what in their view was, a blind eye to wrongdoing; the minority regarded their own stance as one of sensible pragmatism.[11]

(3) POLICY OR LEGAL PRINCIPLE

One year before they heard the appeal in the *Spycatcher* case, the Law Lords had locked horns on another issue which had attracted the attention of the media, and which had also featured Lords Bridge, Brandon and Templeman – again aligned on different sides of the argument. As in the sadomasochism case, what divided the Law Lords was whether or not a specific course of conduct (in this case on the part of doctors) constituted a criminal offence or was otherwise "unlawful".[12] A mother of five daughters all under the age of 16 challenged the legality of a "memorandum of guidance" recently issued to area health authorities by the Department of Health and Social Security, which stated that in exceptional circumstances doctors could prescribe contraceptive treatment for underage girls without first consulting the parents. Two central planks of her case were: first, that it was a criminal offence for a man to have sexual intercourse with an underage girl irrespective of whether she had given her consent; and secondly, that section 8 of the Family Law Reform Act 1969 expressly enacted that "the consent of a minor who has attained the age of 16 years to any ... medical treatment, which in the absence of consent would constitute [an assault], shall be as effective as if he were a full adult." It was argued that therefore by implication a child *under* the age of 16 was unable to give effective consent. Additionally, she relied on a line of nineteenth-century cases culminating in

---

11 The case came on for trial a few months later. The injunction was discharged, but the *Sunday Times* was held liable to account for profits from the publication of a single extract from the book. The Government appealed against the discharge of the injunction; the appeal was dismissed by the Court of Appeal, and there was a further appeal to the House of Lords (differently constituted than before) which too was dismissed. Agreeing with the trial judge and the Court of Appeal, the Law Lords unanimously held that although a third party was bound by a duty of confidence when it knew the information it had acquired was confidential, it ceased to be so bound once that information had become freely available to the general public.

12 *Gillick v West Norfolk & Wisbech Area Health Authority* [1985] UKHL 7, [1986] AC 112.

a late-Victorian decision, in which the Court of Appeal upheld a father's right to prevent his 17-year-old daughter from communicating with her separated mother, and affirming the right of a parent to exercise control over a child in his custody until the child's 18th birthday.

In the first instance the action failed. The judge held that where the doctor exercised his clinical judgment in good faith, he would not render himself liable to criminal proceedings; and that a girl under the age of 16 was in fact capable of giving her effective consent to medical treatment. The mother successfully appealed. The Court of Appeal concluded that a girl under 16 was incapable of either consenting to medical treatment or prohibiting a doctor from seeking the consent of her parents; and that a doctor who treated a girl under 16 without the consent of a parent or guardian would (except in an emergency) be infringing the legally enforceable rights of the parents in regard to the control and upbringing of their children. The Department appealed to the House of Lords, which by a majority of three to two reversed the Court of Appeal. The majority comprised Lords Fraser, Scarman and Bridge; the minority, Lords Brandon and Templeman.

For Lord Scarman, as the guidance only contemplated the prescribing of contraceptive treatment for underage girls in exceptional circumstances, the question which he was required to answer was whether a doctor could in *any* circumstances lawfully prescribe contraception for a girl under 16 without the knowledge and consent of a parent. In his view neither the criminal law nor the statutory provision under which a minor who has attained the age of 16 is deemed capable of giving consent to medical treatment, helped in any way to answer the question. So far as the criminal law was concerned, he entirely agreed with the trial judge that what was critical was the doctor's intention: if the treatment was prescribed or administered with a view to maintaining or restoring the girl's health, no criminal offence has been committed; but if prescribed or administered with the intention of facilitating her having unlawful sexual intercourse, arguably an offence may have been committed. The guidelines necessarily assumed that the doctor would exercise his clinical judgment in good faith and in the interests of the patient. So far as the "effective consent" provision was concerned, this did not imply that a minor *under* the age of 16 was never capable of giving consent: as he, Lord Scarman, understood it, the provision had simply been inserted to remove any doubt as to the position.

In Lord Scarman's view the answer to the question he had posed lay in the search for principle as reflected in "judge-made case law", and against the backcloth of an ever-changing social scene.[13] It was clear that the nineteenth-century line of authority culminating in the "horrendous" decision affirming the right of a father to forbid his 17-year-old daughter any communication with her mother, had to be discarded: the cases reflected different attitudes and assumptions from those prevailing in contemporary society. Nowadays it was recognised that, certainly in sexual matters, young people mature earlier and are more knowledgeable than in previous generations. Crucially, parental rights were not to be treated as "sovereign" and beyond control. They were derived from parental duty and existed only so long as they were needed for the protection of the child and/its property: notably, the Guardianship of Infants Act 1971 made it clear that in any matter relating to the care and upbringing of a child, the welfare of the child was to be treated as "the paramount consideration." In Lord Scarman's view modern case law reinforced the underlying principle that "the parental right yields to the child's right to make his own decisions when he reaches a sufficient understanding and intelligence to be capable of making up his own mind on the matter requiring decision." He concluded, therefore, that "as a matter of law the parental right to determine whether or not [a minor below the age of 16] will have medical treatment terminates if and when the child achieves a sufficient understanding and intelligence to enable him or her to understand fully what is proposed." The position was no different where the medical treatment in question involved contraception or contraceptive advice.

Like Lord Scarman, Lord Fraser did not think that the "consent" provision in section 8 of the Family Reform Act 1969 supported the mother's case. He also shared his view and that of the trial judge that no criminal offence was committed where the doctor exercised his or her clinical judgment in good faith. He also shared Lord Scarman's analysis of the nineteenth-century case law, and of the nature of "parental rights". He argued that once one abandoned (as one must) the notion that parents were entitled to exercise absolute authority over minors in their custody, it was clear that the answer to the question posed by this case "could [not be] found by referring to rigid parental rights at any particular age [but in making] a judgment of what is best for the welfare of this particular child." The key consideration was the girl's ability to understand fully the advice or nature of the treatment in question.

---

13 Lord Scarman was sensitive to changing social trends. He was the very first chairman of the Law Commission, and become known to the wider public when he chaired the inquiry into the Brixton Riots.

Lord Bridge, for his part, questioned whether the guidance, having regard to its nature and purely advisory status, was actually susceptible to a legal challenge, and particularly so when it was "interwoven with questions of ethical and social controversy"; but on the assumption that it was, he agreed with the reasoning and conclusions of Lord Scarman and Lord Fraser.

The minority, Lords Brandon and Templeman, approached the matter from a wholly different perspective. Lord Brandon found it unnecessary to consider the nature and basis of parental rights. For him the issue was one of public policy, and the answer lay in what Parliament had already enacted: namely, the Criminal Law Amendment Act 1985 and the Sexual Offences Act 1956. In Lord Brandon's view "the inescapable inference from [this legislation] is that Parliament has for the past century regarded, and still regards today, sexual intercourse between a man and a girl under 16 as a serious criminal offence so far as the man who has such intercourse is concerned." Lord Brandon concluded that it necessarily followed that "for any person to promote, encourage or facilitate the commission of such an act may itself be a criminal offence, and must in any event be contrary to public policy." In his view the providing of contraceptive advice and treatment involved the promoting, encouraging or facilitating of such intercourse in that it served to remove the one critical inhibiting factor as far as the girl was concerned: namely, the risk of unwanted pregnancy. On his analysis of the issue, it followed that the question of whether or not parental consent to the treatment was required simply did not arise.

Lord Brandon's concluding shot across the bows of the majority was that it had been "open to Parliament in 1956 when the Sexual Offences Act ... was passed, and it ha[d] remained open to Parliament [ever since], to pass legislation providing for some lower age than 16 if it thought fit to do so ...". To hold that girls under the age of 16 can lawfully be provided with contraceptive facilities would, in his view, impermissibly undermine or circumvent the criminal law which Parliament had enacted. The guidance issued by the Department was therefore clearly contrary to public policy and therefore unlawful.

The starting point of Lord Templeman's analysis was rather different: in his view the issue in the case revolved around a consideration of "the independence of a teenager, the powers of a parent and the duties of a doctor." As section 6 of the Sexual Offences Act 1956 made it an offence for a man to have sexual intercourse with a girl under the age of 16, consent not being a defence, Parliament had indicated that a girl under 16 was not mature enough to decide for herself whether to engage in sexual intercourse;

and it followed that as the law presently stood, a girl under the age of 16 was not competent to decide for herself whether to practise sex or contraception.

The legislation was intended to protect the girl from sexual intercourse. But where it was apparent that a girl will not be deterred, and that her sexual activities were uncontrollable, section 6 of the Sexual Offences Act 1956, did *not*, in Lord Templeman's view, prevent a parent or doctor from deciding that contraceptive facilities should be made available; where the doctor and the parent were in agreement, there was no legal bar to such treatment.

So what did Lord Templeman consider to be the position where such agreement was unlikely and where conflict between the views of the doctor and parent was to be assumed? A parent was the natural and legal guardian of a minor and responsible for his or her upbringing. Parental power had to be exercised in the best interests of the child, and the courts could intervene at the request of a third party, but usually the courts would uphold the right of the parent to decide matters which the child was not competent to decide. A doctor was under a duty to act in the best interests of his patient, and it was of course recognised that there were situations in which the advice and judgment of the doctor could override the objection or assumed objection of the parent. But this was not such a situation. "There are many things which a girl under 16 needs to practise", Lord Templeman drily observed, "but sex is not one of them." He therefore concluded that the parent's knowledge and consent was essential. Furthermore, he pointed out that there were practical objections to the statement contained in the Department's guidance that the "decision whether or not to prescribe contraception must be for the clinical judgment of a doctor." Without the input of the parent, the doctor would not be able to get the full picture: he would only know what the girl chose to tell him, and sooner or later the parent will discover the truth, and may do so in circumstances like to rupture good relationships between members of the family.

In many ways this was a remarkable case. The only common ground of any significance shared by all the Law Lords was the frank recognition that what they were being called on to decide was a question of public policy rather than a pure point of law. For Lord Brandon the key consideration (indeed the only consideration) was the fact that it was a criminal offence for a man to have intercourse with an underage girl: the fact that the intention behind the Department's guidance was to assist doctors and other professionals in preventing physical and/or psychological harm resulting from unwanted pregnancies, simply did not enter into the equation. For Lord Templeman the key consideration was the lack of competence of an underage girl to decide these matters for herself, and the right of the parent to make such decisions in the girl's best interests in those circumstances. For Lords Scarman, Fraser and Bridge the key consideration was the underage girl's capacity to understand what was being proposed and why. For them the criminal legislation was a virtual irrelevance: what was relevant was the exercise of a doctor's clinical judgment made in good faith.

(4) CONSTITUTIONAL NICETIES AND A MATTER OF CONSCIENCE

The strength of feeling, and the liberal use of emotive language, which characterised the judgments of Lord Bridge and Lord Templeman in the *Spycatcher* case can fairly be said to be unusual. But some 20 years later it was displayed by a later generation of Law Lords, several of whom have already featured in a number of the cases discussed above, such as Lords Bingham, Nicholls, Steyn, Hoffmann, Hope, Scott, Rodger and Walker. The forum for this illustration of "colliding principles" was the Privy Council, rather than the House of Lords Appellate Committee.[14] In fact it was a nine-member panel – the ninth member being a former appeal judge from Jamaica, whose "vote" proved decisive. The case concerned the constitutionality of the mandatory death penalty under the laws of Trinidad and Tobago.[15]

The Trinidad and Tobago Offences Against the Person Act imposed a mandatory death penalty for murder. The Constitution of Trinidad and Tobago, enacted in 1976, provided that it – the Constitution – shall be the supreme law of the country, "and that any other law shall be void to the extent of the inconsistency." It also proclaimed the "right of the individual to life" and provided that Parliament may not "impose or authorise the imposition of cruel and unusual treatment or punishment." (It was accepted on all sides that the mandatory death penalty was indeed a "cruel and unusual punishment or treatment" in that it failed to allow for individual consideration in the sentencing of a convicted offender.) Critically, however, the Constitution in section 6(1) also provided that "nothing in [those above-mentioned provisions] shall invalidate an existing law or repeal and re-enact

14 The Privy Council hears appeals from certain Commonwealth countries.

15 *Matthew v The State (Trinidad and Tobago)* [2004] UKPC 33, [2005] 1 AC 433. The appeal was heard at the same time as one from Barbados, and with the same issue and of course the same result.

an existing law without alteration": the law imposing the mandatory death penalty was an existing law at the relevant time, having replaced a previous enactment in 1925. It was argued on behalf of the appellant, who had been convicted of murder and sentenced to death, that in fact the Act bringing the Constitution into force (and to which the Constitution was annexed in a Schedule) itself required the existing law so far as possible to be modified in order to conform with those constitutional provisions. (Section 5 of the Act stated that "existing laws shall be construed with such modifications ... as may be necessary to bring them into conformity with this Act.") The phrase "nothing shall invalidate ..." in section 6(1) of the Constitution was to be contrasted with the previous 1962 version: "... shall not apply." It meant that the provisions can indeed apply to existing laws but with appropriate modifications and changes: only their wholesale invalidation was excluded. The legislation was to be interpreted and applied in such a way as to conform, rather than conflict with, international human rights treaties to which the state of Trinidad and Tobago had subscribed. Accordingly the death penalty was to be treated as discretionary and not mandatory. By a majority of 5 to 4 the Privy Council rejected this argument, thereby departing from a previous, albeit recent, decision of the Council.[16]

The majority comprised Lords Hoffmann, Hope, Scott, Rodger and the former Chief Justice of the Supreme Court of Jamaica, Mr Justice Zacca. A single opinion was delivered on their behalf by Lord Hoffmann. He did not mince his words. They – the majority – regarded the argument as "completely untenable [and] incompatible with the status of the Constitution as the supreme law of Trinidad and Tobago, and arbitrary to the point of absurdity in its results." He added, perhaps somewhat lamely, that they naturally respected the views of the minority "who see more merit ... in the argument", but tartly pointed out that since they had not addressed the objections which the majority found insuperable, they – the majority – remained unpersuaded.

In the majority's view the meaning of the words "that nothing shall invalidate ..." in section 6(1) was so clear and unambiguous that they were bound as a court of law to give effect to it irrespective of their own views about the morality and efficacy of the death penalty. When section 6(1) declared that nothing in the "right to life" and "cruel and unusual

---

16 The panel on the previous occasion comprised Lords Bingham, Steyn, Millett, Rodger and Walker, and was also a majority decision. The death sentence was in fact commuted to one of life imprisonment, to enable the appellant to have the benefit of the previous decision.

punishment" provisions "shall invalidate an existing law", it precisely mirrored the effect which those provisions would otherwise have. In the majority's view there was no significance whatsoever in the change of expression from "shall not apply" to "shall not invalidate"; and if the Constitution itself showed a plain intention to preserve existing laws, it was frankly impossible to accept that the Trinidad and Tobago Parliament, by enacting section 5(1) of the 1976 Act could "have created a mechanism outside the Constitution for undermining the effect of its provisions." The irrationality of the argument was demonstrated by the fact that whether or not an existing law (which *ex hypothesi* was inconsistent with the relevant provisions) survived by virtue of section 6(1), depended on its form rather than its substance.

The minority, Lords Bingham, Nicholls, Steyn and Walker, delivered a joint opinion, in which the guiding hand of Lord Bingham was clearly discernible. The opening paragraph set the tone. The minority observed that the Privy Council has in recent years:

> ... brought a broader vision to its task of constitutional adjudication, recognising that a legalistic and over-literal approach may be quite inappropriate when seeking to give effect to the rights, values and standards expressed in a constitution as these evolve over time ... It is such an approach which, in our opinion, vitiates the reasoning of the decision of the majority in this appeal. We consider the decision ... to be unsound in law and productive of grave injustice to a small but important class of people in Trinidad and Tobago. It is clear in our opinion that the interpretation of the 1976 Constitution of Trinidad and Tobago which commends itself to the majority does not ensure the protection of fundamental human rights and freedoms, degrades the dignity of the human person and does not respect the rule of law.

It is unlikely that one can find a stronger condemnation of a decision (majority or unanimous) in the modern law reports. Indeed the minority did not leave it at that. They went on to underline the point that, surprisingly, the State of Trinidad and Tobago had striven to uphold a right to subject its citizens to what it acknowledged and accepted to be a cruel and unusual punishment, and the majority of the Privy Council had now held that this is what indeed it was entitled to do.

Central to the minority's view of the matter was that the interpretation of a constitution did not necessarily involve the same exercise as the interpretation of an ordinary statute. Effect had to be given to its spirit. Significance in this case was to be attached to the principles upon which the new republic was to be founded as set out in the preamble of the

Constitution, including "faith in fundamental human rights and freedoms." And so on the key issue in this case as to the meaning of "shall not invalidate" in section 6 (1) it was right to attach significance to the change in wording from "shall not apply". The change could not have been made simply for no reason, and therefore one must assume that some change of meaning must have been intended. Both the dictionary meanings and the meaning in the context of the Constitution were directed, in the view of the minority, to *total* invalidity, and therefore the modification process required in section 5 of the 1976 Act came into play. In their view "there was nothing strange in requiring a court to interpret an existing law with such modifications ... as may be necessary to bring it into conformity with a human rights instrument, but prohibiting it from annulling that law."

One member of the minority, Lord Nicholls, felt so strongly about the consequences of the stance taken by the majority that he felt constrained to deliver a short supplemental opinion of his own. He did not believe that the framers of the Constitution under appeal ever intended the provision preserving existing laws should operate so as to deprive the country's citizens of the protection afforded by rising standards set by human rights values. The provision was intended to smooth a period of transition, not to freeze standards forever. Lord Nicholls went on, "[s]elf-evidently an interpretation of the constitution which produce[d] such outcome [was] unacceptable. A Supreme Court of a country which adopt[ed] such a literal approach [was] failing in its responsibilities ...", and was failing to carry out is proper role as guardian of the constitution.

Of course the constitutionality of capital punishment, and in particular that of a mandatory death sentence, is always calculated to arouse strong feelings, but in this instance the strength of feeling was reinforced by the nature of the disagreement .The majority were unwilling to look at the big picture and to interpret the critical provisions with something rather less than rigorous orthodoxy: to do so, in their view, would be a breach of duty owed to the commonwealth countries for whom the Privy Council was the court of last resort. For the minority, context made all the difference. Their solution to the problem was not without difficulties, but a strained and somewhat tortuous interpretation of the words "shall not invalidate" was perfectly acceptable in the circumstances. It was a proper function of the court of last resort to ensure that the constitution evolved in accordance with changing values and that the citizens of Trinidad and Tobago benefitted from its declared aspirations.

(5) TAKING LIBERTIES WITH THE WILL OF PARLIAMENT

In a rather less dramatic context, the same contrast in approach which characterised the conflict of views in the Trinidad case re-surfaced some seven years later in the Supreme Court.[17] Parliament, in 2000, implemented the recommendations of the Neill report on the funding of political parties[18] by passing the Political Parties, Elections and Referendums Act 2000, the main purpose of which was to exclude donations from foreign donors with no stake in the life of the UK. The Act prohibits the acceptance by political parties of any donation from anyone who is not a "permissible donor": that is, in the case of an individual, a person who is registered on the electoral register at the time the donation is made; and in the case of a company, a company incorporated in the UK under the Companies Act. The Political Parties, Elections and Referendums Act 2000 required a party, on receiving a donation, to take reasonable steps to verify the identity of the donor and to verify that he was in fact a "permissible donor"; and if it transpired that he was not, the party was required to return the donation within 30 days. If it failed to do so, the Electoral Commission could apply to the court for a forfeiture order under section 58(2) of the Act, which provided that "the court ... may order the forfeiture by the party of an amount equal to the value of the donation."

The facts of this case were that the United Kingdom Independent Party (UKIP) accepted some 691 donations over a period of time from one of its members, a Mr Bown, totalling £349,216. He was the main source of the party's funding. Unbeknown to the party, Mr Bown was not on any electoral register at the time, though neither he nor the party were aware that this was the case, and there was no reason why he should not have been on the register. No checks had been carried out by the party, and the donations were never returned once the party had become aware of the position. The Electoral Commission applied pursuant to section 58(2) to the Westminster Magistrates Court for a forfeiture order in the sum of £349,216. The district judge ordered the forfeiture of the sum of just £14,481, representing the value of some seven donations which the party had accepted after having become aware that he was not on the electoral register. In making the order he did, the district judge took into account that the purpose of the Act was to

---

17 *R (Electoral Commission) v City of Westminster Magistrates Court & Anor* [2010] UKSC 40, [2011] 1 AC 496.

18 The Fifth Report of the Committee on Standards in Public Life, chaired by Lord Neill of Bladen, on "The Funding of Political Parties in the United Kingdom".

ban foreign donations to political parties, and the fact that the donations had been made by someone who was entitled to be registered on the electoral register. The Electoral Commission challenged the propriety of the making of such an order on the ground that it was an improper exercise of the judge's discretion under section 58(2). The Court of Appeal concluded that the sub-section conferred a narrow discretion; there was a strong presumption in favour of forfeiture which could only be displaced by exceptional circumstances; and that an order for forfeiture, if made, could only be made in the full amount. UKIP appealed against this ruling to the Supreme Court.

It was clear that there were two, albeit interconnected, issues for the Supreme Court to resolve: one, the breadth of the discretion conferred on the court in regard to the making of a forfeiture order; and two, whether it was open to the court to order the forfeiture of a lesser sum than an amount equal to the full value of the donation. In the event the Supreme Court was divided on both issues, and by a majority of four to three it reversed the decision of the Court of Appeal and upheld the original order of the district judge. The majority comprised Lord Phillips, the then President of the Court, and Lords Mance, Kerr and Clarke.

For Lord Phillips the background to the legislation was all-important in the resolving of both issues. He noted that the primary object of the legislation was to prevent donations to political parties from foreign sources; and that whilst the Neill report had recommended that *eligibility* for inclusion on the electoral register would be sufficient to qualify as a permissible donor, the Act required actual inclusion on the register, but did so for purely pragmatic reasons: namely, "it was easier to demonstrate that a person is not on an electoral register than it is to demonstrate that he is not entitled to be placed on an electoral register." Furthermore, it was clear that Parliament did not intend that entitlement to vote was of itself an essential quality in a donor: under the Act, companies and other corporate bodies could be donors provided they had a sufficient presence within the United Kingdom; and the Act also permitted bequests from a person who had been on the electoral register at any time five years before his death.

In Lord Phillips's view, it was clear that Parliament intended, by making the power to order forfeiture discretionary, that the magistrates court should discriminate between cases where forfeiture was warranted and cases where it was not, and to consider whether forfeiture was a proportionate response to the particular facts of the case; specifically, the court had to consider whether forfeiture was necessary to prevent retention of a donation from a foreign source, and what kind of sanction was appropriate in the light of the shortcomings which led to the acceptance of the impermissible donation. The fact that a donor was eligible for inclusion on the electoral register was clearly a relevant circumstance, and rebutted the presumption of a foreign donation. Lord Phillips did not accept that "almost automatic forfeiture of the totality of an impermissible donation [was] necessary as a realistic sanction against non-compliance with the requirements of the Act". In his view, in a case where the donor was shown not to be foreign, Parliament must have intended, by conferring a discretion on the court, that there should be a careful evaluation of all the circumstances before such a draconian step as ordering forfeiture of the full amount was taken.

Like Lord Phillips, Lord Mance concluded that the forfeiture provision in the Political Parties, Elections and Referendums Act 2000 was an open discretion, broad enough to be capable of distinguishing "between foreign donations [which the purpose of the legislation was to ban] and donations made irregularly by a person who was entitled to be on a United Kingdom register, but by mistake was not." In his view the conclusion that the discretion was broad and that "partial" forfeiture was possible, was more consistent with the policy of the legislation than that reached by the Court of Appeal and the three dissenting Justices. Although Parliament had departed from the Neill Committee's recommendation that the test should be entitlement to register, preferring the simpler test of actual registration for pragmatic reasons, "the underlying aim of the legislation remained to eliminate inappropriate 'foreign' donations."

Like Lord Phillips and Lord Mance, Lord Kerr regarded the background to the legislation as the key factor in resolving the issues: "The central purpose of the legislation was to prohibit donations from those who did not have a stake in this country ... [following on] the Government's commitment in its manifesto to ban foreign donors." In his view it could never have been intended that forfeiture could be ordered where the donor was someone entitled to be on the electoral register, but who, because of an administrative error, was not; nor could it have been intended that the draconian penalty of the full amount of the donation was to be imposed irrespective of the circumstances.

The minority (Lords Rodger, Walker[19] and Brown) saw things very differently. Thus Lord Rodger, "[n]othing could be clearer than the language used by Parliament, and nothing could be clearer than the intention behind

---

19 Lord Walker expressed his agreement with the judgments of Lords Rodger and Brown.

the language", namely, political parties were not to accept donations from any individual who was not registered on an electoral register, and that necessarily meant that parties were not to accept donations from individuals who were entitled to be registered but who actually were not on the register. The latter situation could be simply remedied by the individual concerned getting himself registered: the party could then accept the donation.

In Lord Rodger's view the analysis of the majority involved the substituting of the ultimate aim of the legislation (the banning of foreign donations) for the means by which the legislation sought to achieve that aim. Parliament had chosen to pursue that aim by prohibiting donations from all but a narrowly defined class of permissible donors. In his view it was axiomatic that where a party had accepted a donation which they were prohibited from accepting and appeared unwilling to return it in defiance of the law, the court must make an order for forfeiture for the whole value of the unlawful donation; and indeed that was exactly what section 58(2) expressly said. He noted that the Government White Paper, which outlined and explained the proposed legislation, had explained why there were good practical reasons for the registration (as opposed to the eligibility) test for a permissible donor, and in those circumstances it was not open to the court "to second-guess Parliament and to proceed on the footing that some impermissible donors are less impermissible than others". There was no hint in the legislation that Parliament intended anything else. Had it in fact been the intention to give the court the power to order the forfeiture of a less amount than the value of the donation, it would have been simple enough to express that intention.

Lord Brown, making the same point, quoted from the Government White Paper:

> Checking that a particular donor appears on the electoral register offers a test that is both conclusive and simple to administer. It would be far less straightforward for political parties to verify that a donor not appearing on the register was nevertheless entitled to do so. It [was] in the interests of the parties to have … a test which offer[ed] certainty as to the eligibility of a donor.

For Lord Brown, it was clear what scheme the legislation was intended to operate, and there was simply no room for the exercise of any discretion by the court once it had been shown that an impermissible donation had been accepted and retained, except arguably where the non-compliance was purely technical, such as in a case where the donation been returned, but out of time – i.e. not within the prescribed 30-day period. However, the presumption of forfeiture simply could not be rebutted by showing that the donor was eligible to be on the register; and the contention that the court could in its discretion order a lesser sum than the full amount of the impermissible donation was an "impossible" one. Where, as in this instance, "the draftsman had explicitly chosen the words 'an amount equal to the value of the donation' it could hardly be thought he intended them to mean an amount 'up to' that value or an amount 'not exceeding' that value …".

This was in a sense a rather curious case. Undoubtedly the court had some kind of discretion under the sub-section: the words, after all, were "the court *may* … order the forfeiture …". The sharp division of opinion centred on the breadth of that discretion. Was it limited to the exceptional circumstance of the kind referred to by Lord Brown, or was it broad enough to embrace the circumstances of this case? The majority evidently felt that the imposition of a "full amount" penalty so grossly disproportionate to the offence that such an outcome could not be properly reconciled with the presumed intention of the legislation. The minority, for their part, regarded such an approach as virtually tantamount to playing fast and loose with the will of Parliament as expressed in the plain language of the relevant provisions of the Political Parties, Elections and Referendums Act 2000. Thus both sides relied on what they regarded as the presumed intention of Parliament, and came to different conclusions. This is by no means unusual. Quite recently the Supreme Court divided four to three on the question whether Parliament, when enacting the legislation which provided for the bringing of claims for unfair dismissal in employment tribunals, intended the compensation awarded by the tribunals to be the only remedy available to the dismissed employee, or whether it was open to the employee to bring an action for damages for breach of contract against the employer in the ordinary civil courts.[20] Needless to say, the tendency is to attribute to Parliament the intention which appears to make the most sense, and unsurprisingly it is often the case that agreement cannot be achieved as to what that should be.

---

20 *Edwards v Chesterfield Royal Hospital NHS Foundation Trust* [2011] UKSC 58, [2012] 2 AC 22. The seventh member of the court preferred to decide the case on an altogether different basis.

PART THREE

PROBLEMS WITH THE MEANING OF ORDINARY WORDS

Although concerned with a question of the interpretation of words in a constitution and a statute, the issue in the Trinidad case was only in a limited sense concerned with the meaning of words. In reality it involved something of a theological dispute as to *how* the exercise in interpretation in a particular context should be approached. Yet research would probably show that the most frequent catalyst for disagreement amongst the Law Lords and their successors, the Supreme Court Justices, would probably turn out to be disagreement as to the meaning or scope of ordinary words: or, to be more specific, as to whether the words in question can apply, or are capable of applying, to particular circumstances. This is not really surprising: the disagreement in such cases is really about what the words *ought* to mean or to what they *ought* to apply. The point was frankly made by Lord Neuberger, now President of the Supreme Court, in a case which will be discussed below:

> Any reasoned decision as to the meaning of [the relevant statutory provision] risks falling foul of circularity, preconception and arbitrariness. The centrally relevant words "functions of a public nature" are so imprecise in their meaning that one searches for a policy as an aid to interpretation. The identification of the policy is almost inevitably governed ... by one's notion of what the policy should be, and the policy so identified is then used to justify one's conclusion.[1]

The cases discussed below illustrate the truth of this observation.

1 *YL v Birmingham City Council & Ors* [2007] UKHL 27, [2008] 1 AC 95, at 142.

(1) SUPPORT FOR THE OLD AND INFIRM: THE DUTY OF COUNCILS

Two cases concerned with the scope of duties of local authorities derived from powers acquired under that great flagship of the post-war Labour Government, the National Assistance Act 1948, illustrate the nature of the problems often posed by the use of ordinary words, and the manner in which those problems tend to be resolved.

In the first case a Mr Barry, who was aged 84 and who suffered from a heart condition, was provided with assistance by his local council pursuant to its responsibilities under the Chronically Sick and Disabled Persons Act 1970.[2] That assistance included cleaning and laundry services. About a year later he was notified by the council that the cleaning and laundry services would be withdrawn. He was told that the reason for this was that there had been a substantial reduction in the funding allocated to the council by central government, and it was no longer possible for the council to meet the demand. Mr Barry applied to the courts for a ruling that the council was not entitled to withdraw those services. Based on the wording of the relevant provision of the 1970 Act (section 2(1)), it was argued on his behalf that the council had been under a duty to make the appropriate arrangements in the light of its previous assessment of his needs. The crucial wording of the relevant provision was as follows:

> Where a local authority ... is satisfied ... that it is necessary in order to meet the needs of [a person eligible for assistance] for that authority to make arrangements for the provision of:
>
> (a) practical assistance for that person in his home [and in respect of other matters listed (b) to (h)], ... it shall be the duty of that authority to make those arrangements in exercise of their functions under [the National Assistance Act].

The key words on which the argument hinged were of course "needs", "necessary" and "duty". Mr Barry's application failed at the initial stage, the court holding that the council was entitled to take into account its resources in its assessment of needs; but the Court of Appeal, by a majority decision, concluded otherwise. The council appealed, and the Law Lords, by a majority of three to two, reversed the decision of the Court of Appeal and ruled in favour of the council.

---

2 *R (Barry) v Gloucestershire CC & Anor* [1997] UKHL 58, [1997] AC 584.

The majority comprised Lords Nicholls, Hoffmann and Clyde. (Lord Hoffmann simply agreed with both his colleagues without delivering a judgment of his own.) Lord Nicholls acknowledged Mr Barry's argument at first sight to be a "compelling" one. His needs depended on the nature and extent of his disability; not on whether the council had more or less money currently available. *His* needs had not changed, even if the council's financial resources had; but Lord Nicholls concluded that this argument was flawed because it failed "to recognise that needs for services cannot sensibly be assessed without having some regard to the cost of providing them. A person's need for a particular type or level of service cannot be decided in a vacuum from which all considerations of cost have been expelled."

Lord Nicholls goes on to develop the point in the context of the services such as home help, meals on wheels and home adaptation listed under (a) to (h) in the relevant provision. An assessment of the extent of a "need" for any of those services by the council's social services committee must depend on the application of its eligibility criteria, and in carrying out its task the council must have regard to the cost of providing a particular service, "[t]he relative cost will be balanced against the relative benefit and the relative need for that benefit". Once it is accepted, Lord Nicholls concluded, that cost is a relevant factor in assessing a person's needs in regard to any of the listed services, some evaluation of the impact the cost is likely to have on the council will have to be made. He rejected the suggestion that such a conclusion would deprive the words "it shall be the duty of the [council] to make those arrangements ..." of any value or force. The council was obliged to carry out its function in a rational and responsible fashion.

Lord Clyde's analysis was essentially the same, but he made the point in a slightly different way. He emphasised that the "duty" only arose if or when the council was "satisfied" that it was "necessary" to make the appropriate arrangements to meet the eligible person's "needs". If, or once, that duty did arise, then he would agree that shortage of resources would not excuse a failure to make the arrangements, but the crucial point was that this did not preclude consideration of resources at the earlier stage of the process envisaged by the Chronically Sick and Disabled Persons Act 1970 when the assessment had to be carried out. The words "necessary" and "needs" were both relative expressions, "admitting in each case a considerable range of meaning." There was, for example, no clear distinction between what was necessary and what was desirable. Everything depended on the criteria set by the council. Cost and resources would always be an element in determining whether a service was "necessary".

Lord Lloyd, with whom Lord Steyn agreed, roundly rejected the majority's analysis. He pointed out that the relevant provision – section 2(1) – contemplated three separate stages. First, the council had to assess the needs of the eligible person. Second, having identified those needs, the council had to decide whether it was necessary to make arrangements for those needs to be met. (There could be any number of reasons why it might not be necessary to make such arrangements, e.g. the person may have adequate means of his own or his needs were being met by family and friends.) Finally, if the council decided that it was indeed necessary to make arrangements for those needs to be met, the council was under a duty to do so. It was clear that once the council had so decided, the duty was absolute and could not be evaded by pointing to lack of money.

For Lord Lloyd, as indeed was the case for Lord Clyde, it followed that the real question was whether lack of financial resources was a relevant consideration when assessing the needs of the person. He recognised that the word "need" had different shades of meaning; for example, one might say of an overworked colleague that he was in "need" of a holiday, but that was clearly not the sense in which the word was to be understood in the present context: "need" in this context was intended to mean the lack of what is essential for the ordinary business of living. What a disabled person needs would in the simple case be decided by the individual social worker, and in the more complex case there may have to be a so-called comprehensive assessment. In either case the standard against which the social worker assesses the person's needs are those set by the council's social services committee, and reflect the standards and views of contemporary society. Lack, or otherwise, of resources simply did not enter into the equation. Resources could of course operate to impose a cash limit on what is provided, but they could not help to measure the need.

Lord Lloyd goes on to illustrate the point by way of a simple example. Suppose there are two people living in different parts of the country with identical disabilities and needs. Council A provides for his needs by arranging meals on wheels four days a week. Council B declines to provide the same service because they say they do not have the money: it cannot be open to them to say that they are going to reduce the person's needs. His needs remain exactly the same, "[e]very child needs a new pair of shoes from time to time. The need is not the less because his parents cannot afford them." Lord Lloyd was perfectly happy to read into the word "needs" in section 2(1) the concept of "*reasonable* needs"; but what he could not accept was that the reasonable needs of the individual required consideration of the council's ability to meet those needs. There was nothing, he concluded, in the language of the relevant provision which permitted or even suggested that external resources were to be taken into account. There was no halfway house.

It would be naive to suppose that in this case the Law Lords fell out over what was simply a problem of language. The majority thinking was that it was essential to feed into the concepts of "need" and "necessary" a balancing consideration of cost in order to make the legislation workable, and in order to ensure that local authorities functioned on a rational and responsible basis. For the minority, it was nothing of the kind. There was no case for diluting the ordinary and natural meaning of "needs" and "necessary" in the context of the relevant provision: problems of funding were simply something to be worked out by the council or by the council in tandem with central government. The nature of the council's statutory social welfare obligations should not depend on the state of its finances.[3]

The second case concerns the responsibility of local authorities in the provision of residential care for those unable to care for themselves.[4] The claimant was an 84-year-old lady suffering from Alzheimer's who was placed by Birmingham City Council in a privately run residential care home pursuant to its "contracting out" powers under the National Assistance Act 1948 (in its amended form). Except for a small top-up fee paid by the claimant's family, this arrangement was publicly funded. (Eighty per cent of the residents in the home were similarly funded by local authorities.) Friction developed between the family and those running the home, as a result of which the care home company gave notice of its intention to terminate the arrangement. An action was brought on the claimant's behalf against both the City Council and the care home company alleging that the termination would be unlawful on the grounds that it would breach certain provisions, including the right to a private and family life, of the European Convention for the Protection of Human Rights. The Human Rights Act 1998 provides that it is "unlawful for a public authority to act in a way which is incompatible with a Convention right ...". The Act goes on to

---

3 Although regarded as highly controversial at the time (1997), this majority decision has so far survived unscathed, and represents the existing law as to the relevance or otherwise of financial resources in this area. However, in a recent case in which the Supreme Court applied the decision, Baroness Hale, "confessed" to finding "the reasoning of the minority much more convincing, both as a matter of statutory construction and as a matter of everyday life, than the reasoning of the majority": *R (McDonald) v Royal Borough of Kensington and Chelsea* [2011] UKSC 33, [2011] PTSR 1266, at 1292.

4 *YL v Birmingham City Council and Others* [2007] UKHL 27, [2008] 1 AC 95.

define a "public authority" for these purposes as including "any person[5] certain of whose functions are functions of a public nature", and the nature of the particular act is not a private one. (This extended meaning recognised the fact that an ever increasing number of governmental functions were being contracted out to commercial organisations, e.g. the prison service.)

The case therefore hinged on whether the care home, by virtue of its contract with Birmingham City Council, was carrying out in relation to the claimant "functions of a public nature." Previously the Law Lords had declared that there was "no single test of universal application" but that factors such as whether the body in question was publicly funded or exercising statutory powers or providing a public service were all relevant: in the case with which they were concerned they rejected the proposition that a parochial parish council, in seeking to impose on certain landowners liability for the repair of a parish church, was performing a "function of a public nature."

Both the court which initially ruled on the issue, and the Court of Appeal, decided that the care home company was not exercising a public function within the meaning of the Human Rights Act 1998, and that therefore Convention rights could not be relied upon by residents in respect of its operations. An appeal was launched against this decision, with the Government (through the Secretary of State for Constitutional Affairs, no less) intervening in support of the claimant. The appeal was heard by Lord Bingham, Lord Scott, Baroness Hale, Lord Mance and Lord Neuberger, who by a majority of three to two upheld the decision of the "first instance" court and the Court of Appeal. The majority comprised Lords Scott, Mance and Neuberger.

Lord Scott summarised his reasons for concluding that the care home company did not carry out functions of a public nature in the following manner. The company carried on a "socially useful" business for profit: it was neither a charity nor a philanthropist. It entered into private contracts with its residents or with the local authorities with whom it did business. It received no public funding nor enjoyed any special statutory powers.

In his view it was a misuse of language to describe the company as publicly funded just because the majority of residents were placed in the home by local authorities: there was no element whatever of any subsidy from public

---

5 The expression "person" in this context means, of course, a legal person or entity such as a corporate body.

funds. He cited the example of cleaning and catering contractors to illustrate his point:

> If an outside private contractor is engaged on ordinary commercial terms to provide the cleaning ... or catering services at a local authority owned care home, it seems to me absurd to suggest that the private contractor, in earning its fee for its business services, is publicly funded or is carrying on a function of a public nature. It is simply carrying on its private business with a customer who happens to be a public authority.

A care home company taking local authority funded residents was in no different position, he concluded.

In terms of the running and management of care homes, there was, Lord Scott pointed out, a clear distinction between a private and a local authority owned care home. The duties and liabilities of the former were governed by private law and the latter by public and statute law, even if the management and control in the running of the home were essentially the same in both cases. For the purposes of the Human Rights Act 1998, he concluded, the nature and functions of a private care home were no different from that of a privately owned school or hospital.

For Lord Mance, his focus was apparent from the way he chose to pose the question raised by the case: "Does a privately owned, profit earning care home providing care and accommodation for a publicly funded resident, have 'functions of a public nature'?" For his part, he drew what he thought was a clear distinction between a local authority with a statutory duty to arrange care and accommodation, and a private company providing services with which the local authority contracts on a commercial basis in order to fulfil its duty to arrange care and accommodation. He did not regard "the actual *provision*, as opposed to the *arrangement*, of care and accommodation for those unable to arrange it for themselves as an inherently governmental function" [emphasis added]. In providing care and accommodation the care home company simply acted as a private, profit-earning company. He agreed with the reasoning, analysis and conclusions of Lord Scott.

Lord Neuberger agreed. It will be recalled that his point about the impreciseness of the expression "functions of a public nature" and the search for a policy which could throw light on its meaning was previously referred to at the beginning of this section on the problems with the meaning of ordinary words.[6] Furthermore, he recognised the question of whether the extended definition applied might often turn on a number of factors, the weight to be accorded to each factor being "inevitably a somewhat subjective decision." Nevertheless he had no difficulty in dismissing some of the suggested factors in this case as rather less than compelling. The fact that care homes were subject to the 2001 Care Homes Regulations and the fact that the public interest required their close regulation, did not mean that the provision of the service was a function of a public nature. Like Lord Mance, in his view it did not follow that because the statutory duty on a local authority to make arrangements to provide care and accommodation was a function of a public nature, then likewise the provision of such care and accommodation through the means of a private care home was of a public nature. "If the Ministry of Defence", Lord Neuberger argued, "placed an order for military [equipment] with a private manufacturer, the Ministry could fairly be said ... to be carrying out a function of a public nature in placing the contract, but it does not follow ... that the manufacturer would be carrying out [such] function in performing the contract."

He recognised there was force in the point that if a person had the protection of Convention rights if a service was provided by a local authority, she should not lose that protection simply because the service was contracted out by that authority to a private company. But this case was not concerned with the contracting out of a duty: Birmingham City Council had a duty to arrange for the provision of care and accommodation for the claimant, but it had no duty to provide such care and accommodation itself. He was unable to identify any policy consideration which militated against concluding that the provision of care and accommodation by the care home company was not "a function of a public nature" within the meaning of the Human Rights Act 1998.

Lord Bingham and Baroness Hale strongly disagreed. As in the case of the majority, a clue to their thinking lay in the way in which they chose to formulate the issue. For Lord Bingham the question was whether a care home, when providing care and accommodation to a resident pursuant to arrangements made with a local authority under the provisions of the National Assistance Act 1948, is performing "functions of a public nature" for the purposes of the Human Rights Act 1998. "I venture to think," observed Lord Bingham, "that the answer to this question was clear."

6 See p. 51.

Citing in support a passage from the leading judgment of Lord Nicholls in the church repairs case, he was at pains to emphasise that since the purpose of the Human Rights Act 1998 in general, and the extended statutory definition in particular, was to give effective domestic protection of Convention rights, it was appropriate to give the expression "public function" a generously wide meaning. It was important to consider with some care the nature of the function and the nature and extent of any statutory power or duty, including the state's willingness to pay, so that one could gauge the extent of the state's concern and responsibility. It was not in doubt in this case that the state had accepted a social welfare responsibility towards the old and infirm who were unable to care for themselves. The intention of Parliament was that residential care should be the responsibility of local authorities in such cases. In Lord Bingham's view the means by which that should be provided was not significant: he did not regard the fact that in this instance the actual provider was a private care home as of any particular relevance. It could scarcely be supposed that Parliament, when enacting the Human Rights Act 1998, could have intended residents of private care homes, placed in such homes by local authorities pursuant to the National Assistance Act 1948, would be unprotected in regard to Convention rights.

Baroness Hale emphasised, as had Lord Bingham, that it was nature of the function being performed rather than the nature of the body performing it which was critical. She reiterated what had been emphasised in the church repairs case, namely, that the phrase used in the Human Rights Act 1998 was a *public* function, not a *governmental* function, and reiterated the factors listed in that case as relevant in providing an answer. She acknowledged there could not be a single litmus test, but it was clear in her view that "the underlying rationale must be that it [was] a task for which the public, in the shape of the state, [had] assumed responsibility, at public expense if need be, and in the public interest". Furthermore, in this instance there was the additional point of the closeness of connection between the provision of residential care for the vulnerable and the core values underlying the Convention rights, "and the undoubted risk that rights will be violated unless adequate steps are taken to protect them."

All these considerations led Baroness Hale "inexorably to the conclusion" that the home care company was performing a function of a public nature. "This was a function performed ... pursuant to statutory arrangements, at public expense, and in the public interest. I have no doubt that Parliament intended it to be covered ...”.[7]

Just as in the contraceptive advice case, what is striking about this case is that the majority and the minority looked at the issue in completely different ways. The majority drew a distinction between the *arrangement* of residential care on the one hand, and its actual *provision* on the other. Their focus was on the provider, the commercial character of the transaction, and the absence of any element of public subsidy. In their view, in terms of legal analysis there was no essential difference between cleaning contractors providing a service for a local authority, and a private care home providing a service for such authority. The focus of the minority, on the other hand, was on the local authority's statutory duty to make the appropriate arrangements and to fund them. The care home company was simply the means of discharging that duty. It simply could not be the case that residents in a local authority run home had the protection of Convention rights, whereas residents placed by that authority in a private care home had no such protection.

(2) DISCRIMINATING “ON GROUNDS OF [HER OR HIS] SEX” AND “ON RACIAL GROUNDS”

Two cases separated by some 20 years illustrate problems posed by the simple words “on the ground of” and “on racial grounds” in respectively the Sex Discrimination Act 1975 and the Race Relations Act 1976, the provisions of which have now been absorbed into the Equality Act 2010. The division of opinion in these cases reflect sharply differing views as to how the aims of this legislation were best promoted and implemented.

In the first case a council operated a policy of free use of the swimming pool at its leisure centre for persons of pensionable age, i.e. 60 in the case of women and 65 in the case of men.[8] A local resident, a Mr James, who was aged 61 and was retired, found that he therefore had to pay for admission to the pool, whereas his wife, who was the same age, did not. He brought a

---

7 Both she and Lord Bingham must have felt vindicated when less than a year later Parliament passed the Health and Social Care Act 2012, which contained a provision (s. 145) that care home companies providing residential care pursuant to contractual arrangements with local authorities, are public authorities for the purposes of the Human Rights Act 1998.

8 *James v Eastleigh Borough Council* [1990] UKHL 6, [1990] 2 AC 751.

claim in the local county court alleging unlawful discrimination by the council in the provision of its leisure services, contrary to the Sex Discrimination Act 1975. The Act, which applied equally to both men and women, provided that "a person discriminates against a [man] in any circumstances relevant for the purposes ... of this Act if ... on the ground of [his] sex he treats him less favourably than he would treat a [woman]."[9]

The county court judge rejected the claim and, supported by the Equal Opportunities Commission, Mr James appealed to the Court of Appeal. The Court of Appeal also rejected the claim, albeit on a different basis, concluding that the words "on the ground of" in the above definition required the court to look at the subjective reason why the alleged discriminator acted as he did, and in this instance it was to benefit those with limited or reduced resources: Mr James had been denied free admission to the pool not because he was a man, but because he had not reached "pensionable age". On behalf of Mr James it had been argued that the subjective reason or intention of the discriminator was irrelevant: what mattered was the objective cause of the less favourable treatment, and this was because he was a man. Mr James, again with the support of the Equal Opportunities Commission, appealed to the House of Lords. An indication that the position might be rather less than straightforward had come in the shape of a recent House of Lords' decision,[10] in which there had been a challenge to a policy operated by a local authority relating to its selective secondary schooling. The facts were that there were more single sex grammar schools for boys than for girls, and therefore there were more places for boys than for girls. Admission was by examination. Because there were fewer places available, the council required higher marks from the girls than for the boys in order to gain a place. The council argued that this measure, for financial and administrative reasons, was necessary in order to deal with the gender imbalance, and it was not operated with a view to discriminate against girls simply because they were girls. Nevertheless, the Law Lords unanimously held this policy to be discriminatory and unlawful: the motive and intention of the council were irrelevant, except in regard to remedies. There was no such unanimity in the case of Mr James, however. The Law Lords (who included two who had sat in the grammar schools case) by a majority of three to two ruled in his favour, reversing the decision of the Court of Appeal.

---

9 This definition applies to what is known as direct discrimination. The Act goes on to define what is known as indirect discrimination: the imposition of conditions or the adoption of practices which have a disproportionate impact on the one sex or the other.

10 *Birmingham City Council v Equal Opportunities Commission* [1989] 1 AC 1155.

The majority comprised Lords Bridge, Goff and Ackner. Lord Bridge regarded as fallacious the view expressed in the judgment of the Court of Appeal that the statutory definition of discrimination required one to "look at the case where, subjectively, the defendant has treated the [claimant] less favourably because of his or her sex: [w]hat is relevant is the defendant's reason for doing an act, not the causative effect of the act done by the defendant." The fallacy, he pointed out, was the "failure to recognise that the statutory pensionable age, being fixed at 60 for women and 65 for men, is itself a criterion which ... discriminates between men and women in that it treats women more favourably than men 'on the ground of their sex'." It therefore followed that any other differential treatment of men and women that adopted the same criterion would equally involve discrimination "on the ground of sex."

Dealing with the argument that the council was simply basing its policy on the statutory concept (in the Social Security Act 1975) of "pensionable age" rather than on any differentiation between men and women, Lord Bridge remarked that that "this simply will not do." The expression "pensionable age" was no more than "a convenient shorthand expression" which referred to the age of 60 in a woman and to the age of 65 in a man. In Lord Bridge's view, in equating "on the ground of" with the subjective reason of the alleged discriminator, the Court of Appeal adopted an interpretation which was contrary to what had been decided in the grammar schools case. That case, in his view, was indistinguishable from this one. In the schools case it would have been no answer to the complaint that the pass mark was set at different levels for boys and girls to say that the condition for admission to the grammar schools was the same for both: namely, to pass the entrance examination. By precise parity of reasoning in this case it was no answer for the council to a complaint of allowing free admission to its swimming pool at different ages for men and women that the condition was the same for both: namely, the attainment of "pensionable age". The subjective reason for the differential treatment in both cases was irrelevant. The councils in both cases had the best of motives, but this was not the point. "The purity of the discriminator's subjective motive, intention or reason cannot save the criterion applied from the objective taint of discrimination on the ground of sex."

Lord Goff, who happened to give the leading judgment in the grammar schools case, strongly and, in the circumstances unsurprisingly, approved the reasoning in Lord Bridge's judgment. He did not read the words "on the ground of sex" as referring only to the reason why the alleged discriminator acted as he did, "but as embracing cases in which a gender based criterion

[was] the criterion upon which the complainant [had] been selected for the relevant treatment". Lord Goff considered that such a conclusion was consistent with the policy of the Act, "which was the active promotion of equal treatment of men and women." In his view the intention of the alleged discriminator was only relevant to the extent that there was an intention to administer the treatment complained of; neither did the existence of a benign motive enable the defendant to escape liability. However, in most cases, he pointed out, it would be unnecessary to consider either intention or motive, because whether any specific "treatment" came within the statutory definition could be resolved by posing the simple question: would the complainant have received that treatment from the defendant *but for his or her sex*?

The remaining member of the majority, Lord Ackner, expressed his full agreement with the reasoning of Lords Bridge and Goff. Lord Griffiths (who was himself a party to the unanimous decision in the grammar schools case) and Lord Lowry profoundly disagreed.

For Lord Griffiths, the reason why the council acted as it did went right to the heart of the matter. In his view the council was following the "wholly admirable practice of treating old age pensioners with generosity". He could not believe "that it was the intention of Parliament that this benevolent practice should be declared to be unlawful – but such [was] the result of [this majority] decision." He appreciated that in adopting state pensionable age as a criterion to determine whether a person was living on a pension the council was adopting a broad brush approach, but failing the applying of a means test in each individual case it was the only practical criterion to adopt. In his view "the reference to 'pensionable age' carried with it the unmistakable intention of the council to give ... free swimming facilities to people because they are pensioners and not because they are men or women." Had the council instead resolved to allow free swimming to everyone living on a pension, that surely would not have been discriminating "on the ground of sex"; and the position would surely be the same if the council had added that it regarded proof of pensionable age as proof of living on a pension.

Lord Griffiths did not consider the question whether a person treated another less favourably "on the grounds of sex" as a question which permitted of much refinement. "It means did they do what they did because she was a woman (or a man). It is a question of fact which [had] to be answered by applying common sense." He agreed that the motive behind the treatment was not necessarily determinative of the answer. In his view the grammar schools case was plainly distinguishable. In that case it was indisputable that it was more difficult for girls to get places than for boys because they were girls. Thus there clearly was discrimination within the meaning of the statutory definition: the application of the "but for" test inevitably led to that result. The fact that the council were very unhappy about the situation and did not wish to discriminate did not alter the fact they were indeed discriminating. The question in the present case was whether the council refused Mr James free admission to the pool because he was a man, to which the answer was: no, they refused him free admission because he was not an old age pensioner, and presumably could afford to pay.

Lord Griffiths recognised that imposing a retirement age of 60 on women and 65 on men was discriminatory on the ground of sex, but what he would not accept was that an attempt to redress this unfairness by offering free facilities to those disadvantaged by the prior act of discrimination was itself discriminatory "on the ground of sex."

Lord Lowry rejected the interpretation of the words "on the ground of" which equated those words with "by reason of" or "due to", and involved applying the test of causation. The structure of the key sentence pointed to a subjective test: was the reason for the alleged discriminator acting as he did the sex of the complainant? He analysed the syntax in the following terms: "The words 'on the ground of sex' ... constitute an adverbial phrase modifying the transitive verb 'treats' in a clause of which the discriminator is the subject and the victim is the object; it is the reason which has caused him to act." In his view the meaning of the key words, at the point at which they occur, could not be expressed by saying that the victim receives treatment which on the ground of his or her sex is less favourable to him or her than to a person of opposite sex. Furthermore, his conclusion that the natural meaning of "ground" in this context meant "reason" was supported by the definitions supplied by Oxford English Dictionary, 2nd edition. Whilst he appreciated that the causative test had the merit of simplicity in that it eliminated irrelevant mental ingredients such as malice, prejudice and motive, and indeed the need to investigate at all the discriminator's mental processes, it nevertheless eliminated an essential ingredient, namely, the *ground* on which the discriminator acted. To adopt this approach, argued Lord Lowry, would be to reduce the words "on the ground of" in their natural meaning to insignificance. For his part, he endorsed the observation (previously quoted) in the judgment of the Court of Appeal that "what is relevant is the defendant's reason for doing an act, not the causative effect of the act done by the defendant."

Like Lord Griffiths, Lord Lowry regarded the key question in this case to be: why did the council act as it did; and in answering that question, like Lord Griffiths, and for the reasons Lord Griffiths gave, he did not consider that the statutory "pensionable age" was itself discriminatory critical to the answer. "The council were providing free swimming for a certain group of people because they were of pensionable age and not because they were men and women of specific but different ages. Therefore, the council did not use the expression 'persons who have reached the state pensionable age' as a convenient way of describing women over 60 and men over 65." That this was in fact the foreseeable result was not, in his view, a relevant consideration. Furthermore, the policy of the council would not change even if the state pensionable age changed.

And like Lord Griffiths, he considered the grammar schools case clearly distinguishable:

> Because there were fewer places available for girls, they had to achieve higher marks than the boys and accordingly the council, when considering the performance of a girl ... was obliged to demand from her a higher mark than if she had been a boy. In so doing the council treated a girl less favourably than it treated a boy and did so "on the ground of her sex".

This sharp divergence of opinion as to the meaning of the statutory definition of direct discrimination can best be summarised as saying that in the view of the majority the aims of the Act could more sensibly be promoted and realised by adopting the causative, "but for" test; and to treat the words "on the ground of" as embracing not only the reason for the treatment but any underlying discrimination giving rise to that treatment, was to ensure that treatment reflecting underlying discriminatory treatment would not slip through the net and that liability would not be evaded by focusing narrowly on the discriminator's immediate intention. For Lord Griffiths, such an approach – certainly in this particular case – was productive of injustice and of a result which Parliament, when enacting the legislation, could not have intended. For both Lord Griffiths, and in particular Lord Lowry, the approach of the majority did violence to the natural meaning of the words "on the grounds of [his or her] sex". "Ground" was to be equated with "reason" and therefore a consideration of the alleged discriminator's "mental processes" was highly relevant. (The minority view on this aspect of the problem did not in fact go unheeded; later, in more than one discrimination case, it was recognised by the House of Lords that where the reason for the less favourable treatment was not readily apparent, *some* consideration of the alleged discriminator's "mental processes" was clearly necessary.)

Remarkably, this divergence of opinion on a fundamental aspect of discrimination law re-surfaced some 20 years later in the Supreme Court in another case concerning school admissions.[11] A voluntarily aided Jewish comprehensive school, which was heavily oversubscribed, gave priority under its oversubscription policy to children who were recognised as Jewish by the Office of the Chief Rabbi (the OCR) – namely, that the mother was Jewish either by matrilineal descent or by conversion in accordance with Orthodox Jewish doctrine. The school refused admission to the claimant's son because he did not satisfy these criteria: the mother was Italian and formerly a Catholic who had converted to a Jewish denomination which was not recognised by the OCR. The claimant, who was Jewish by birth, alleged that the refusal by the school to admit his son amounted to direct racial discrimination. The Race Relations Act 1976 declared that "a person discriminates against another in any circumstances relevant for the purposes ... of this Act if ... on racial grounds he treats that other less favourably than he treats or would treat another person."[12] Under the Act "racial grounds" included any of the following: "... colour, race, nationality or ethnic or national origins." The school argued that the refusal was for religious reasons: it simply reflected the OCR's criteria as to who was or was not Jewish. The High Court judge who heard the case at first instance ruled that the school, in refusing the boy admission, did indeed act on religious and not racial grounds. This decision was reversed by the Court of Appeal, which held that since Jews constituted a racial group defined mainly by ethnic origin, the refusal had been on racial grounds, and that therefore there had been direct discrimination within the meaning of the Act. The school appealed. The appeal was heard by a nine-member Supreme Court,[13] which by a majority of five to four upheld the decision of the Court of Appeal. The majority comprised Lord Phillips, Baroness Hale, Lord Mance, Lord Kerr and Lord Clarke.

Lord Phillips found the reasoning of the majority in the swimming pool case "compelling" and to be applicable in the present case. He concluded that the

---

11 *R (E) v Governing Body of JFS & Anor* [2009] UKSC 15, [2010] 2 AC 728.

12 As in the case of the Sex Discrimination Act 1975, this is a definition of *direct* discrimination. Indirect discrimination also happened to be an issue in this case, but irrelevant for present purposes.

13 The Supreme Court can sit with five, seven or nine members, depending on the perceived importance, difficulty or sensitivity of the case.

religious motive behind the school's decision to refuse admission was irrelevant; what was critical was whether the criteria applied by the OCR, and on which the refusal was based, were themselves racially discriminatory. In his view it was clear that the matrilineal test was a test of "ethnic origin": the test was applied irrespective of religious practice and belief. He noted that the expert evidence underlined the fact that conversion to Judaism embraced not only conversion to a set of religious beliefs but to shared customs and culture characteristic of a particular ethnic group.

Baroness Hale identified the issue in similarly narrow terms: "... do the criteria used by [the school] to select [its] pupils ... treat people differently because of their 'ethnic origins'?" Like Lord Phillips, in her view the reasoning in both the grammar schools case and the majority reasoning in the swimming pool case were applicable. It was not in doubt that both the school and the Chief Rabbi thought they were solely concerned with religious considerations, but their motives in so acting were irrelevant.

Unquestionably, in her view, the criterion adopted by the Chief Rabbi and by the school were based upon the child's ethnic origins. The ethnic origins of the mother in this case were Italian and Roman Catholic. "The fact that the OCR would have overlooked [her] Italian origins had she converted by a procedure which they would recognise, makes no difference to this fundamental fact." The boy was rejected not because of who he is but because of his mother's ethnicity." It was because his mother was not descended in the matrilineal line from the original Jewish people: in other words, "lack of descent from a particular ethnic group."

Lord Mance agreed. Although the school's motivation may well have been religious, "the treatment derived from a test which was substantially based on inherently ethnic grounds." In his view his conclusion that the school's refusal of admission amounted to discrimination on racial grounds was consistent with the policy of the Race Relations Act 1976. "To treat individual applicants to a school less favourably than others because of the happenstance of their respective ancestries, is not to treat them as individuals, but as members in a group defined in a manner unrelated to their individual attributes."

Like his colleagues, Lord Kerr thought it was necessary in this case to recognise there was a clear distinction "between, on the one hand, the grounds for the decision (what was the basis on which the decision was taken) and on the other, what motivated the decision-maker to make that decision." In this instance the school had refused to admit the boy because an essential part of the required ethnic make-up was missing: the reason they took the decision on those grounds was a religious one – the OCR had declared he was not a Jew. But the reason he was not a Jew was because of his ethnic origins, "or more pertinently, his lack of the requisite ethnic origins." It followed that the school had made its decision on grounds which the Act had decreed to be racial.

Lord Clarke, agreeing with the rest of the majority, concluded that the criteria were both religious and ethnic, and it was sufficient for the purposes of the Race Relations Act 1976 that they had an ethnic element. He thought the analogy adopted by the Court of Appeal of the Dutch Reformed Church in South Africa directly in point: their belief that God had made black people inferior to white, and had destined them to live separately from whites, was no answer to a charge that such belief was discriminatory on racial grounds.

The minority comprised Lords Hope, Walker, Rodger and Brown. Lord Hope (with whose reasoning Lord Walker agreed) took the view that the approach adopted by the majority was misconceived: it was a mistake to adhere to a rigid distinction between motive and the underlying criteria on which the treatment complained of was based; Lord Goff's rejection in the swimming pool case of the relevance of a subjective test needed to be reconsidered. In this case the Chief Rabbi gave the guidance he did because he concluded that this was required of him by Orthodox Jewish religious law. "The question whether or not [the claimant's son] was Jewish in the secular sense was of no interest to him at all. His advice was based simply and solely on his understanding of Jewish law … To say that the ground was a racial one [was] to confuse the effect of the treatment with the ground itself." In Lord Hope's view it was a complete misconception to categorise the ground as a racial one.

Lord Rodger was brutally dismissive of the line of reasoning of the majority. The whole point of the school was its Jewish character, providing education within an Orthodox religious framework. The decision of the majority meant that there could in future be no Jewish faith schools which gave preference to children because they were Jewish according to Jewish religious law and belief. Their decision "leads to such extraordinary results, and produces such manifest discrimination against Jewish schools in comparison with other faith schools, that one can't help feeling that something has gone wrong."

In Lord Rodger's view "to reduce the religious element in the actions of those concerned to the status of mere motive" was to misrepresent what they were doing. He disagreed with Baroness Hale's assertion that the claimant's son was rejected because of his mother's ethnic origins, which were Italian and Catholic. "His mother could have been as Italian in origin as Sophia Loren and as Roman Catholic as the Pope for all that the governors cared: the only thing that mattered was that she had not converted to Judaism under Orthodox auspices." What was critical was her non-Jewish religious status in the eyes of the OCR. The suggestion that her son was rejected because of his ethnic origins was rebutted by the fact that as far as the school was concerned, the son of an Italian and Catholic mother who had converted to Orthodox Judaism *would* have qualified for admission.

Lord Brown was equally robust. In reality, in his view, the real complaint underlying the claimant's case was that in deciding who is a Jew the OCR's approach to conversion was misguided. This was not a dispute which should concern the courts. The criteria reflected Jewish religious doctrine according to Orthodox Judaism: it was quite unrealistic, given that those treated less favourably and those treated more favourably were within the same ethnic group, to regard the school's admissions policy as discriminatory on racial rather than religious grounds. (The treatment of blacks and whites by the Dutch Reformed Church was not analogous.) Like Lord Rodger, he pointed to the practical consequences of the majority decision: a Jewish faith school would never be entitled to give preference to those who are members of the Jewish religion under Jewish law. Furthermore, the decision implied that Orthodox Judaism was a directly racially discriminating religion, an implication he greatly regretted.

It could hardly have been foreseen when the legislation was introduced that the scope of the meaning of the simple expressions "on the ground of sex" and "on racial grounds" would have provoked such sharp and repeated disagreement at the top of our judicial hierarchy. The majority in both these cases not only clearly thought that their decision reflected the policy and aims of the legislation, but that a decision to the contrary would in fact undermine the statutory purpose. The minority in both cases clearly thought that what they perceived to be resultant unfairness of the decision was such that it could not have been intended or contemplated by the legislation, and that to disregard the subjective reason for the decision-maker acting in the way he did was calculated to produce injustice.

(3) COMPENSATING THE INNOCENT

The meaning and scope of a simple phrase caused yet again a nine-member Supreme Court to divide five to four, the phrase being "a miscarriage of justice".[14] The Criminal Justice Act 1988 (section 133(1)) provided that a person who had been convicted of a criminal offence, and whose conviction was subsequently reversed because a new or newly discovered fact had shown "beyond reasonable doubt" that there had been a miscarriage of justice, was entitled to receive compensation from the Secretary of State. (The wording of the provision followed closely that set out in Article 14.6 of the International Covenant on Civil and Political Rights 1977, to which the UK was a signatory, the only difference being that the latter used the word "conclusively" rather than the phrase "beyond reasonable doubt".) In this case the claimant, Mr Adams, had been convicted of murder and sentenced to life imprisonment. Some four years later his conviction was quashed as unsafe: it transpired that the legal team which represented him at his trial, through their incompetence, had failed to discover and to deploy unused evidence made available to them by the prosecution, which had it been deployed may, but not inevitably, have resulted in his acquittal. He applied for compensation, which was refused. His claim for judicial review of the Secretary of State's refusal was dismissed, as was his subsequent appeal to the Court of Appeal, on the ground that he had failed to show that there had been a miscarriage of justice within the meaning of section 133(1). In a case heard by the House of Lords some seven years earlier, which had turned on a different point, the Law Lords (specifically Lord Bingham and Lord Steyn) were divided on whether conclusive proof of innocence was necessary in order to establish that there had been a miscarriage of justice: both Law Lords had expressed differing views as to the meaning of the expression in the context of Article 14.6 of the International Covenant and section 133. The Court of Appeal, in dismissing Mr Adams' appeal, found it unnecessary to express its own view on this issue; as far as they were concerned, what was critical was that even if the unused evidence had been deployed at the trial, the acquittal of Mr Adams was by no means a certainty; therefore it could not be shown beyond reasonable doubt that a miscarriage of justice had occurred.

Mr Adams appealed to the Supreme Court. The importance of finally resolving what the expression "miscarriage of justice" in the context of claiming compensation for a wrongful conviction was intended to mean, led to the convening of a nine-member court. Although unanimous in

---

14 *R (Adams) v Secretary of State for Justice* [2011] UKSC 18, [2012] 1 AC 48.

dismissing Mr Adams' appeal in the light of the particular facts of his case, the Court divided five to four as to what was the appropriate test to be applied, the majority ruling that the phrase "miscarriage of justice" was not confined to circumstances where conclusive proof of innocence had been established.

The majority comprised Lord Phillips, Lord Hope, Baroness Hale, Lord Kerr and Lord Clarke. Both Lord Phillips and Lord Hope recognised, as had the Court of Appeal, that the expression "miscarriage of justice" was capable of having different shades of meaning in the context of section 133. In addition to cases where the fresh evidence showed clearly that the defendant was innocent, it was capable of embracing cases where, had the fresh evidence been available at the trial, a properly directed jury simply would not have convicted the defendant, or may or may not have convicted him. It could also embrace a case where something had gone seriously wrong in the investigation of the offence or the conduct of the trial which resulted in the conviction of someone who should not have been convicted.

Lord Phillips and Lord Hope also both recognised that in order to ascertain the meaning of the phrase in the context of section 133, it was helpful to consider its meaning in the context of Article 14.6 of the International Covenant, on which the statutory provision was based. They agreed with the view expressed by Lord Bingham in the earlier case that the phrase in Article 14.6 had a broader meaning than one which simply equated with innocence – the meaning favoured by Lord Steyn. They both noted that the French text used the phrase "*une erreur judicaire*"; and that significantly both the French and other European legal systems allowed for the recovery of compensation in circumstances short of proof of innocence, namely, where the conviction had been quashed because the fresh evidence had given rise to serious doubt about the defendant's guilt. In their view, what had to be demonstrated conclusively under Article 14.6 was not innocence but a miscarriage of justice in the sense that the correctness of the conviction had been seriously undermined.

Reverting to section 133(1) and to the scope and meaning of "miscarriage of justice" in that context, Lord Phillips pointed out that the primary object of this legislation was to compensate a person who has been convicted and punished for a crime which he did not commit, but that there was a subsidiary object: namely, that compensation should not be paid to a person who has been convicted and punished for a crime which he *did* commit. A balance had to be struck between those two objectives. In his view this could best be accomplished by adopting as a test for determining whether a miscarriage of justice had occurred whether "the new fact ... so undermine[d] the evidence against the defendant that no conviction could possibly be based on it." Whilst this test would not guarantee that all those entitled to compensation are innocent, it would at least ensure that when those who are in fact innocent have been convicted on evidence which has been subsequently discredited, they are not precluded from getting compensation because they are unable to prove their innocence beyond reasonable doubt.

Lord Hope agreed that this test met the case. It would, he said, quite properly include cases where the prosecution had depended on a confession statement subsequently shown to have been inadmissible because, as the defendant had always maintained, it had been obtained by improper means. Whilst it was impossible to say that the defendant was beyond reasonable doubt innocent, it could nevertheless be shown beyond reasonable doubt that a miscarriage of justice had occurred because he should not have been prosecuted at all.

Baroness Hale also agreed with the test as formulated by Lord Phillips, and with his reasoning. In her view "the phrase [miscarriage of justice] is clearly capable of bearing a wider meaning than conclusive proof of innocence. Both the inspiration for section 133(1) in Article 14.6 of the [International Covenant] and the meaning of 'miscarriage of justice' in domestic law ... support a wider meaning."

Lord Clarke likewise agreed with the test proposed by Lord Phillips. He made the additional point that if Parliament had intended to limit miscarriages of justice to cases where the claimant could prove his innocence, it would have been easy to say so.

Lord Kerr expressed himself "content" with Lord Phillips's formulation, although the test he himself would have proposed was: "whether on the facts as they now stand revealed, it can be concluded beyond reasonable doubt that the [claimant] should not have been convicted."

Lord Judge (the present Lord Chief Justice) and Lord Brown delivered the dissenting judgments, with which both Lord Walker and Lord Rodger agreed. Lord Judge emphasised that section 133(1) was enacted in fulfilment of the UK's treaty obligations as signatory to the International Covenant, and that consequently the phrase "miscarriage of justice" must be intended to bear the same "autonomous" meaning in section 133(1) as it bore in Article 14.6 of the Covenant. The only textual difference, he noted, was the use in the latter of the word "conclusively" instead of "beyond reasonable doubt." When one examined Article 14(1) and section 133(1) it was apparent that there was a distinction between the concepts of the reversal of the conviction and a miscarriage of justice: the former being an essential precondition to, but not conclusive of, the entitlement to compensation. Therefore more than a reversal of conviction was required before compensation became payable: namely that a "miscarriage of justice" had been conclusively demonstrated. Obviously the phrase was not relevant to whether a conviction had been reversed, or to any particular aspect of the investigation or trial processes. Instead, argued Lord Judge, the phrase:

> ... describes the characteristics or attributes of the 'miscarriage of justice' which must be established ... Accordingly, for section 133 to apply ... the emergence of a newly discovered fact should demonstrate not only that the conviction was unsafe or that the investigative or trial processes were defective, but that justice had surely miscarried. In the present context, the ultimate and sure miscarriage of justice is the conviction and incarceration of the truly innocent.

For Lord Judge the conclusion was inescapable that the compensation scheme under section 133 was confined to miscarriages of justice in which the defendant was convicted of an offence of which he was completely innocent. In his view, nothing less would do. There could be no halfway house or compromise solution consistent with what he regarded as a "clear statutory provision".

Lord Brown agreed with Lord Judge's textual analysis and conclusion, which in his view was reinforced by the following points. In fulfilling its treaty obligations, it was perfectly open to the UK to introduce legislation intended to compensate only those shown to be clearly innocent of the crime of which they were convicted. This would be consistent with the explanatory report issued in relation to Article 3 of Protocol 7 to the European Convention of Human Rights (the text of which is virtually identical to that of Article 14.6 of the Covenant), which stated: "The intention is that states would be obliged to compensate persons only in clear cases of miscarriage of justice, in the sense that there would be an acknowledgement that the person concerned was clearly innocent."

The question raised in section 133 was not one for a criminal court to answer but one for the Secretary of State: the question for the court is: was the verdict unsafe? The question for the Secretary of State, on the other hand, is: has there been a miscarriage of justice? That invited different considerations. Lord Brown repeated what he had said on a previous occasion (when sitting as a member of the Court of Appeal) that in the context of section 133 the phrase "miscarriage of justice" meant the wrongful conviction of an innocent person; compensation should only go to those proved to be innocent. He had difficulty in reconciling the language of section 133 – specifically the requirement of establishing a miscarriage of justice *beyond reasonable doubt* – with the test proposed by the majority. And whilst the application of the proof of innocence test would inevitably exclude from compensation a few who were indeed innocent, this was preferable, in his view, to compensating a considerably greater number who were in fact guilty. It was, he thought, perfectly reasonable for the state to operate a scheme which compensated generously the comparatively few who could demonstrate their innocence rather than a larger number who may or may not be innocent.

The sharp divergence of view in this case as to the meaning of the phrase "miscarriage of justice" in section 133 is a perfect illustration of Lord Neuberger's comment in the care home case that the difficulty in ascertaining the meaning of an imprecise word or phrase in a statute is usually resolved by reference to a subjective policy decision as to what the word or phrase *ought* to mean. The view of the majority was that it would be unfair, and therefore inconsistent with the intention of Parliament, to exclude from the compensation scheme those who had been wrongly convicted but were unable to prove conclusively their innocence. The view of the minority was that it was not acceptable that the scheme should operate in such a way as to run the risk that a significant number of applicants would receive compensation whose convictions had been quashed but were in fact guilty. (For the purposes of entitlement to compensation, Lord Judge in particular could not see how the phrase "miscarriage of justice" could properly apply other than to those who were "truly innocent".)

(4) A PROBLEM WITH THE WORD "KNOWLEDGE"

Ever since the sixteenth century there has always been, in some form or another, legislation designed to prevent the litigation of stale claims, a policy enshrined in the well-known aphorism "Justice delayed is justice denied." However, it will happen not infrequently (particularly in cases involving personal injury such as an industrial disease) that at the relevant time claimants were unaware, through no fault of their own, of facts which could reasonably have led them to bring a claim in negligence. The Limitation Act 1980 specifically deals with this problem. The Act provides that in respect of negligence, nuisance and breach of duty claims involving personal injury, those claims must be brought within three years from the date the cause of action arose, or the date, if later, the person injured "had knowledge of the following facts: that the injury was significant; and was attributable wholly or in part to the acts or omissions [alleged to amount to] negligence, or nuisance or breach of duty; and the identity of the defendant." The Act also provides that in this context "a person's knowledge includes knowledge which he might reasonably have been expected to acquire from facts observable or ascertainable by him or from facts ascertainable by him with the help of medical or other expert advice."

For many years judges have experienced difficulty in applying these provisions; in particular there has been uncertainty as to whether "knowledge" equated to a reasonable belief, or whether something more solid was required. The competing views were expressed by two distinguished judges in the following terms:

> "Knowledge" is an ordinary English word with a clear meaning to which one must give full effect: "reasonable belief" or "suspicion" is not enough. The relevant question [is]: When did the [claimant] first know that his [illness] was capable of being attributed to his conditions at work?
> (Lord Justice May in a 1985 case)

> "Knowledge" clearly does not mean "know for certain and beyond possibility of contradiction". It does, however, mean "know with sufficient confidence to justify embarking on the preliminaries to [commencing proceedings] ... Suspicion, particularly if it is vague and unsupported, will indeed be not enough, but reasonable belief will normally suffice.
> (Lord Donaldson, the then Master of the Rolls, in a 1990 case.)

The issue was ultimately resolved by a sharply divided seven-member Supreme Court. The facts of the case which produced this conflict were these.[15] Between 1952 and 1958 the Ministry of Defence carried out certain nuclear tests in the atmosphere above Australia and the South Pacific, involving a large number of servicemen. A claim form was issued on behalf of many of these servicemen or their dependents as a group action in 2004, alleging that the servicemen had been exposed to radiation causing illness, disability and, in some cases, death. At the time there was no objective, scientific evidence to support the allegation that these symptoms were caused by exposure to radiation. The action thereafter stalled, but an attempt was made to revive it several years later after a new scientific study was

[15] *Ministry of Defence v AB & Ors* [2012] UKSC 9, [2013] 1 AC 78.

produced which suggested that certainly in some cases a causal connection could be established. Other former servicemen, and in some instances their dependants, joined in the action at this stage. By agreement some 10 claims were selected for consideration by the court as to whether they were "time-barred" under the Limitation Act 1980. The judge ruled that five of the claims were time-barred, having applied the subjective "reasonable belief" test. The Court of Appeal upheld that ruling, approving the judge's application of the subjective test. The Supreme Court decided by a majority of four to three that they were right to do so.

In this instance, in order to appreciate the full flavour of the debate and the divergence of views, it is best to start with the minority judgments. The minority comprised Lord Phillips, Baroness Hale and Lord Kerr.

Lord Phillips thought that the object of the statutory provision was perfectly clear: namely, time will begin to run when the claimant has, or ought reasonably to have, knowledge of the facts on which his claim based. It is about *knowledge*, actual or constructive, of *facts*, and not law. The test of knowledge which the provision lays down is what the claimant ought *reasonably* to have been expected to acquire either from facts "observable or ascertainable" by or ascertainable by him with the aid of *appropriate* expert advice which it was *reasonable* for him to seek. It was therefore clear, in Lord Phillips's view, that objective standards had to be applied. The wording and the scheme of the provision did not permit the substitution of the test of actual or constructive knowledge of the specified facts with a test of subjective belief.

Lord Phillips thought it eminently sensible that this should be the case. Firstly, it was undesirable that a claimant should bring an action on the basis of a subjective belief that was not reasonably founded on a basis of fact. Secondly, it would not be fair to discriminate between two claimants who had identical knowledge of the relevant facts "on the ground that one believed that they demonstrated attributability while the other formed the view they did not."

In the present case, Lord Phillips pointed out, the distinction between knowledge and belief was critical. When the majority of claimants started proceedings "there were no known facts capable of supporting a belief that their injuries were attributable to exposure to ionising radiation." Absent scientific evidence, the belief was not a reasonable one. Prior to the study released in 2007 there was simply no evidence that demonstrated that the injuries were in any way attributable to radiation. The action commenced prior to the release of the study had been commenced on a purely speculative basis.

Baroness Hale, who agreed with the analysis of Lord Phillips, noted that the view of the Court of Appeal was that "a strong but completely irrational belief that an injury was attributable to the act or omission of the defendant equated with 'knowledge' of that fact for the purposes of [the provision]." In her view this was not what the Limitation Act 1980 provided. The prescribed three-year period did not start until the claimant had "knowledge" of the essential "facts" and the strength of a claimant's subjective belief was not a sensible basis for deciding whether he had a right to pursue his action. "Knowledge and belief [were] different concepts, and there was no reason to believe that Parliament intended to equate the two."

Like Lord Phillips and Baroness Hale, Lord Kerr concluded that the plain language of the provision pointed in only one direction. In his view it was impossible to suggest that it was intended to convey that the test should be that a claimant would have the required knowledge when he *believed* (or even firmly believed) that the injury was attributable to the defendant's act or omission. For Lord Kerr, the natural meaning of the language was that the claimant needed to *know* it rather than to believe it. The phrase "knowledge of the facts" permeated the provision.

Lord Kerr argued that if the phrase "knowledge of the facts" was to be interpreted as a firm belief in a state of affairs, it would have to bear the same meaning in respect of each of the circumstances in which the phrase was employed. In other words a claimant needed only to have a belief in the identity of the defendant rather than knowing who he was, and to have a belief that his injury was significant rather than knowing that such was the case. In his view it was inherently unlikely that Parliament could ever have intended that claimants should be encouraged to commence litigation "when all they had to go on was a belief, however strongly held."

The majority comprised Lords Wilson, Walker, Brown and Mance. Lord Wilson was forthright: in his view the approach of the minority to the meaning of the word "knowledge" was "misconceived and would throw the practical application of the [provision] into disarray." It was apparent that knowledge of attributability in this statutory context was predicated on the *assumption* that the claimant had a good cause of action, and on the *assumption* that the relevant facts were true: the defendant may well go on to deny this was case, and equally may turn out to be right if the action were to proceed. Significantly, a claimant had to verify his claim form with a statement that he "believed" the facts stated in it were true. He rejected the contention on behalf of the claimants in this case that the requisite knowledge was only acquired after the release of the scientific report: he thought it "a legal impossibility" to assert lack of knowledge at the time the claim form was issued (in 2004) and that the necessary knowledge was acquired only after the contents of the report had been disclosed. The statement of verification at the bottom of the claim form requires that the claimant "believes" rather than "knows". In his view it would be heretical that a claimant could escape the conventional three-year requirement for bringing an action for personal injury by successfully asserting that even after the claim had been brought "he remained in a state of ignorance entirely inconsistent with it."

For his part Lord Wilson strongly approved the subjective test as defined by Lord Donaldson, i.e. a belief held with sufficient confidence so as to justify embarking on the preliminaries prior to a formal commencement of legal proceedings, and that a "reasonable belief" would suffice for these purposes. One of the objects of the legislation was "to protect defendants from being vexed by stale claims." In Lord Wilson's view the approach of the minority would undermine that object.

Lord Walker, agreeing with Lord Wilson's conclusions, pointed out that the practical result of the minority's approach would result in a situation which Parliament could not have intended when it enacted the provision. It would mean, he thought, that persons (and, as in this case, large groups of persons) who believed, without any real prospect of proving liability, they had suffered injuries through the fault of a government department or local authority or any other large body, would be able to keep their claims on ice for an indefinite period in the hope that one day the right evidence might turn up. Lord Walker agreed with the conclusion of the Court of Appeal in this case that in the context of the provision in question it was knowledge of the *possibilities* that mattered.

The remaining two Justices, Lord Brown and Lord Mance, also agreed with both the analysis and conclusions of Lord Wilson. It is clear that for the majority, the spectre of stale claims being pursued or re-activated on the basis of new evidence emerging many years down the line was not something which they were prepared to view with equanimity. For the minority, their view that the word "knowledge" was to be given its ordinary meaning, and therefore did not equate with mere "belief", was underpinned by a conviction that it was unfair to penalise litigants who had exercised justifiable caution. One could not have a clearer illustration of the point made by Lord Neuberger (in the care home case) that the interpretation of the critical words on which the argument is focused tends to be governed by one's subjective sense of what the words *ought* to mean.

PART FOUR

DIFFERING RESPONSES TO CONSTITUTIONAL AND HUMAN RIGHTS ISSUES

The six cases chosen to illustrate this theme have all been decided within the last five years: two concern what can be described as constitutional rights; two concern Convention rights; and two concern rights that can best be classified as "hybrid." All happen to raise the kind of issues one is more readily inclined to associate with the Supreme Court of the US. Although the figure of "the serial dissenter" does not, unlike in the Supreme Court of the US or, arguably, the High Court of Australia, feature in either the House of Lords or our own Supreme Court, it will not escape the reader's attention that Lord Mance delivered a strong dissent in three of these cases. They, and other recent decisions, also illustrate the point made by the Supreme Court Justice and former Law Lord, Lord Kerr, in a recent lecture on dissenting judgments, that:

> ... the resolution of competing policy arguments or even moral choices is far more frequently the staple diet of judicial decisions than previously ... the court must now confront claims of fundamental importance [where] often vital societal issues are at stake.[1]

At times, it must be said, this "confrontation" has taken on a distinctly theological character.[2]

---

1 The Birkenhead lecture delivered in Gray's Inn Hall on 14 October 2012.

2 A good example is a recent case in the Supreme Court concerning the exercise of the Home Secretary's statutory power to detain prisoners of foreign nationality following completion of their sentences pending their deportation. The majority held that the Home Secretary was liable for the tort of false imprisonment in detaining two foreign nationals pending their deportation on completion of their sentences, on the ground that she had applied the criteria laid down in accordance with an unpublished and "secret" policy, even though they would have been inevitably and legitimately detained under the criteria laid down in accordance with the previously published and lawful policy which it purported to

(1) IS THE "RIGHT OF ABODE" A FUNDAMENTAL RIGHT?

The facts and historical background to this case[3] – decided exactly one year before the Supreme Court came into operation – are worth fleshing out in a little detail. In the early nineteenth century the Chagos islands in the Indian Ocean were ceded by France to Great Britain, and were subsequently administered as a dependency as part of Mauritius. The local economy revolved around coconut plantations operated by a Seychelles company. In 1965 the islands were constituted an independent colony by virtue of the British Indian Ocean Territory Order,[4] which empowered the newly appointed Commissioner to "make laws for the peace, order and good government of the territory" – the traditional words by which the UK conferred the power to legislate for its colonies. In 1971, under the terms of an "Immigration Ordinance" issued by the Commissioner, purportedly pursuant to his powers under the 1965 order, the inhabitants were compulsorily removed and resettled elsewhere to enable the US, which had been negotiating with the UK since 1964, to acquire the largest of the islands – Diego Garcia – as a military base. The 1965 order conferring the independent colony status had been made specifically in contemplation of this development.

In 2000 a former inhabitant successfully challenged the legality of the 1971 removal ordinance in the Divisional Court. The Government accepted the decision, choosing not to appeal, and the then Foreign Secretary, Robin Cook, made a statement in the House of Commons in which he said that a study of the feasibility of resettlement was under way, and that "[the Government would] put in place a new Immigration Ordinance which

---

replace, but that in the circumstances they were only entitled to recover nominal damages. One of the three dissentients, Lord Brown, whilst acknowledging "the beguiling simplicity and apparent purity of the majority's approach", concluded that it was "nothing short of absurd that assuming the inevitability of detention in any event ... to hold [that] the tort of false imprisonment [was] nevertheless made out." Furthermore, in his view so to hold was inconsistent and incompatible with the award of merely nominal damages. The case occupied a nine-member Supreme Court for four working days, and occupied some 115 pages of the law reports: *Lumba (WL) v Secretary of State for the Home Department* [2011] UKSC 12, [2012] 1 AC 245.

3 *R (Bancoult) v Secretary of State for Foreign and Commonwealth Affairs* [2008] UKHL 61, [2009] 1 AC 453.

4 Such an order is made by the Privy Council on the advice of ministers in the exercise of the Royal Prerogative. It is therefore not subject to the scrutiny of Parliament or parliamentary debate.

[would allow the Chagos islanders] to return to the outer islands [i.e. excluding Diego Garcia] ... ." Following further court proceedings, compensation was paid out to the Islanders, and pending the completion of the feasibility study, no attempt was made by any of them to return and resettle.

Some four years later, in 2004, the Government, without prior warning or consultation with the Islanders, made an order called the British Indian Ocean Territory (Constitution) Order, section 9 of which declared:

> (1) Whereas the territory was constituted and is set aside to be available for the defence purposes of the Government of the United Kingdom and the Government of the United States of America, *no person has the right of abode in the territory.* [Emphasis added]
>
> (2) Accordingly, no person is entitled to enter or be present in the territory except as authorised by or under this Order or any other law for the time being in force in the territory.

The legality of this order was likewise challenged in the courts. This challenge was resisted essentially on the ground that the order, being a "prerogative" order, and therefore not the subject of normal legislation, was immune to judicial scrutiny and, specifically, was not susceptible to the process of judicial review. The Divisional Court quashed the order, primarily on the ground that it was irrational, not having been made in the interests of the Islanders but in the interests of the UK and the US; and that they did not serve the purpose of ensuring "the peace, order and good government of the territory." The Court of Appeal upheld the decision on the grounds that the order was made without proper regard for the interests of the Islanders; and the Islanders, in the light of the 2000 statement, had a legitimate expectation[5] that the ban on their return and resettlement would be removed.

On the further appeal to the House of Lords, the primary argument for the Government continued to be that a prerogative order, not being part of the Parliamentary legislative process, was not subject to judicial scrutiny or judicial review. The secondary argument was that the power of the Crown to

---

[5] It is now a firmly established doctrine that where a public authority or Government Department makes a promise or representation which is intended to be relied upon, a person who has acted in reliance on that representation or promise and has "a legitimate expectation" that it will be adhered to, is entitled to a remedy should the promise or representation be broken or breached, as the case may be.

legislate "in Council" was not subject to any limitation. The primary argument for the claimant was that the Islanders' right of abode was a fundamental right integral to British citizenship, and was not capable of being removed by the exercise of a prerogative power. (The illustrious eighteenth-century judge, Lord Mansfield, had stated in a well-known case that although the Crown had the power to introduce new laws to conquered or ceded countries "[it] could not make any new change contrary to fundamental principles.") Secondly, it was argued that any order made pursuant to the original 1965 Order was required to be made for the purpose of ensuring of "peace, order and good government of the territory", and to be made in the interests of the Islanders. Thirdly, it was argued that since the order was not made in the interests of the Islanders and was made without any consultation, it lacked rationality and proportionality – familiar grounds for a judicial review. And lastly, Robin Cook's statement to the House of Commons explaining why the Government chose not to appeal on the previous occasion, gave rise to a "legitimate expectation" that the Islanders would be allowed to return and resettle.

Despite there being unanimity on the part of the Law Lords in condemning the behaviour of successive governments as "disgraceful", and in confirming that prerogative orders could be subject to judicial scrutiny, the appeal resulted in a three to two majority in the Government's favour. The majority comprised Lords Hoffmann, Rodger and Carswell. There were clear differences in both tone and approach.

Lord Hoffmann did not regard the "right of abode" either as "fundamental" or necessarily a "constitutional right". He accepted that the position was as declared in the 29th Chapter of Magna Carta: "No freeman shall be taken, or imprisoned ... or exiled ... but by the law of the land." "[B]ut by the law of the land" being the operative words; and as in Blackstone's *Commentaries on the Laws of England*: "But no power on earth, except the authority of Parliament, can send any send any subject of England *out* of the land against his will ... ." At common law any subject of the Crown had the right to enter and remain in the United Kingdom whenever and for as long as he pleased, Lord Hoffmann pointed out, and this right could not be removed by the exercise of prerogative powers; but the position was different in regard to a ceded colony where the Crown had the authority "to make or unmake the law of the land". In his view the citations from Magna Carta and Blackstone demonstrated that the right of abode was a creature of law, "the law gives it and the law may take it away": there was no basis for saying that the right of abode was in its nature "so fundamental that the legislative powers of the

Crown simply [could] not touch it." He added that it did not "assist the argument to call it a constitutional right."

He was equally emphatic on the "peace, order and good government" point: the prerogative power of the Crown to legislate for a ceded colony had never been limited by the requirement that legislation should be for the peace, order and good government or otherwise for the benefit of the inhabitants of that colony. The Crown was entitled to legislate solely in the interests of the UK. Furthermore, there was ample authority in the case law to demonstrate that the words "peace, order, and good government" were not to be interpreted as words limiting the power of a legislature. The courts had previously declined to inquire whether legislation within the territorial scope of that power was in fact for the benefit of the inhabitants in question.

Lord Hoffmann went on to reject the argument that the orders lacked rationality and proportionality because they were not made in the interests of the Islanders, and without consulting them. Whilst he agreed with what Lord Bingham, when Master of the Rolls, had once said in another judicial review case to the effect that where a measure affected fundamental rights, or had profoundly intrusive effects, the public body in question would be required to demonstrate a most compelling justification, it had to be borne in mind precisely what fundamental rights and "profoundly intrusive effects" one was considering in this context. Effects which would have been "profoundly intrusive" in 1968 would not necessarily have been so in 2004:

> If we were in 1968 and concerned with a proposal to remove the [Islanders] … with little or no provision for their future, that would indeed be a profoundly intrusive measure affecting their fundamental rights. But that was many years ago, the deed had been done, the wrong confessed, compensation agreed and paid.

He pointed out that without financial support from the UK Government it would simply not be possible to live on the outer islands, as evidenced by the fact that following the decision of the court and the statement in 2001 no one had ever returned with the intention of living there. In Lord Hoffmann's view the whole of this litigation was simply "the continuation of protest by other means." Taking into account questions of public expenditure and economic viability, the 2004 order could not be described as irrational, unreasonable or otherwise an abuse of power.

Finally, as for the "legitimate expectation" point, Lord Hoffmann did not think the promise contained in the 2000 statement met the requirement of being clear, unambiguous and devoid of qualification: the outcome of the feasibility study would have been critical to any future decisions. Furthermore, even if it were capable of being interpreted as an unambiguous promise, there was sufficient "public interest" justification for the adoption of a new policy in 2004, which recognised and reflected the economic realities.

Unlike Lord Hoffmann, Lord Rodger thought it was "certainly arguable" that it was a fundamental principle of English law that no citizen should be exiled or banished from a British colony and sent to a foreign country. However, he understood the statement of Lord Mansfield that the Crown was not empowered to change the law of a conquered or ceded territory "contrary to fundamental principles" to mean in the particular context of that case, that the Crown could not use its power to legislate for a ceded colony without the consent of Parliament so as to exempt an inhabitant of the colony from import duty or taxes, or to confer on him some exclusive privilege. It was a mistake to read too much into Lord Mansfield's statement. Furthermore, in the late 1960s, the Privy Council (comprising eminent Law Lords of the day) specifically rejected an argument that a particular law passed in Ceylon was void because it was repugnant to the fundamental principles of justice. Lord Rodger regarded this as compelling authority for the proposition that the legislature was "unfettered." He therefore concluded that the order was not open to challenge on the ground that it was repugnant to any fundamental principle of English common law by preventing or restricting the return of the Islanders.

Like Lord Hoffmann, Lord Rodger did not regard the time-honoured phrase "... for peace, order and good governance of the territory" as amounting to words of limitation. There was persuasive case law demonstrating that fact. There was no requirement that the interests of the Islanders were paramount. In his view the remedy for countering an oppressive Order in Council was political, not legal – for example, by securing the involvement and scrutiny of Parliament. It could not be said that no reasonable Secretary of State would have enacted the two Orders in 2004. There was no prospect of the Chagos Islanders living on the outer islands in the foreseeable future, and there were no grounds for impugning the Government's good faith in concluding that immigration control was necessary in the interests of security and defence considerations.

Finally, like Lord Hoffmann, he felt unable to spell out of Robin Cook's 2000 statement a clear and unambiguous promise that the Islanders would be allowed to return. The outcome of the feasibility study was critical.

Lord Carswell, agreeing with much that had been said by Lords Hoffmann and Rodger, did not regard the right of abode as inviolable: he thought it could be as much the subject of a prerogative order as ordinary legislation by Parliament; and he pointed to the danger of stepping into the political arena were one to treat the mantra "... for peace, order and good governance" as a fixed term of reference in judging the legality of a prerogative order. So far as grounds for judicial review were concerned, since in the light of the fact that over the years the whole of the substructure of the Islands' economy had disappeared, it was not possible to characterise the 2004 orders as being in any way irrational; and like Lord Hoffmann and Lord Rodger he felt unable to read into the 2000 statement an unambiguous promise.

The minority comprised Lord Bingham and Lord Mance. Lord Bingham was forthright and succinct, summarising his conclusions within the confines of a mere two and a half pages, whilst expressing his complete agreement with the much fuller analysis of Lord Mance. He noted that there had been no previous instance in which the royal prerogative had been exercised "to exile an indigenous population from its homeland. Authority negates the existence of such a power." The relationship between the citizen and the Crown was based on reciprocal duties of allegiance and protection: the duty of protection, he added dryly, could not ordinarily be discharged by removing and excluding the citizen from his homeland. Lord Bingham concluded there was no royal prerogative power to make the 2004 order; the fact that the same result could have been achieved by legislation through Parliament, but not without public debate, was neither here nor there. The order was accordingly void.

Additionally, in Lord Bingham's view, the Islanders' claim based on ordinary judicial review principles succeeded because "there was simply no good reason" for making the order. Resettlement was clearly not perceived back in 2000 as a threat to the security of Diego Garcia, and the position had not changed in 2004. "It was not said", commented Lord Bingham, "that Osama Bin Laden was planning to be active in the Indian Ocean." Finally, in the making of the orders no consideration had been given to the interests of the Islanders, and in making those orders the Government had contradicted "a clear representation" made by the Secretary of State. That the right of return was of little practical value was no answer: it could not be doubted that it was of tangible value, "and the smaller its practical value the less reason to take it away."

Lord Mance set the tone for his dissent in distancing himself from some of Lord Hoffmann's factual observations. In particular he did not accept that the Islanders were engaged in a mere campaign to obtain support for resettlement or to embarrass the UK or US Governments. In his view "their wish for recognition of their historic connection, and ... of their rights of abode [was] deeply felt, longstanding, and understandable." Arguments that any right of abode was really only symbolic, missed the point: they simply indicated that the right claimed would have no practical effect on the Islands. Those islands, apart from Diego Garcia, appeared to be "an unspoilt nature paradise to which an increasing number of long-distance yachtsmen venture[d] to spend ... months without noticeable disturbance to the operations of the United States base at Diego Garcia many miles away."

Lord Mance pointed out that whilst there was no express definition of the Crown's powers over ceded territories in terms of "peace, order and good government" a sense of their practical meaning could be got from the British Settlements Act 1887, which conferred on "the Queen in Council" the power to make such laws as appeared to her "necessary for the peace, order and good government of Her Majesty's subjects and others within any British settlement." The Act was intended to equate the position of settlements with that of ceded colonies. Both Lord Mansfield's statement and his decision in the eighteenth-century case, argued Lord Mance, clearly pointed to limitations on the power to legislate in the absence of Parliament. Once the British Indian Ocean Territory had become an independent British colony in 1965, the Islanders were, in Lord Mansfield's words, under the protection of the Crown. Unsurprisingly there was no precedent for legislating for the removal of an entire population. It was accepted that so far as the UK was concerned, and as the citations from Magna Carta and Blackstone's *Commentaries* made clear, a British citizen certainly had the common law right of abode; and in his view there was no basis for distinguishing in this respect between the UK and a ceded colony: the reciprocal relationship of allegiance and protection was the same. The contention that the Islanders had no right of abode in the territory from which they had been removed came close, in Lord Mance's view, to treating them as if they were aliens; and the Government's alternative case that the Islanders' common law right of abode could be overridden by a prerogative order, effectively treated the territory as if it was nothing more than bare land, and as if the inhabitants were a mere inconvenience. He concluded that there was no prerogative power to enact a constitution by an Order in Council, which had the aim of depopulating the whole of a habitable territory in the interests of the United Kingdom and its allies: "A constitution which exiles a territory's inhabitants is a contradiction in terms." Any of the orders which purported to achieve this between 1965 and 1973 were void.

Like Lord Bingham, he thought the 2000 statement amounted to an unconditional assurance that the Islanders had a legal right to return: there was not the slightest indication that it was conditional on the outcome of the feasibility study. Agreeing with the approach of both the Divisional Court and the Court of Appeal, he concluded that the 2004 order was void. The Government had failed to give any weight to the Islanders' right of abode or to the legitimate expectation on their part of the right to return generated by Robin Cook's statement; and the outcome of the feasibility study had been known two years previously without it being thought necessary to take any further steps, and during which time no strategic or security threat had been identified.

To characterise this remarkable case as an instance of "differing responses to constitutional rights issues" is perhaps to understate what was going on here. There was no agreement as to whether a British citizen had a fundamental right of abode: Lord Hoffmann thought he did not: merely a common law right not be removed from the UK; Lord Rodger thought that "arguably" he did; Lord Carswell was agnostic on the point; and Lords Bingham and Mance thought he most definitely did. And of course critically there was no agreement as to whether the Government, through the exercise of the royal prerogative, had the power to legislate for the removal of British citizens from the country or territory in which they lived. What was common to all three of the majority Law Lords was that they were disposed to treat the litigation as essentially a political and symbolic gesture not rooted in reality; and the conviction that to affirm the decision in favour of the Islanders would involve making a judgment on the merits of the reasons put forward by the Government for the making of the order, and thereby inevitably entering into the political arena. The minority, on the other hand, did not shrink from treating those reasons as either implausible or absurd, and therefore from concluding that here was a clear abuse of power which should not go unchecked and for which there should be a legal sanction.

(2) PRIVATE SMITH AND THE REACH OF ARTICLE 1

One of the unintended consequences of the Iraq war was that it gave rise to a series of important human rights cases in the English courts. In one case the claimants were relatives of six Iraqi civilians who had been killed by British troops during the period following the conclusion of major hostilities and prior to the installation of the Iraqi interim government. Five had been shot in the course of operations in separate incidents, and the sixth had been beaten to death whilst detained in a British military detention unit. The claimants sought independent enquiries into those deaths, relying on the Human Rights Act 1998 and Article 2 of the European Convention, "Everyone's right to life shall be protected by law." The House of Lords decided that there was no jurisdiction in regard to the five civilians shot dead in the course of military operations, but that there *was* jurisdiction in regard to the civilian beaten to death in the British military detention unit.[6] In another case two mothers of servicemen killed in action in Iraq brought claims alleging a breach by the UK Government of Article 2 in exposing their sons to the risk of death by failing to make proper enquiries and to take appropriate advice as to whether the invasion of Iraq would be lawful. A nine-member panel of the House of Lords held that there was no procedural obligation implied by Article 2 for the Government to have carried out such an enquiry.[7] The case to be discussed continued in the tradition of this litigation.[8]

Private Smith had served less than two months in Iraq, during which time he had complained of experiencing problems with the extreme heat. Whilst on operational duties, and away from his base, he died of heat stroke. At the inquest the coroner, who was sharply critical of the military authorities, declined to disclose certain information classified by the Ministry of Defence as confidential, on the ground that, contrary to the contention put forward by lawyers representing the mother of Private Smith, the procedural obligations to be implied under Article 2 of the European Convention (the protection of the right to life), scheduled to the Human Rights Act 1998, did not apply. The coroner's refusal was challenged in judicial review proceedings. The judge ruled that a member of the armed forces was within the jurisdiction of the UK for the purposes of the European Convention wherever he might be, and that therefore Article 2 applied to the inquest. The Court of Appeal upheld that decision. The Secretary of State (Defence) duly appealed to the Supreme Court. Jurisdiction under the Convention hinged on the application of Article 1: "The High Contracting parties shall secure to everyone within their jurisdiction the rights defined in Section 1 of this Convention." The central issue, therefore, was whether a member of the armed forces, whilst on active service in Iraq, was under the jurisdiction of

6 *Secretary of State for Defence v Al-Skeini & Ors* [2007] UKHL 26, [2008] 1 AC 153.

7 *R (Gentle) & Anor v The Prime Minister & Anor* [2008] UKHL 20, [2008] 1 AC 1356.

8 *R (Smith) v Secretary of State for Defence & Anor* [2010] UKSC 29, [2011] 1 AC 1.

the UK within the meaning of Article 1 for the purpose of benefitting from Convention rights such as under Article 2. A nine-member Supreme Court decided by a majority of six to three that he was not.

Central to all the judgments was a 2001 decision of the Grand Chamber of the European Court of Human Rights.[9] That case concerned the air strikes carried out by members of NATO on the radio and TV centre in Belgrade at the time of the Kosovo conflict, and had been brought against the member states involved by relatives of civilians killed in those raids and by one injured survivor. The issue was whether the claimants and their deceased relatives came within the jurisdiction of the respective states (all signatories to the Convention) within the meaning of Article 1. The Court ruled that they did not. In its view it was clear that the framers of the Convention intended the word "jurisdiction" in Article 1 to have the same *territorial* connotation as it had in public international law; and as the scope of Article 1 was determinative "of the scope and reach of the entire Convention system of human rights protection", it was desirable to stick to the original meaning and not to allow that meaning to change over the course of time. However, the Court recognised there could be exceptions to the territorial principle but that these would require "special justification in the particular circumstances of each case." In essence these were where one state exercised effective control over the territory of another state; where there was territorial extension by analogy, an embassy or consulate, for example; and what has been compendiously described as "common sense extensions of the notion of jurisdiction to fit cases which should plainly be within the scope of the Convention."[10]

It was accepted by all nine Justices that jurisdiction within the meaning of Article 1 was primarily territorial, and that the facts of Private Smith's case did not fit neatly into any of the exceptions contemplated by the judgment of the European Court: the UK did not exercise "effective territorial control".

Equally important, at least as far as the majority was concerned, was the House of Lords decision involving the killing of the six Iraqi civilians. There, a majority of the Law Lords had concluded that they should follow and apply the decision of the European Court on the basis that the scope of

---

9 *Bankovic & Ors v Belgium & Ors* [2001] ECHR 890, (2001) 11 BHRC 435.

10 As an illustration of the latter, the Court referred to a case involving a complaint under Article 6 – the right to a fair trial – where the claimants had been tried in proceedings in an Andorran court presided over by a French judge. Andorra was not a signatory to the Convention, but the claimants were treated as falling within the jurisdiction of France.

the Convention in terms of jurisdiction was pre-eminently a matter for that court, and it was desirable that the word "jurisdiction" in the context of Article 1, should have a fixed and permanent meaning.[11] What divided the Supreme Court was the question whether operating as part of the armed forces overseas (and not on premises under military control) should be a recognised exception to the territorial principle for the purposes of Article 1.

The majority comprised Lords Phillips, Hope, Rodger, Walker, Brown and Collins. (Lords Hope, Rodger and Brown were all parties to the decision in the Iraqi civilians case.) Lord Phillips, whilst he recognised that it was "unattractive to postulate that once [members of the armed forces] are outside the territorial jurisdiction in the service of their country they lose the protection accorded by the Convention and the Human Rights Act", thought the approach taken in the House of Lords (and spelt out in the leading judgment of Lord Brown) was correct: namely, that it would not be appropriate to extend jurisdiction within the meaning of Article 1 beyond the scope of what had been previously decided by the European Court in the Belgrade bombing case. Furthermore, he thought the European Court was right to apply the "original meaning" principle in that case. There were also obvious difficulties in extending Article 1 jurisdiction to the armed forces when serving abroad: it was "not practicable for a state to secure many of the Convention rights and freedoms for troops in active service abroad ... The proper tribunal for resolving this issue [was] the Strasbourg court itself."

Lord Hope's stance was precisely the same: it would be inappropriate to go beyond the scope of the decision by the European Court. In his view there were no policy grounds for extending the scope of the Convention to members of the armed forces serving abroad "simply because they [were] under the authority and control of the United Kingdom"; and he reiterated the concern expressed in the course of an interview by the recently retired President of the European Court in regard to any extra-territorial extension to jurisdiction as had been argued for in the Belgrade bombing case; namely, that the court could not function effectively as a court when there was no prospect of obtaining reliable evidence as to events beyond the frontiers of member states, and that it would risk turning itself into a campaigning organisation, making allegations without solid evidence. He thought there

---

11 The Human Rights Act 1998 requires that the British courts "take into account" decisions of the European Court, though not necessarily follow them. However, it has become the practice to follow decisions of the European Court which are decisions of the Grand Chamber and which reflect clearly established principles.

was a clear distinction between recognition of "a member state's jurisdiction over persons within an area beyond [its] frontiers over which [its] armed forces have established total and exclusive *de facto* control such as a military base [or] a detention centre", and withholding such recognition in regard to areas where the armed forces do not have exclusive control and "where the safeguarding of Convention rights cannot be guaranteed, and where reliable evidence about the circumstances of alleged violations could be hard to come by because the state over whose territory these operations are being conducted is not a party to the Convention."

Of the majority, Lord Collins provided the most detailed analysis of the issue. (Lord Brown saw no reason to depart from the view he had expressed in the Iraqi civilians case – namely, to follow the European Court's approach in the Belgrade bombing case. Lords Walker and Rodger endorsed the analysis and conclusions of Lord Collins.) Lord Collins was at pains to demonstrate that there was nothing in either the drafting history or the case law that gave "the slightest credence to the proposition that the Convention was to apply to the relations of the state with its armed forces abroad." It was entirely sensible that jurisdiction should be territorially based and be extended extra-territorially only in very limited and exceptional circumstances.

Like Lord Hope, he saw no good policy reasons for extending the scope of the Convention to armed forces engaged in military operations abroad. In his view there were good reasons for not extending its scope in this way: the courts would ultimately become involved with issues relating to the conduct of hostilities which were essentially non-justiciable. Jurisdiction could not be established simply on the basis that the armed forces abroad were under the authority and control of the UK or that there was some kind of freestanding jurisdictional link between the UK and those armed forces. Such reasoning would be inconsistent with the decision of the European Court in the Belgrade bombing case.

The minority comprised Baroness Hale (who, like Lord Brown, was a party to the House of Lords decision in the Iraqi civilians case) and Lords Rodger and Mance. Lord Mance emphatically rejected the premise underlying the majority view that acceptance of the thrust of the respective decisions of the European Court and the House of Lords led inescapably to the conclusion that members of the armed forces on active service abroad were outside the jurisdiction for the purposes of Article 1. Both cases concerned *civilians* killed outside the territories of member states, who had no pre-existent relationship or connection (e.g. nationality) with the member states in question: there was a one-off interaction between the two. Therefore neither case was directly in point.

For Lord Mance there were compelling reasons for treating the facts of the present case as falling within a recognised exception to the territoriality principle. The exceptions recognised by the European Court all involved the exercise of power and authority by state A over individuals – particularly its own nationals – by consent, invitation or acquiescence of state B. At the relevant time the civil administration of Iraq was being carried out by what was called the Coalition Provisional Authority, an emanation of the two main occupying powers, the UK and the US. Whilst it did not have complete and effective control over parts of Iraq such as to equate with territory of the UK, it had complete control over its armed forces, and did so with the consent or acquiescence of the state of Iraq. If the UK did not have jurisdiction under international law over its armed forces in Iraq, then *no* state did. Lord Mance argued that it could not sensibly be the case that once a member of the armed forces was operating outside his base, he then ceased to be under the jurisdiction of the UK and to have the benefit of any Convention rights.

In Lord Mance's view, the practical difficulties in enforcing Convention rights in relation to a state's armed forces operating outside its territory was no justification for giving a more limited meaning to the concept of jurisdiction than that which followed from the guidance provided by the European Court. The "clear answer" to the question posed by this case was that:

> where the United Kingdom was present in Iraq, both with the consent of the only administrative authority that existed and in any event as an occupying power recognised under international law ... there [was] an irresistible case for treating the United Kingdom's jurisdiction over its armed forces for the purposes of Article 1 as extending to soldiers [wherever they were] serving in Iraq ...

Lord Kerr expressed his "complete agreement" with the judgment of Lord Mance, as did Baroness Hale. In particular, like Lord Mance, and for the same reasons, he saw no basis for concluding that the decision either in the Belgrade bombing case or in the Iraqi civilians case precluded the extending of jurisdiction to the armed forces of the UK serving abroad, or limiting the exceptions to the territorial principle to the examples expressly referred to in the judgment of the European Court.

It is tempting to characterise the division of opinion in this case as a divide between the cautious and the bold. What in fact appears to have accounted for the uncompromising stance of the minority is their greater willingness to recognise as an unacceptable anomaly a situation in which members of the armed forces on active service abroad lose the protection of their Convention rights, and indeed are not subject to the jurisdiction of *any* state, once they are operating away from their base. Clearly, the minority regarded what they perceived to be the moral imperative as outweighing in importance considerations such as the potential difficulties in enforcing Convention rights or the obtaining of evidence in such situations.[12]

(3) USING A SLEDGEHAMMER TO CRACK A NUT

From time to time disagreement in the House of Lords and the Supreme Court has been confined to the dissent of just one member of the panel, and which has been expressed in the form of a single dissenting judgment. Perhaps the most striking instance of this in recent years has been the dissent of Baroness Hale in a nine-member Supreme Court decision concerning the weight to be attached to ante-nuptial agreements, in which she pointed out that there was "a gender dimension to the issue which some may think ill-suited to a decision by a court consisting of eight men and one woman."[13] The case to be discussed is one such case where the disagreement was confined to the dissent of a single member of the panel: it concerned the

---

[12] Their approach in fact appears to have been vindicated by the more recent decisions of the Grand Chamber of the European Court. The Court has since reversed the House of Lords decision in regard to the Iraqis killed by British troops in operational incidents, adopting a broader based jurisdiction than that applied by the House of Lords. The Court concluded that during the period between the removal of the old regime and the accession of the Interim Government, the UK "assumed the exercise of some of the public powers normally ... exercised by a sovereign government ... In these exceptional circumstances, the United Kingdom, through its soldiers engaged in security operations ... exercised authority and control over [the] individuals killed in the course of such ... operations, so as to establish a jurisdictional link between the deceased and the United Kingdom for the purposes of Article 1...": *Al-Skeini and Others v The United Kingdom* [2011] ECHR 1093. This decision has now been very recently applied by the Supreme Court in ruling there was jurisdiction within the UK for the purposes of enforcing Convention rights in regard to claims brought by families of soldiers killed by roadside bombs when travelling in inadequately protected vehicles: *Smith & Others v Ministry of Defence* [2013] UKSC 41.

[13] *Radmacher (formerly Granatino) v Granatino* [2010] UKSC 42, [2011] 1 AC 534, at 577.

introduction of an amendment to the immigration rules by the Home Secretary with a view to reducing the risk of forced marriages.[14]

The claimants were a young couple who had married in the UK. The husband was an 18-year-old Chilean who had entered the UK on a student visa, and the wife was a 17-year-old British girl. The husband was refused permission to remain in the UK because the immigration rules did not permit leave to enter or remain in the UK as a spouse of a person lawfully

---

14 *R (Quila & Anor) v Secretary of State for the Home Department* [2011] UKSC 45, [2012] 1 AC 621. The question is not infrequently asked: why bother to deliver a fully reasoned judgment when you are in a minority of one? Why risk complicating even more what may already be a complicated case? Isn't it really a pointless exercise? In some cases the explanation clearly lies in the need to register a protest; in other cases it is the need felt by the lone dissenter to flag up what he or she considers to be potential difficulties arising from the majority decision: in other words, a duty to warn. A good example of the former is when Lord Millett dissented on whether the extended meaning given in the Rent Act 1977 to the spouse of a deceased tenant as a person who has lived as "his wife or her husband" can include the surviving partner of a gay couple. Section 3 of the Human Rights Act 1998 requires the courts, "*so far as possible*", to interpret domestic legislation in a way that is compatible with Convention rights. It was accepted that the ordinary and natural meaning of the phrase would not include a gay couple, (and therefore on its *ordinary* meaning the legislation was incompatible with Article 8), but Lord Millett alone concluded that, even when taking into account the underlying principle of the legislation, it was simply not possible to give the phrase this extended meaning. "I have given long and anxious consideration", he said, "to the question whether in the interests of unanimity I should suppress my dissent, but I have come to the conclusion that I should not. The question is of great constitutional importance, for it goes to the relationship between the legislature and the judiciary, and hence ultimately to the supremacy of Parliament." In his view the majority decision "subverted" the will of Parliament: *Ghaidan v Godin-Mendoza* [2004] UKHL 30, [2004] 2 AC 557, at 583. A good, and very recent, example of the latter is when Lord Reed dissented on the question whether an honest belief by a defendant that his pursuit of the course of conduct alleged to be harassment was in order to prevent or detect the commission of a crime, could be a defence within the meaning of section 1(3) of the Protection from Harassment Act 1997, when there was no rational basis for such belief. The majority concluded that it could not be a defence: they drew a distinction between behaviour which was irrational and that which was simply unreasonable. Lord Reed thought it wrong that criminal liability should turn on a subtle distinction between irrationality and unreasonableness, and pointed to the difficulties which a trial judge would inevitably experience when attempting to explain the distinction to a jury: *Hayes v Willoughby* [2013] UKSC 17. The lone dissenter in the case to be discussed is Lord Brown, who since his recent retirement has contributed an essay to a volume published in memory of the late Lord Rodger on the subject of dissenting judgments. He explains that there are simply occasions when one feels obliged to dissent because one's conscience tells one to. He also makes the point that a dissenting judgment performs the useful function of demonstrating to the losing party that the arguments advanced on his behalf have been carefully listened to and have been found at least by one member of the court to be persuasive.

present and settled in the UK if either party to the marriage was under the age of 18. (There was no dispute that the couple were in love with each other.) After the wife's 18th birthday, the husband re-applied for permission, but this was again refused, this time because the immigration rules had been amended to increase the minimum age to 21. The claimants challenged the legality of this rule change, contending that it breached Article 8(1) of the European Convention – the right to respect for private and family life.

As the background to the change in the minimum age from 18 to 21 ultimately proved to be of critical importance to the outcome of the case, a brief summary is necessary. The change followed the acceptance by the then Home Secretary of recommendations contained in a report of the Home Affairs Select Committee of the House of Commons, and responses to a consultation paper which she had issued prior to the publication of the Select Committee's report. For some time forced marriages had been identified as a growing problem, and in view of the fact that countries with a significant number of immigrants, such as Germany and the Netherlands, had recently increased the minimum age from 18 to 21, the Home Secretary had previously commissioned a report from a specialist unit at Bristol University to examine whether the minimum age should be increased in this country as well. The report recommended there should be no increase, concluding that to raise the minimum age would be likely to have a detrimental effect and, in particular, would be "discriminatory on racial and ethnic grounds and with regard to arranged and love marriages." The report was not published, as the Home Secretary and two of the external peer reviewers were critical of some aspects of the research which had been undertaken, and of some of its contents. Prior to introducing the change in the minimum age requirement, the Home Secretary explained that raising the age to 21 would provide an opportunity for individuals: (i) to develop maturity and life skills which would help them resist pressures of being forced into marriage; (ii) complete education and training; and (iii) seek help and advice, and to delay the making of a decision to sponsor the spouse living abroad.

Initially the claimants failed in their application for judicial review, but the Court of Appeal reversed the decision on the ground that the Home Secretary's application of the amended rule to the claimants was indeed an unjustified interference with their rights to respect for their family life within the meaning of Article 8. The Home Secretary appealed to the Supreme Court. The Court, comprising Lord Phillips, Baroness Hale, Lord Brown, Lord Clarke and Lord Wilson, dismissed her appeal by a majority of four to one.

The majority judgments were given by Lord Wilson and Baroness Hale. Lord Wilson recognised that forced marriages were a serious problem for the UK, and that the change had been introduced to combat that problem. However, in his view there was no doubt in this case that Article 8 was "engaged": there was an interference by a public authority with the exercise of a person's right to respect for his private and family life, and the gravity of the consequences were such as "to engage the operation of the Article". (He in fact described the interference as "colossal".) The issue was whether the Home Secretary could justify that interference within the meaning of Article 8(2), i.e. on the grounds that it was necessary for the protection of, *inter alia*, health and morals and of "the rights and freedoms of others".

In the light of settled legal principles, Lord Wilson argued, the critical questions were: (1) was the introduction of the new minimum age requirement no more than was necessary to achieve its objective; and (2) did its introduction strike a fair balance between the rights of the individual and the interests of the community? Furthermore, the question of proportionality – for that is what it was – was one which had to be judged objectively by the court; and, citing from a leading judgment of Lord Bingham, he emphasised that in so doing, it was not appropriate in such a case for the court to accord the views of the Secretary of State any special deference.

In Lord Wilson's view the Home Secretary had failed to provide any evidence supporting the reasons which she had cited for introducing the change. Those reasons raised a number of questions – he proceeded to list 10 – which remained unanswered. He noted that the Deputy Director of Immigration Policy, in her written evidence in the case, had stated that the question of proportionality, in terms of impact upon couples entering into unforced marriages where one or both of the couple were under 21, had been "considered carefully when drafting the policy"; and that the evidence demonstrated that the rates of forced marriage in the years 2005–2008 were highest among those aged 17–20. In fact, Lord Wilson observed, the evidence relied upon demonstrated nothing of the kind, and then proceeded to explain in some detail why this was the case.

Having analysed the background, Lord Wilson concluded that the Home Secretary had failed to establish that the change in the minimum age was no more than was necessary to achieve her, albeit laudable, objective; and that she had likewise failed to establish that it struck a fair balance between the rights of parties to an unforced marriage and the interests of the community in preventing forced marriages. The amended rule, he drily commented, was on any view "a sledge-hammer", but the Secretary of State had "failed to identify the size of the nut."

Baroness Hale identified the issue in the case in the same way as Lord Wilson. For her the only question was whether "the colossal interference" with the claimants' rights to respect for their private and family life was objectively justified, bearing in mind that the object of deterring, preventing or delaying forced marriages was a legitimate aim within the meaning of Article 8(2).

Having observed that in "today's world it is recognised that everyone has the right to decide whether or not to enter a particular marriage" but that "the right to marry [was] just as important as the right not to marry", Baroness Hale went on to state that in her view there were a number of reasons for concluding that the change in the minimum age was not a proportionate response to the problem.

Firstly, although nobody knew the figures, it was clear that the rule would interfere with more voluntary marriages than it would prevent, deter or delay forced marriages, yet "the scale and severity of the impact upon these unforced marriages [had] scarcely been considered." One was here concerned with the imposition of a blanket restriction: the European Court of Human Rights, in the prisoners' votes case, had ruled that "a general, automatic, indiscriminate restriction" on a vitally important Convention right fell outside any margin for discretion.

Secondly, if the rule proved ineffective in preventing a forced marriage, it may do a great deal more harm than good. Thus, "a young woman may be sent abroad and forced to marry against her will, and kept there until she can sponsor her husband to come here", during which time she could be subjected to repeated sexual abuse.

Thirdly, like Lord Wilson, in her view none of the evidence relied upon by the Secretary of State supported the reasons she had given when introducing the new rule, and certainly it did not amount to the "conclusive evidence" which had been called for by the Home Affairs Select Committee at the time it reported.

Lord Brown dissented. He fundamentally disagreed with the whole approach of the majority to the issue. As he saw it, the duty of the court was to decide the case not by reference to the quality of the research and related matters before the new rule had been introduced, "but by reference to the proportionality as perceived today between the impact of the rule change on such 'innocent' young couples as are adversely affected by it, and the overall benefit of the rule in terms of combating forced marriages." The stark facts were that the extent of the "forced marriages" problem was impossible to gauge, and it was simply not possible to answer the 10 questions which Lord Wilson had identified as having been raised by the reasons for the rule change given by Secretary of State. So at the end of the day it was largely a matter of judgment; and such judgment, unless it was demonstrably wrong, should be one for the Government to make, and not the courts.

He pointed out that Germany, Austria and the Netherlands had imposed the same minimum age requirement as the UK Government, and that Denmark had in fact imposed a minimum age requirement of 24. It could surely not be plausibly argued, commented Lord Brown, that simply because the evidence was uncertain and the whole problem a difficult one, the Secretary of State was disabled from making a policy judgment and from increasing the minimum age to that imposed by other EU countries.

Lord Brown was dismissive of the relevance of the European Court's ruling in the prisoners' votes case referred to by Baroness Hale. He thought the real parallel to this case would have been if the UK Government had legislated to give all prisoners the vote who were serving less than a four-year term. It surely could not be then seriously argued that in denying the vote to those serving four years or more, the Government would fall foul of the principle against "a general, automatic, indiscriminate restriction". He was likewise dismissive of Baroness Hale's comment that the right to marry was just as important as the right not to do so: she could not possibly have meant by this, he said, that the postponement by up to three years of a couple's wish to live together as man and wife in this country was just as much a violation of human rights as a forced marriage.

Whilst the question of proportionality in the context of Article 8 was ultimately for the courts to decide, in Lord Brown's view in a case such as this the Government should be accorded "a very substantial area of discretionary judgment." He concluded his judgment in the following terms:

> In a sensitive context such as that of forced marriages it [would be] not merely impermissible but positively unwise for the courts ... to frustrate Government policy except in the clearest of cases. To my mind this cannot be regarded as the clearest of cases.

The nature of the sharp disagreement between the majority and Lord Brown which emerged in this case is in fact symptomatic of an increasing cause of tension and unease within the higher judiciary. The underlying position of the majority was that there was absolutely no reason to hold back from conducting a rigorous analysis of the merits of the Government's case for raising the minimum age: what was involved was indisputably an interference with an important Convention right; the burden was on the Government to justify that interference; and it was for the court to decide whether, looked at objectively, that burden had been discharged. Lord Brown's position was that in a case involving Government policy in a highly problematical and sensitive area, even though the facts involved an interference with Convention rights, the court had no business to substitute its own judgment for that of the Secretary of State. Rather, it should stick to its traditional role in judicial review cases of interfering with a decision only when the procedure employed in the decision-making process had been shown to be flawed or unfair, or the decision itself is shown to be wholly irrational. To do otherwise (as the majority had seen fit to do) would be to encroach on the exclusive preserve of the Government to make policy and make policy judgments, and would only help to fuel existing tensions between it and the judiciary.[15]

---

[15] Since the majority decision in this case, there have in fact been signs that the courts are less inclined to subject the reasons for any amendment to the immigration rules to such rigorous analysis. Recently the Court of Appeal, albeit not unanimously, upheld the rejection of a challenge to an amendment to the rules requiring foreign spouses wishing to settle in this country to produce a certificate of knowledge of the English language to a prescribed standard *prior* to entry. The majority view was that the degree of interference with Article 8 rights, although significant, was not "colossal"; that the introduction of this requirement as a means to facilitate the social integration of non-English speaking spouses was proportionate, despite the absence of empirical evidence to show that such a difficulty in achieving social integration was in fact a significant problem; and the test should be whether the Government's policy choice was "manifestly without reasonable foundation": the test laid down in a decision of the European Court of Human Rights concerned with discriminatory treatment. The dissenting appeal judge questioned whether, in the absence of *any* empirical evidence, ignorance of the English language by a foreign spouse on entry posed a significant social problem which justified this degree of interference with the right to respect for family life under Article 8: *R (Bibi & Anor) v Secretary of State for the Home Department* [2013] EWCA Civ 322.

(4) HOW SACROSANCT IS THE CONSTITUTIONAL RIGHT TO PURSUE A PRIVATE PROSECUTION?

Remarkably, it is a historical fact that until the late eighteenth century all criminal prosecutions were private, brought by or on behalf of the victim of the alleged crime; and the right to bring a private prosecution has survived the advent of the Metropolitan Police Force, the constabularies created by the County and Borough Police Act 1856, the office of the Director of Public Prosecutions created by the Prosecution of Offences Act 1879, which expressly declared that "nothing in [this] Act shall interfere with the right of any person to institute, undertake or carry on any criminal proceeding"; and finally the creation of the Crown Prosecution Service established under the Prosecution of Offences Act 1985. Subsequently, the right was qualified only to the extent that legislation in the early twentieth century provided that the Director of Public Prosecutions could, if he thought fit, at any stage take over the conduct of such a prosecution. It was accepted that as the Director had the power to take over such a prosecution, he also had the power to discontinue it. The Prosecution of Offences Act 1985 (in section 6) expressly preserved the right to bring a private prosecution, whilst at the same time expressly conferring on the Director (effectively the Crown Prosecution Service, of which the Director is the head) the power to take over a prosecution at any stage. Although some eminent judges have questioned the practical value of the right, regarding it as something of an anomaly, others have described it in terms such as a "useful constitutional safeguard against capricious, corrupt, or biased failure of … authorities to prosecute offences against the criminal law". Nowadays the right tends usually to be exercised by organisations such as the RSPB or the RSPCA, or retail stores in regard to shoplifting offences, and only very occasionally by individuals: the private prosecution several years ago arising from the murder of Stephen Lawrence was of course such a case.

The present case[16] arose from private prosecutions brought by the claimant against two men for common assault, and against a third for threatening and insulting behaviour. The Crown Prosecution Service (CPS) decided to take over these prosecutions, and then to discontinue them. It did so because it regarded the evidence as insufficient, although the claimant's lawyers took a different view. In making its decision, the CPS applied the test laid down in the Code for Crown Prosecutors applicable to all prosecutions for which it was responsible for initiating; namely, was it more likely than not that the

---

16 *R (Gujra) v Crown Prosecution Service* [2011] UKSC 52, [2012] 3 WLR 1227.

prosecution would result in a conviction.[17] This was popularly known as "the better than evens" or "the reasonable prospect" test. In fact until 2009 the CPS, when considering whether to take over a prosecution and continue or discontinue the proceedings, had adopted the policy of taking over and discontinuing such a prosecution *only* when in its view there was clearly no case to answer, and/or a prosecution was clearly *against* the public interest. A few years previously the then Director of Public Prosecutions had gone on record in explaining that it had "been considered that to apply the Code tests to private prosecutions would unfairly limit the right of individuals to bring their own cases." Thus, as one Justice of the Supreme Court put it, the Director had performed a *volte face*.

The claimant brought proceedings for judicial review of the decision by the CPS on the ground that the policy it had applied was unlawful and, in the alternative, on the ground that it was irrational. He was unsuccessful, but was given permission to appeal to the Supreme Court. The Supreme Court, by a majority of three to two, dismissed the appeal.

The majority comprised Lords Neuberger, Kerr and Wilson. The main issue, declared Lord Wilson, (and on this point everyone was agreed) was whether, in applying the "reasonable prospect" and public interest tests to a decision to intervene in a private prosecution in order to discontinue it, the Director (effectively the CPS) frustrated the policy which underpinned the express right to bring a private prosecution re-enacted in section 6 of the Prosecution of Offences Act 1985. He dismissed the suggestion by an Appeal Court judge in an earlier case, in which there had been an unsuccessful attempt to challenge a decision of the *refusal* by the Director to intervene in a private prosecution, that to apply the "reasonable prospect" test was effectively to emasculate the right. He pointed out that bodies such as the RSPCA and the RSPB routinely applied the test, as did other organisations such as retail stores.

There were a number of reasons, thought Lord Wilson, why the application of the new test to interventions was perfectly consistent with the policy underpinning section 6. Firstly, in focusing on the prospects of obtaining a conviction, the Director was posing a far more relevant question than by posing the question whether at the close of the prosecution case there was a case to answer. Secondly, Parliament did not choose to limit the discretion conferred on the Director in section 6 by any qualifying words. Thirdly, the

---

17 The code also required the CPS to consider whether or not a prosecution was in the public interest.

very purpose of establishing the CPS in the Prosecution of Offences Act 1985 was to remedy the apparent lack of consistency nationwide in the decisions as to whether to prosecute. Fourthly, a prosecution which has no reasonable prospect of success "draws inappropriately upon the resources of the court." And lastly, a defendant would have a legitimate grievance were he subjected to a prosecution to which, by the application of the usual criteria enshrined in the Code, he would not have been subjected. It was worth noting, Lord Wilson pointed out, that in Australia the Director of Prosecutions has always applied the "reasonable prospect" test when intervening to discontinue a private prosecution, which is the same test he applied to all other prosecutions.

Lord Neuberger was at pains to point out that the discretionary power conferred on the Director under section 6 was "unfettered". Like Lord Wilson he saw no basis for concluding that the application of the "reasonable prospect" and public interest tests frustrated the underlying policy of section 6. The presumption had to be that the new policy was lawful: it was hard to quarrel with a policy that required that a prosecution would not be initiated or conducted by the Director unless: (i) there was a better than evens prospect of securing a conviction; and (ii) it was in the public interest to continue with the prosecution.

In Lord Neuberger's view, so far as public prosecutions were concerned, the "reasonable prospect" test made good sense. It would be unfair to potential defendants to subject them to criminal proceedings unless there was a good chance of securing a conviction; court time should not be occupied by prosecutions which were speculative; and public money would be better spent on cases which were likely to prove successful. Whilst he recognised that these considerations did not by themselves "ineluctably mean" that the Director was justified in applying the test to private prosecutions, there were, he thought, additional factors which suggested that this was in fact the case. Firstly, like Lord Wilson, he was impressed with the fact that the primary purpose of the Prosecution of Offences Act 1985 was to introduce some consistency in the approach to initiating and conducting prosecutions. Secondly, where the Director had taken over a prosecution with the intention of continuing it, and fresh evidence emerged which significantly undermined the strength of the case, it was clearly right he would be entitled to apply the reasonable prospect test and discontinue the prosecution; and if that was right, there was an obvious logic in his applying the same test when considering whether to take over a prosecution with a view to discontinuing it. Thirdly, the considerations which he had mentioned as favouring the application of the reasonable prospect test rather than a less stringent test in the case of public prosecutions – avoidance of unfairness to defendants, use of court time and cost implications – were all highly relevant to private prosecutions as well.

Lord Neuberger, like Lord Wilson, rejected the notion that the new policy would effectively emasculate the right of an individual to bring a private prosecution: the evidence and available statistics suggested that a significant number of privately initiated prosecutions were capable of surviving the application of the reasonable prospect test. And whilst he accepted that one:

> should not be relaxed about a code, or rules or guidelines promulgated by any branch of the Executive, which ha[d] the effect of cutting down individuals' right of access to the courts, … the right to [bring] a private prosecution is not quite in the same category of rights as a right to seek a remedy or compensation for a wrong by bringing a claim in the civil courts.

Lord Kerr, in agreeing with the reasoning of both Lord Wilson and Lord Neuberger, pointed out that access to justice was "not always an unqualified right of the citizen." In judicial review proceedings, for example, the permission of the court was first required. Critically, in his view, the inference to be drawn from the Prosecution of Offences Act 1985 was that Parliament, in conferring on the Director the power to take over the conduct of a private prosecution without circumscribing that power in any way, intended that he should apply the same test to public and private prosecutions alike.

The minority judgments were those of Lord Mance and Baroness Hale. In Lord Mance's opinion the reluctance of a former Director of Public Prosecutions to apply the "reasonable prospect" test and to permit private prosecutions to proceed only if to do so could be shown to be in the public interest, was soundly rooted in "constitutional principle". That was the right of access to justice, a right granted by section 6 of the Prosecution of Offences Act 1985, and which the re-enactment of the right of the Director to take over the conduct of a private prosecution could not have been intended to subvert. As a matter of general principle, Parliament must be taken to have legislated against the background of rights "which the common law treats as fundamental or constitutional." If, pointed out Lord Mance, the intention behind the Prosecution of Offences Act 1985 had been, among other things, to apply the same test to both public and private prosecutions, it was remarkable that this fact remained unnoticed for some 24 years until the change in policy in 2009.

It had not been suggested at any time prior to the policy change, Lord Mance observed, that the Director could exercise the power to take over and discontinue "on the simple basis of evidential weakness" short of an abuse of process involving the pursuit of a hopeless case. In his view the policy and objects of the Prosecution of Offences Act 1985 could not have been intended to undermine the right to bring a private prosecution, "long recognised as fundamental", the manner which the Director's new policy would undoubtedly achieve. That right had always been a safeguard against the feeling of injustice that arises when, in the eyes of the public, the authorities failed to take steps to bring "culprits" before a criminal court.

There were cogent reasons, argued Lord Mance, why a different and less stringent test should be applied in the case of a private prosecution. Such a case was brought in the exercise of a constitutional right and not within the statutory framework of a public prosecution service, and at private expense. And it was a fact of life that it was possible for lawyers to hold differing but perfectly reasonable views as to the strength of a case or of a particular piece of evidence, and specifically whether there was a reasonable prospect of securing a conviction or whether the public interest test had been satisfied. Why, in such circumstances, should the Director's view prevail?

Baroness Hale agreed completely with Lord Mance. She could not accept that it was the intention of Parliament, when setting up the CPS in 1985, "to allow the Director to reduce the centuries-old right of private prosecution almost to vanishing point: in effect, to a right to pursue those prosecutions which the CPS are content to have pursued but would prefer to have pursued by someone else." In her view the right of access to a court to prosecute an alleged offender was as much a constitutional right as a right of access to a court to bring a civil claim. The cutting down of such a right could only be achieved by clear and express words. Furthermore, how in relation to a case where there may be differing but reasonable views on the part of the lawyers as to the likelihood of a conviction, could it conceivably have been the intention of Parliament to allow the CPS to take over and prevent a private prosecution?

It is very obvious that the disagreement in this case reflected wholly contrasting views as to the nature of the "right" which was at its centre. The majority treated it in what was essentially a pragmatic manner. In other words, despite its historical provenance, it had to be seen in its modern setting. We now had a national prosecution service governed by a sensible and workable Code. To perpetuate the previous distinction in regard to evidence and the public interest between public and private prosecutions would have amounted to the perpetuating of an anomaly which was unacceptable, unacceptable because it would be wrong to let a private prosecution proceed in circumstances where a publicly conducted prosecution would not have been allowed to do so. The minority's position was that the right was indisputably both a constitutional and fundamental right, and had to be seen from the individual citizen's point of view, namely as a safeguard of historical importance. There was nothing in the legislation, and specifically the Prosecution of Offences Act 1985, which hinted at the whittling down of that right. To do so would in fact violate another constitutional right: namely, access to justice.

(5) ARE THERE LIMITS TO THE RIGHT TO KEEP LEGAL ADVICE CONFIDENTIAL?

The right of a person not to be compelled to disclose to third parties legal advice which he has requested and received has for more than two centuries been recognised as a playing a crucial public interest role in ensuring that people who need advice and help on legal matters can communicate with their legal advisers in absolute confidence and with total candour. In other words, a person should not be discouraged from obtaining proper advice for fear that the information contained in any communication passing between himself and his legal adviser may come into the hands of others. This right, known as legal advice privilege, attaches to the client and not to the person providing the legal advice, and is one which the client may waive if he wishes to do so – even if the legal adviser objects. It has been described in an appeal heard by the House of Lords a few years ago as a "fundamental human right long established in the common law ... [and] a necessary corollary of the right of any person to obtain skilled advice about the law."[18] It had until now been assumed that legal advice privilege was confined to communications between clients and their lawyers. However, it is now a fact of modern life that members of other professions, such as chartered accountants, also provide expert legal advice – particularly on tax law; and in 2003 the then Government rejected a proposal from the Director-General of Fair Trading that legal advice from accountants should be subject to the same privilege as advice from members of the legal profession. Recently,

---

[18] Lord Hoffmann in *R v Special Commissioner and Another, ex p Morgan Grenfell & Co Ltd* [2002] UKHL 21, [2003] 1 AC 563.

the question whether the privilege can indeed apply to legal advice obtained from accountants was tested all the way to the Supreme Court.[19]

The facts of the case were simple. A tax inspector, with the consent of a special commissioner, served a statutory notice on a company requiring it to deliver to the inspector documents containing information relevant to the company's tax liability. They included communications passing between the company and its accountants which both related to, and contained, legal advice. The company, by way of judicial review proceedings, applied to quash the notice on the ground that it included documents which were subject to legal advice privilege. (The statutory provisions under which the notice had been served exempted from disclosure "items subject to legal privilege", defined as "communications between a professional legal adviser and his client ... made in connection with the giving of legal advice to the client.") The judge who heard the company's application considered that the case for extending legal advice privilege to advice by accountants was "compelling, indeed unanswerable", and that "in modern conditions accountants have the expertise to advise on tax law, and it is firms of accountants, rather than firms of solicitors, who do give such advice and represent clients in disputes with the revenue ... ." However, both he and later the Court of Appeal refused the application, largely on the ground that since the issue was one which concerned matters of policy, and since Parliament had from time to time legislated on the assumption that the privilege was in fact confined to advice from members of the legal profession, the matter was one which only Parliament could properly resolve. The Supreme Court, by a majority of five to two, agreed.

The main judgment for the majority was given by Lord Neuberger. He readily acknowledged that as a matter purely of principle and logic the case for extending the scope of the privilege to legal advice from accountants was indeed "compelling"; but, the point was that what would be involved would indeed be an *extension* to the existing scope of the privilege, and not simply a clarification of the existing boundaries: "judicial statements of high authority" and underlying assumptions made in different pieces of legislation, as well as a number of official reports, made it clear that the privilege was confined to advice from members of the legal profession. Furthermore, an extension could not just apply to accountants and matters of tax law: it would have to apply to legal advice given by members of other professions.

---

19 *R (Prudential plc & Anor) v Special Commissioner of Income Tax & Anor* [2013] UKSC 1, [2013] 2 WLR 325.

In Lord Neuberger's view there were a number of reasons for exercising caution. Firstly, the proposed extension would involve a lack of clarity and a degree of uncertainty where previously there had been no lack of clarity and no uncertainty. Even if the court were to decide to extend the privilege to a member of a profession of which it could be said that it ordinarily included the giving of legal advice, it was by no means clear whether such occupations as town planners, engineers or pension advisers would be members of such a "profession" for this purpose. Nor, for that matter, was it clear how a court would decide whether a profession is one which "ordinarily" includes the giving of legal advice in the first place. What criterion should be applied to determine this? And typically with many professions the legal advice would be included with advice on other and, sometimes, from the client's point of view, more important matters. How in such circumstances would one determine which, if any, of the documents concerned could be covered by legal advice privilege? With the privilege presently confined to legal advice from members of the legal professions, these problems simply do not arise.

Secondly, in Lord Neuberger's view, the scope of legal advice privilege was an area into which the court should be reluctant to tread. The issues raised were largely issues of policy, and sensitive ones at that. This was pre-eminently a matter for Parliament. Parliament, for example, would be able to impose conditions and restrictions in extending privilege to other professions which the courts would be unable to. An example was the recommendation of Lord Keith's Committee in 1983 that privilege should be overridden where it would otherwise have the effect of unreasonably impeding the ascertaining of facts necessary for determining a taxpayer's tax liabilities. Furthermore, legal advice privilege had been the subject of discussion by a Parliamentary committee and the subject of reports from two other committees. And perhaps most tellingly, the statutory provisions under which the notice in this case had been served on the company drew a distinction between a "barrister, advocate or solicitor" on the one hand, and a "tax adviser" on the other. It was therefore clear, as far as Parliament was concerned, that legal advice privilege was confined to the legal profession.

Finally, Lord Neuberger pointed out, Parliament had legislated "relevantly" on other occasions;[20] had done so on the basis that legal advice privilege was confined to members of the legal profession; and had shown no inclination to extend the privilege to other professions.

---

[20] Legal advice privilege was at various times extended to, respectively, patent attorneys, trade mark agents and licensed conveyancers.

Lord Hope, agreeing with Lord Neuberger, said that his starting point was that the reason why the issue was before them at all in this case was because legal advice privilege was generally understood to apply only to advice given by lawyers. If they were to declare that the question of privilege had to be determined by reference to the function which the adviser was performing rather than to the profession to which the adviser belonged, they would be extending the ambit of the privilege. And were they to extend the privilege to chartered accountants, why not to other members of the accountancy profession or indeed to other professions. In his view, no pressing need had been demonstrated to make this change. If reasons of public policy did emerge to justify the change, then it was clearly a matter to be left to Parliament.

Agreeing also with Lord Neuberger, Lord Mance likewise emphasised the difficulty, were the privilege extended to other professions, of distinguishing between privileged and non-privileged "activities". He attached, again like Lord Neuberger, considerable importance to the fact that Parliament had on a number of occasions "not only treated lawyers as the only persons whose advice [gave] rise to [the privilege] on behalf of their clients, but also decided specifically to maintain a distinction between lawyers and tax advisers" in this respect.

Lord Reed, also agreeing with Lord Neuberger, observed that he was "unpersuaded" by the argument advanced by the minority that "existing legal principle already recognises" the privilege claimed by the company. In all of the historic cases in which the privilege had been held to exist, the relationship of the persons between whom the privileged communication passed was that of client and professional lawyer. The court was being asked to make a policy decision, which was a decision which Parliament was better equipped to make.

The minority members of the court were Lord Sumption and Lord Clarke. Lord Sumption had no doubt as to what the law as to legal advice privilege actually was. The privilege attached to any communication between a client and his legal adviser which was made for the purpose of enabling the client to receive legal advice; and when the advice was being given in a professional capacity and the adviser belonged to a profession an ordinary function of which involved the giving of skilled legal advice on the subject in question. The privilege was the substantive right of the client, and its availability did not depend on the status of the adviser but on the nature of the advice. That proposition was borne out by the notable decisions in the late eighteenth and mid-nineteenth centuries, which shaped the law on the subject. The rationale underlying legal advice privilege has always been well understood, and has remained unchanged. That its existence is also essential to the administration of justice has always been recognised.

In Lord Sumption's view it was clear that what was critical in determining whether privilege attached to an advice or to communications relating to such advice was the *function* which the adviser was performing, not his *status*. Advice on tax law from a chartered accountant should attract the privilege in the circumstances where it would have done had it been given by a barrister or solicitor. They were performing the same function. The complexities of modern tax law had made it increasingly common for accountants, as part of their everyday lives, to give legal advice to their clients. Once it was appreciated that the privilege was the privilege of the client; that it depended on the public interest in promoting the client's access to legal advice on the basis of absolute confidence – and was not dependant on the status of the adviser – then it followed that there could be no principled reason for distinguishing between the advice of solicitors and barristers on the one hand, and the advice of accountants on the other.

Lord Sumption was unimpressed by the kind of considerations which prompted the majority to conclude that difficult policy issues were in play, and that it was pre-eminently a matter for Parliament to decide whether to intervene rather than the courts. Those considerations were founded on the false premise that to recognise legal advice privilege as attaching to legal advice from accountants would be to extend its scope. In his view the existing law already covered the position. The fact that there could be a substantial increase in the number of claims for privilege, or that there could be practical difficulties in resolving them, was not a good reason for failing to apply general principles coherently, or for "justifying an arbitrary distinction between different professions performing exactly the same function."

He did not think it was of any particular significance that Parliament had previously legislated in regard to legal advice privilege. Here one was concerned with legal principle: legal advice privilege was a creature of the common law and one which was wholly shaped by the common law. One was not concerned with social and economic or macro issues which were the domain of Parliament. It was therefore the function of the courts of common law, and not Parliament, to resolve the issue. Nor was it of particular significance that the very legislation under which the statutory notice had been served by the tax inspector in this case, expressly referred to barristers, advocates and solicitors in regard to legal advice privilege, and referred elsewhere to "tax advisers". These statutory provisions, Lord Sumption argued, did not purport to provide a complete code governing the applicability of the privilege, still less redefine it.

Lord Clarke agreed with both Lord Sumption's analysis and his conclusion. In his view, a simple example illustrated the point of principle involved. Two individuals have the same problem in an area of tax law. One seeks advice from a firm of city solicitors and the other seeks advice from a firm of city accountants. To the question: are both entitled to claim privilege and refuse to disclose to HMRC the information and advice, the only principled answer was, "yes". Lord Clarke noted that legal advice privilege also applied to advice given by foreign lawyers. Such being the case, he could not see how it was possible to deny that privilege in the case of an accountant qualified to give advice on the law of tax.

The cause of the disagreement in this case is very easy to identify. The majority resorted to what it considered to be a dose of healthy pragmatism. The problems which could arise from conferring legal advice privilege on other professions could be considerable in terms of defining both scope and application. Life had until now proceeded on the assumption that the privilege was confined to advice from members of the legal profession, and there was no evidence to suggest that this had proved to be a source of any significant difficulty. If it transpired that something should indeed be done about it, then that surely should be the job of Parliament. Thus, for the majority caution was the order of the day. The minority, on the other hand, were not disposed to treat the issue other than one of principle, and accordingly did not shrink from applying what they perceived to be the logic implicit in the facts of this case. The present position was anomalous and unacceptable. Legal advice privilege was a common law right, and it was for the courts and not Parliament to define its boundaries.

It is something of an irony that the majority and minority judgments in this case in fact represent a neat reversal of the position which arose some 18 months previously, when the Supreme Court decided by a majority of five to two that there were no good policy reasons for continuing the immunity of expert witnesses from negligence claims brought by aggrieved litigants, the minority arguing that such a radical decision involving a departure from what had been understood for many years to be settled practice, should, in the absence of any empirical evidence, better have been left to Parliament to take if it thought it appropriate.[21] The difference in outcomes certainly

---

21 *Jones v Kaney* [2011] UKSC 13, [2011] 2 AC 398.

illustrates how capricious and subjective the process of assessing where the public interest lies really is.

(6) A CASE OF OVER-REACTION BY THE TREASURY?

Questions of proportionality, as can be seen from the foreign spouses cases, tend to divide judicial opinion. They did so quite spectacularly in a recent case where the Supreme Court held by a majority of five to four that a restriction imposed by the Treasury on an Iranian bank with a UK-based subsidiary from all access to UK financial markets because of its alleged links to Iran's nuclear and ballistics programme, was not a proportionate response to the risk to the national interest of nuclear proliferation. In the same case the Court further divided (by six to three) in holding that the Treasury acted unfairly in not giving the bank (Bank Mellat) prior notice of its intention to impose the restriction, and in not giving the bank the opportunity to make any representations before doing so.[22] The background and facts giving rise to this impressive degree of disunity within the ranks need to be described in a little detail.

Iran has a large banking sector, comprising 26 banks, eight of which are large commercial banks. Four of those, including Bank Mellat, are privately owned. Bank Mellat is one of five Iranian banks which carry on business through subsidiaries in the UK, but was the only one "targeted" by the Treasury, although some of them were subject to restrictions under other legislation, for example, assets frozen under the Iran (Financial Sanctions) Order pursuant to a Security Council resolution, and similar asset freezing orders under EU legislation. Prior to the Treasury's intervention, Bank Mellat had a substantial international business, much of which was transacted in London. As a result of the intervention it sustained substantial losses.

Under Schedule 7 to the Counter-Terrorism Act 2008 the Treasury is empowered to make a direction (laid before Parliament in the form of a statutory instrument) preventing a "designated person"[23] from operating in the UK financial sector if it reasonably believes that such person is facilitating the development of nuclear weapons by a foreign country outside the EU which poses a significant risk to the national interest of the UK. The direction is required to be "proportionate" to the perceived risk.

---

[22] *Bank Mellat v Her Majesty's Treasury (No. 2)* [2013] UKSC 39.

[23] The expression includes a legal person such as a corporation or company.

Furthermore, it ceases to have effect after 28 days unless it has been approved by Parliament by an "affirmative resolution"; and by virtue of section 63 of the Act it is open to any person affected by the direction to apply to the High Court to have it set aside in accordance with ordinary judicial review principles.

The written ministerial statement, issued three days after the direction in this instance had been laid before Parliament, explained that:

> Bank Mellat has provided banking services to UN listed organisations connected to Iran's proliferation sensitive activities, and has been involved in transactions related to financing Iran's nuclear and ballistic missile programme … The direction to cease business will therefore reduce the risk of the UK financial sector being used, unknowingly or otherwise, to facilitate Iran's proliferation … activities.

The direction was subsequently approved by Parliament.

Some weeks later Bank Mellat applied to the High Court to have the direction set aside, contending that the decision to make the direction was irrational, discriminatory, disproportionate and procedurally unfair. The court dismissed the application, but nevertheless accepted that the bank had conscientiously applied a system to ensure that it did not provide banking services to Security Council listed entities and individuals connected with Iran's nuclear industry. It further accepted that the bank had ceased to supply banking services to a particular company once that company had become listed under a Security Council resolution. The court did, however, find that the bank held the accounts of one company which had played a part in Iran's nuclear programme, but that it had acted in good faith. The basis on which the court dismissed the bank's application was that there was an obvious risk that "however careful the bank may be, [its] facilities are open to use by entities participating in Iran's nuclear weapons programme"; that "even as an unknowing and unwilling actor, [it] is by reason of its international reach, well placed to assist entities to facilitate the development of nuclear weapons by providing them with banking facilities, in particular trade finance ..."; and that although the bank was not controlled by the Iranian government, nevertheless some pressure would be brought to bear on it by virtue of the direction.

The decision, and the basis on which it had been reached, were upheld by the Court of Appeal. The bank then appealed to what transpired to be a nine-member Supreme Court. For the purposes of the appeal it was accepted that the Treasury had reasonable grounds to believe that Iran's nuclear and ballistic missile programmes posed a significant risk to the national interests of the UK.

The proportionality/rationality issue

There was agreement between the majority and the minority as to the criteria to be applied in determining whether the direction was "proportionate", namely:

(i) Was the objective of the measure in question of sufficient importance to justify the limitation of a fundamental right?

(ii) Was it rationally connected to that objective?

(iii) Could a less intrusive measure have been used?

(iv) In the light of these considerations, had a fair balance been struck between the rights of the person or entity affected and the interests of the community?

The problem, of course, lay in the application of these criteria to the particular facts.

The majority comprised Lady Hale and Lords Kerr, Clarke, Sumption and Carnworth, with Lord Sumption delivering the leading judgment. He identified the essential question as being whether "the interruption of commercial dealings with Bank Mellat in the UK's financial markets bore some rational and proportionate relationship to the statutory purpose of hindering the pursuit by Iran of its weapon programmes." He concluded that it did not.

In his view, the reasoning and decision of the courts below presented serious difficulties. First, in his view, "[they] do not explain, let alone justify, the singling out of Bank Mellat, if, as both courts [accepted was the case], the problem is a general problem of international banking." Second, "the justification for the direction which they have found was not the one which ministers advanced when laying the direction before Parliament, and was in some respects inconsistent with it."

The impression which ministers created when justifying the targeting of Bank Mellat, pointed out Lord Sumption, was that the bank had knowingly collaborated in transactions relating to the Iranian nuclear and ballistics programmes, or at least had turned a blind eye to them, or had unacceptably low standards of customer due diligence, which made it especially liable to let through such transactions. None of this was found to be the case by the courts below: what they had concluded was that there was an inherent risk common to all Iranian banks engaged in international trade.

In Lord Sumption's view, the position was analogous to that considered by the House of Lords in the celebrated case[24] in which it held that the detention of foreign nationals whose presence in the UK was considered by the Home Secretary to be a risk to national security but who could not be deported, was a disproportionate response to the terrorist threat which had provoked it. It was disproportionate and discriminatory because the same threat was posed by identified UK nationals, who remained free and whose movements could be monitored. Likewise:

> the distinction between Bank Mellat and other Iranian banks, which was at the heart of the case put to Parliament by ministers, was an arbitrary and irrational distinction and … the measure as a whole was disproportionate. This is because once it is found that the problem is not specific to Bank Mellat but an inherent risk of banking, the risk posed by Bank Mellat's access to those markets is no different from that posed by the access which comparable banks continued to enjoy.

Even allowing for a wide margin of judgment to which the decision maker was entitled, in Lord Sumption's view there was nothing in the Treasury's case to explain why the statutory objective could not simply have been sufficiently achieved by requiring all Iranian banks carrying on business in London to observe "relevant sanctions and risk warnings."

A contrasting picture emerges from Lord Reed's (minority) judgment, with which Lords Neuberger, Hope and Dyson agreed. There was no doubt, he pointed out, that in applying the proportionality test to the facts of this case, the first criterion had been satisfied: the objective of inhibiting the development of nuclear weapons by Iran and thereby reducing the risk to the national interests of the UK was sufficiently important to justify an interference with Bank Mellat's operations. The question, he acknowledged, was whether the remaining criteria were satisfied; and in considering that

---

24 *A and Ors v Secretary of State for the Home Department* [2004] UKHL 56, [2005] 2 AC 68.

question he did not think that the case concerning the detention of foreign nationals was particularly helpful. The case, in his view, had not been decided on the basis that the different treatment of UK nationals and foreign nationals was discriminatory and that detention of foreign nationals alone could only be a partially effective measure: it had been decided on the basis that the interference with the rights of foreign suspects had been shown not to be necessary.

Lord Reed rejected the criticism founded on the fact that Bank Mellat alone amongst the Iranian banks engaged in business in the UK has been singled out by the Treasury notwithstanding that the problem was acknowledged to be common to the entire Iranian banking sector. There was clear evidence of Bank Mellat's involvement, albeit unwittingly, with "listed entities", whereas there was no such evidence in relation to the other banks. Furthermore, most of the remaining UK subsidiaries were already subject to restrictions – such as freezing orders – and there was, he thought, substance in the Treasury's view that the direction might lead to the UK banking sector winding down business with Iran generally. "In these circumstances", concluded Lord Reed, "an order directed specifically against Bank Mellat and its UK subsidiary was far from being pointless or arbitrary."

He flatly disagreed with Lord Sumption that both the Treasury and ministers, in explaining the making of the direction, created the impression that Bank Mellat was knowingly involved in transactions related to Iran's nuclear and ballistic missile programme. The statements which were made were of objective fact. And, in his view, even if the point had substance, it had no real bearing on the issue of proportionality and rationality.

Finally, he disagreed with Lord Sumption that the objective could have been achieved by "less intrusive" means. He was disposed to attach considerable weight to the Treasury's view that making the direction was the most effective way of exerting pressure on Iran in reducing the use of UK financial markets in connection with its nuclear and ballistic programme. He did so because the court:

> did not possess expertise or experience in international relations, national security or experience in international regulation … In a complex situation of this kind, where the stakes are so high, the court has to attach considerable weight to the Government's assessment that the requirements are necessary and proportionate to the risk.

The "fairness" issue

Again, as was the case in regard to the issue of proportionality, the majority and minority were agreed as to the principles to be applied: namely, in general, unless the relevant legislation under which the action or decision is taken expressly or impliedly provides otherwise, a person adversely affected should have an opportunity to make representations before that action or decision is taken, and that fairness usually requires that he is informed of the gist of the case against him. It was common ground that there could indeed be circumstances where the giving of prior notice would deprive the action or decision of any effectiveness.

Lord Sumption (with whom Lady Hale and Lords Neuberger, Kerr, Clarke, and Dyson agreed), concluded that Bank Mellat was "entitled to succeed on the ground that it received no notice of the Treasury's intention to make the direction, and therefore had no opportunity to make representations." He started from the premise that unless the relevant legislation (i.e. the Counter-Terrorism Act 2008) expressly or impliedly excluded any duty of consultation, obvious fairness required that Bank Mellat should have had the opportunity to make representations before the direction was made. The direction took immediate effect, and the effect on business could well have proved to be irreversible. The direction was based on specific factual allegations "of a kind plainly capable of being refuted, being for the most part within the special knowledge of the Bank." The Act certainly did not expressly exclude the duty to consult. Did it impliedly do so? The basis on which it was suggested that it did was that Schedule 7, in conjunction with sections 62–65, expressly provides for the right to apply to the High Court to set aside a direction, and prescribes the procedure for such application, including the use of "closed material", that is, documents and intelligence-related information of a sensitive nature. This was, Lord Sumption pointed out, hardly an effective remedy: the direction takes immediate effect, and by the time the application is heard by the High Court considerable damage has already been done.

Nor was Lord Sumption impressed by the suggestion that because the Act expressly contemplated the use of "closed material" in the making of such an application, it impliedly ruled out the use of such material in other circumstances, such as representations in response to notice of the Treasury's intentions to make the direction. If it was practicable to use such material in the course of the court proceedings (as in fact proved to be the case here), then it was practicable to use such material in any consultation process before a final decision was made. Nor was he impressed with the suggestion that had Bank Mellat been given prior notice of the Treasury's intentions, it would have had the opportunity to make alternative arrangements with a view to concealing the nature of the transactions affected. The bank was equally capable of making such arrangements *after* the direction was made.

Both Lord Hope and Lord Reed delivered judgments reflecting the minority view. (Lord Carnworth agreed with both judgments.) For them the crucial point was that the legislation contained an elaborate scheme, including several safeguards, which provided for this kind of intervention. The direction or order had to be laid before Parliament for approval, and would cease to have effect unless approved within 28 days; and an application could be made at any time to the High Court in accordance with a prescribed procedure to have the direction or order set aside, which included provision for dealing with "closed material", and for which permission was not necessary. The clear inference, in their view, was that the omission in the Act of any reference to the making of representations or the need to consult was deliberate, and reflected the importance of the fact that there would be occasions where the Treasury would be required to act swiftly and without warning.

Both Lord Hope and Lord Reed questioned the practical value of consultation or representations in the kind of circumstances being considered: inevitably, only limited information could be disclosed by the Treasury for that purpose. And both took the view that the majority were unduly dismissive of the risk that prior notice of the Treasury's intentions would enable the proposed "designated person" to take some form of avoiding action. Exceptionally, they thought, this was one of those cases where the duty to consult and the right to make representations did not arise.

The explanation for the differing responses to the issue of proportionality clearly lay in the very nature of the exercise in which the court was engaged: that is, to make a value judgment on whether or not the Treasury's intervention was excessively heavy-handed and unnecessarily draconian. Or to put it in more formal language, it had to consider whether a fair balance had been struck between the rights of the person or entity affected and the interests of the community. Clinical legal analysis does not help much in such circumstances, and it is hardly surprising that three members of the court each made a point of stating that they found the issue in this case particularly difficult, and one on which their views had wavered over the course of time.

So far as the "fairness" issue was concerned, the explanation for the division of opinion was equally clear. The majority thought that the difficulties said to confront the Treasury were it required to give notice of its intentions and to consult prior to taking the proposed action, were overstated. The minority, for their part, thought that the majority minimised the difficulties facing the Treasury were it required to give notice of its intentions, and that were it in fact required to do so, this would deprive the intervention of much of its effectiveness. Again, this was not an issue capable of resolution simply through clinical legal analysis. Ultimately, everything depended on what weight one was disposed to attach to what particular piece of evidence.

PART FIVE

WHAT DO THESE DISAGREEMENTS REVEAL ABOUT DECISION-MAKING IN OUR COURT OF LAST RESORT?

Before considering what can be gleaned from the nature of the disagreements which have been discussed in this book, it is worthwhile at this point to take a brief sideways glance at the workings of the Supreme Court of the US, and see what kind of disagreements tend to occur in that particular jurisdiction. After all, the example of the US Supreme Court loomed large in the debate which preceded the decision to create a Supreme Court in the UK and to jettison the former Appellate Committee of the House of Lords, and had been prayed in aid by both supporters and opponents of the change. On the one side of the debate fears had been expressed that, like in the US, the Supreme Court would become a polarising institution, and act as a buffer or brake on executive and governmental powers; and were this indeed to happen, it would be a development of great constitutional importance and one which would pose great dangers. On the other side of the debate, it had been argued that on the basis of the US experience, the creation of a Supreme Court would bring transparency, democracy and accountability into a part of our constitutional arrangements hitherto occupied by the distinctly anomalous and – from the general public's point of view – relatively obscure Appellate Committee of the House of Lords.

(1) DISAGREEMENTS IN THE US SUPREME COURT

Several factors have combined to make the US tradition and experience rather different from our own. The US Supreme Court has pre-eminently served the function of being a constitutional court, being, together with the Presidency and Congress, one of the three so-called pillars of the Federal constitution, and as such has been commonly regarded as a source of political power. (Unlike our own court of last resort, it has the power, which it has frequently exercised, of striking down primary legislation.) Its members are appointed by what is perceived to be very much a political process, having been nominated by the President and confirmed by the Senate following a public hearing. Nominations have invariably reflected the thinking and political complexion of the President who happens to be in office at the time the vacancy has arisen, and have quite frequently provoked controversy and, on some occasions, a certain amount of ridicule.[1] Indeed it has long been customary to characterise members of the Court as either "Republican friendly" or "Democrat friendly". The cases which have come before the Court frequently involve challenges to the "constitutionality" of federal legislation and federal policies and decisions, and occasionally challenges to state legislation, all of which tend to have stark political or social implications: for example, abortion, positive discrimination, compulsory prayers at publicly funded schools, the death penalty and, more recently, the legal status of detainees at Guantanamo Bay and gay marriages. Inevitably, the members of the Court become nationally known figures.

Against this background, it is not surprising that disagreement and dissent are taken for granted as characteristic features of the Court, and that such dissent is acknowledged as an important part of the democratic process. Nor is it surprising that disagreements have in the main tended to be on predictable ideological lines.[2] For many years there has been a division in approach amongst the members of the Court between the "originalists" (the Republican-leaning faction) on the one hand, and the "activists" or "pragmatists" (the Democrat-leaning faction) on the other. The originalists believe that the Constitution should be both interpreted and applied in the way which its framers intended or would have intended, if necessary in the light of historical evidence. The activists, or pragmatists, regard the Constitution as a "living instrument", capable of being adapted to modern and ever-changing conditions in society, whilst remaining true to its spirit. In a sense the argument has also been, and continues to be, about whether or

---

1 A *Times* Washington correspondent once memorably wrote of a particular nominee, when describing the controversy surrounding his nomination: "He will not of course be the first inadequate man to serve in the Supreme Court. The country and the Court will learn to live with him." (6 October 1969).

2 Indeed so much so, that in the recent challenge to President Obama's healthcare legislation, Chief Justice Roberts, who unexpectedly sided with those of his colleagues who upheld the legislation and who otherwise would have formed the minority, was widely criticised for engaging in something akin to treachery. In the celebrated case of *Bush v Gore*, which effectively decided the outcome of the 2000 Presidential election, Justice Bryer was critical of the fact that the majority had approached the issue in such a way as to give the public the impression their decision had been overtly political. Their decision, in his view, was a "self-inflicted wound".

not there should be strict limits to judicial law-making in a democracy such as that of the US. Two recent decisions of the Court illustrate the continuing relevance of these rival schools of thought.

In 2002 Congress passed the Bipartisan Campaign Reform Act. This prohibited, within 30 days of a primary election and 60 days of a general election, corporations and unions funding – from their own sources of revenue – televised election advertisements which mentioned a candidate's name. In 2009 the constitutionality of this ban was challenged in the Supreme Court on the ground that it violated the First Amendment (the amendment which guarantees freedom of speech). By a majority of five to four the Court held the ban was indeed in violation of the First Amendment.

Justice Kennedy, delivering the lead judgment on behalf of the majority, declared that there was:

> simply no support for the view that the First Amendment, as originally understood, would permit the suppression of political speech by media corporations, The Framers may not have anticipated modern business and media corporations, [but] television networks and major newspapers owned by media corporations have become the most important means of mass communication in modern times.

In his view, the First Amendment could not be understood to condone the suppression of freedom of speech "in society's most salient media." The Amendment had been a response to the repression of speech and the press that had existed in England, and the heavy taxes that were imposed on the press in the colonies. When the founding document was published, "speech was open, comprehensive and vital to society's definition of itself ... ." Because the Framers did not have certain types of "speakers" or modern forms of communication in mind, it did not mean that those speakers and media were entitled to less First Amendment protection than those speakers and forms of communication which existed when the Bill of Rights was adopted. The prevention of corruption was not a sufficiently powerful consideration to displace freedom of speech.

The lead judgment on behalf of the minority was delivered by Justice Stephen. He dismissed as having simply "rhetorical appeal" the proposition that the First Amendment precluded regulatory distinctions based on a speaker's identity, and specifically its identity as a corporation. That proposition failed, for example, to answer the question: when can a corporation engage in electioneering that some of its shareholders oppose? It was fallacious to equate corporations with natural persons: case law had already established a distinction between corporate and individual campaign spending. There was not the slightest doubt that what the Framers had in mind was the free speech of individual Americans: "Unlike our colleagues", observed Justice Stephen tartly, "they had little trouble from distinguishing corporations from human beings." Outside the corporate form an individual shareholder could do as much electioneering as he pleased. The prohibition under challenge hardly amounted to a categorical ban on corporate speech. Furthermore, the Government has routinely restricted freedom of speech when it was perceived to be in the public interest to do so, as in the case of the Armed Forces and its own employees. The legislation which the majority had declared to be unlawful reflected the common sense of the American people, who recognised a need to prevent corporations from undermining the integrity of both federal and local government. It was, he said, "a strange time to repudiate that common sense".

Thus, according to the originalist majority, the Framers did not allow for, or even hint at, any distinction to be drawn in the drafting of the First Amendment between corporations and individuals, and that is what really mattered. The "pragmatic" minority on the other hand argued that freedom of speech had to be tempered with what could clearly be shown to be in the public interest, and banning the funding by corporations of television advertising over a specified period of a campaign was hardly a case which called for the invoking of the First Amendment.

The second case was the unsuccessful challenge in 2012 to President Obama's healthcare legislation. There were in fact two issues to be determined, but for present purposes it is sufficient to focus on just the one: this was whether the provision in the Affordable Care Act, which provided that those who did not comply with the mandate to purchase health insurance cover had to make a "shared responsibility payment" to the Federal Government, came within the ambit of Article 1.8 of the Constitution. This empowers Congress "to regulate Commerce … among the several States." The Court divided five to four in deciding that the provision fell outside the ambit of Article 8.1.[3]

Chief Justice Roberts, rejecting the proposition that the legality of the provision was underpinned by Article 8.1, was disposed to give the wording

---

3 However, it decided – again by a majority of five to four – that the provision did fall *within* the ambit of Article 1.8.1 of the Constitution (the power of Congress to "lay and collect Taxes") – Chief Justice Roberts "switching sides" on this issue.

of Article 8.1 a literal interpretation. "The language of the Constitution", he argued, "reflects the natural understanding that the power to regulate assumes there is already something to be regulated." In his view, to construe the clause in such a way as to permit Congress to "regulate" individuals precisely because they were doing nothing would open up "a new and potentially vast domain" to congressional authority. In this case people could not be said to be actually participating in the healthcare scheme unless or until they were physically doing so.

Justice Scalia, agreeing with Chief Justice Roberts, observed that whilst the Federal Government can prescribe what the quality of the food we consume should be, and even how much we must pay, the mere fact that we all consume food and are sooner or later in "the market" for food, does not empower the Government to say when and what we will buy. In Justice Scalia's view, that "is essentially what this Act seeks to do with respect to the purchase of health care. It exceeds federal power."

Justice (Ruth) Ginsberg, by contrast, as was the case with her colleagues in the minority on this issue, was disposed to give the wording of Article 8.1 a wider and more flexible meaning. In her view the expression "Commerce" embraced a healthcare system. She argued that the Framers well understood that the "general interests of the Union" would change over the course of time, and in ways which they could not anticipate. It was the role of Congress, not the courts, to delineate the boundaries of the market the legislature sought to regulate. Congress could reasonably have viewed the market from a long-term perspective, encompassing transactions virtually certain to occur over the next decade.

The third case is the recent well-publicised clash over the legal status of same sex marriages. The factual background makes interesting reading.

The oddly named Defense of Marriage Act (1996) provided for federal estate tax exemption for a surviving spouse who has inherited the estate of her/his deceased partner. However, section 3 of the Act provided that in this context the expression "spouse" only applied to a marriage between a man and a woman. Edith Windsor and Thea Spyer, a same sex couple residing in New York, were lawfully married in Ontario, Canada, in 2007 in accordance with the provisions of the Canadian Civil Marriage Act. The validity of their marriage was subsequently recognised by the state of New York. Thea Spyer died in 2009, leaving her entire estate to Ms. Windsor. Because her claim to tax exemption was barred by section 3 of the Act, Ms. Windsor filed a lawsuit against the federal government alleging that the Act had singled out legally married same sex couples "for differential treatment compared to other similarly situated couples without justification."

The Obama administration was strongly sympathetic to this argument, and in due course the US Attorney General, Eric Holder, announced that the federal government did not intend to contest the proceedings. However, an interest group called the Bipartisan Legal Advisory Group chose to intervene and to contest Ms. Windsor's claim. She eventually obtained a ruling in her favour on the ground that section 3 was unconstitutional by virtue of the due process guarantees in the Fifth Amendment, this ruling being later upheld on appeal. Eventually, the case made its way to the Supreme Court. By a majority of five to four the Court declared section 3 to be unconstitutional.

Justice Kennedy delivered the opinion on behalf of the majority. Essentially, section 3 was unconstitutional because it is "deprivation" of the equal liberty of persons protected by the Fifth Amendment:

> [The Act] seeks to injure the very class New York seeks to protect. By doing so it violates basic due process and equal protection principles applicable to the Federal Government … The class to which [the Act] directs its restrictions and restraints are those persons who are joined in same sex marriages made lawful by the State. [It] singles out a class of persons deemed by a State entitled to recognition and protection to enhance their own liberty.

Justice Kennedy went on to point out that this was an unusual departure from the tradition of recognising and accepting a state definition of marriage, with the result that it deprived same sex couples of the benefits and responsibilities which come with a deferral recognition of their marriage. It contrived to create two contradictory marriage regimes within the same state, and thereby diminished the "stability and predictability of basic personal relations [which] the State has found it proper to acknowledge."

Dissenting, the famously outspoken Justice Scalia (with whom Justice Thomas agreed, and Chief Justice Roberts agreed in part) surpassed himself. In his view, the Court had no business to be interfering with legislation borne of a democratic process which expressed a view reflecting popular opinion. "It is one thing for a society to elect change"; observed Justice Scalia, "it is another for a court of law to impose change by adjudging those who oppose it *hostes humani generis*, enemies of the human race." By declaring anyone opposed to same sex marriage "an enemy of human decency" the majority has provided valuable ammunition to anyone wishing to challenge any state law which confines the concept of marriage to its traditional definition. Furthermore, in the absence of a uniform federal definition of marriage, difficult choice-of-law issues are likely to arise, with some states recognising same sex marriages and others not.

Justice Alto echoed Justice Scalia on the function and power of the Court. "Members of this court have the authority and responsibility to interpret and apply the Constitution", he observed:

> Thus, if [it] contained a provision guaranteeing the right to marry a person of the same sex, it would be our duty to enforce that right. But the Constitution does not speak to the issue of same-sex marriage. In our system of government, ultimate sovereignty rests with the people, and the people have the right to control their own destiny. Any change on a question so fundamental should be made by the people through their elected officials.

In his view, the equality framework of the Fifth Amendment was ill-suited for use in evaluating the constitutionality of laws based on the traditional understanding of marriage.

Very clearly, what one sees in these cases is the clash of two competing philosophies or schools of thought which, by virtue of their impact on landmark decisions of the Court, have had over many years significant implications for the shaping of the modern history of the United States. Both are inextricably associated with national politics. The originalist position feeds into the "minimalist" non-interference or "small government" ideology of the Republicans – specifically non-interference by the Federal Government. The activist position feeds comfortably into the "dynamic" approach to Government favoured by the Democrats, treating the Constitution as the proverbial "living instrument".

(2) DISAGREEMENT IN OUR OWN COURT OF LAST RESORT

With the example of the US Supreme Court in mind, what conclusions can be drawn from the sample cross-section of appeals chosen for this study, and which have been heard by, successively, the House of Lords and the UK Supreme Court over the last 25 years or so? One conclusion must surely be that in none of these cases did anything resembling a process of legal analysis lie at the heart of what actually divided opinion so sharply.

Individual *a priori* assumptions, moral judgments and instinctive responses all played a critical role. It is interesting to note that one distinguished academic writer, when discussing the work of the Law Lords back in 1998, commented with just a slight hint of disapproval on their willingness to engage "with complex issues [all] dependant on empirical assumptions and sociological analyses."[4]

In the cases discussed in Part One (the disappointed beneficiaries, damages for a disabled mother, failure by a surgeon to warn a patient of a 2 per cent risk and the effect of unforeseen events on the loss recoverable on a repudiation of a contract) the disagreements were largely shaped by differing notions of what was perceived to be a just, fair and reasonable solution to the particular problem. The respective issues which divided opinion all reflected this. Was it just and fair to deny the intended beneficiaries compensation when the solicitor acting for the testator had failed to comply with his client's instructions? Was it "distributive justice" to give or to deny a disabled mother damages for the birth of an unwanted but healthy child resulting from a negligently performed sterilisation? Was it "corrective justice" to hold a neurosurgeon liable to pay damages for failing to warn a patient of a 2 per cent risk of partial paralysis in regard to proposed surgery, where there was no evidence that had the warning been given it would have made any difference, only evidence that had it been given, the operation would not have been performed when it was? Was it fair and reasonable to require a party to a contract which he had wrongfully repudiated, to pay damages to the innocent party on the basis of the loss he would have been likely to incur at the time of the repudiation, even though subsequent events showed that the loss would in fact have been much less?

In the cases discussed in Part Two (sadomasochistic practices, *Spycatcher*, contraceptive advice to underage girls, the mandatory death sentence in Trinidad and Tobago and political donations from impermissible donors) the disagreements were largely shaped by differing notions of what the public interest or a moral judgment required. Again, the issues which ignited these disagreements very much reflected this. Was it acceptable in terms of public policy that sadomasochistic practices, involving a significant degree of violence and resulting in bodily harm, should be untouched by the criminal law because they were consensual, and for mutual sexual gratification? Did the public interest require that an injunction should be granted to prevent the

---

4 D. Robertson, (1998) *Judicial Discretion in the House of Lords*, Clarendon Press, p. 400.

publication of *Spycatcher* in the UK on the ground of breach of confidence, even though its contents were already widely known, and the book had already been published in the US? Did the public interest require that advice contained in a Department of Health memorandum issued to health authorities, stating that in exceptional circumstances doctors could prescribe contraceptive treatment for underage girls, be declared unlawful? Was it appropriate to interpret provisions in the new constitution of Trinidad and Tobago in such a manner as to avoid the continuing sanction of the mandatory death penalty for murder, even though such interpretation could not be regarded as a natural or ordinary one? Can it really be right that by virtue of the Political Parties, Elections and Referendums Act 2000, a political party should forfeit a donation received from a donor who was resident in the UK, and who neither the party nor he himself was aware that he was not on the electoral register, when the purpose of the legislation was to prohibit donations from persons living abroad?

In the cases discussed in Part Three (lack of council funding for support services, convention rights in regard to residents of private care homes, free use of a council swimming pool at pensionable age, a racially discriminating school admissions policy, compensation for a miscarriage of justice and "knowledge" of a cause of action) the outcome was largely determined by notions of what the problematical words in the particular statute *ought* to mean, or as to what set of circumstances they *ought* to apply. Looking at the issues on which opinion was sharply divided, this was inevitably the case. Was it really the law that a council was obliged under the provisions of the Chronically Sick and Disabled Persons Act 1970, to provide an 84-year-old man suffering from a heart condition with support services, when it had insufficient financial resources to enable it to do so? Did it make sense to interpret the words "public authority" and specifically the words "functions of a public nature" in the Human Rights Act 1998 in such a way as to allow persons placed by local authorities in private residential care homes the benefit of rights under the European Convention? Was it right to treat a council as discriminating unlawfully on the ground of sex when it allowed women to use its swimming pool free of charge at the age of 60, but men to have free use only at the age of 65, when the intention of the council was simply to allow persons free use when they reached pensionable age? Was it right to regard the Jewish Free School as discriminating on racial grounds, when its admissions policy precluded the admission of the son of an Italian mother who was a convert from Catholicism to a Jewish sect not recognised by the Office of the Chief Rabbi? Did it really make sense to allow a person sentenced to a term of imprisonment, but who later had the conviction quashed because of the emergence of fresh evidence, to apply for statutory compensation on the ground that he or she had suffered a "miscarriage of justice", *even though that person was not in a position to demonstrate that he or she was innocent beyond any reasonable doubt*? Was it fair and just that for the purposes of pursuing a personal injury claim within the prescribed three-year period of acquiring the *knowledge* that he or she had a cause of action, time started to run against a claimant from the moment he or she merely *believed* that this could be the case, and when the evidence at the time was inconclusive?

And, finally, the disagreement evident in the six cases discussed in Part Four (the "right of abode", the Convention rights of Private Smith, age restriction for admission of spouses to the UK, the right to bring a private prosecution and the limits to legal advice privilege, and the targeting by the Treasury of Bank Mellat) clearly reflect differing views on policy, the need to adopt a principled position, and differing views as to what is a "proportionate" response to a particular problem. Again, the issues on which opinion divided show why inevitably this was so. Did the removal of the Chagos Islanders by the UK Government violate their "right of abode" and amount to an abuse of power? Did members of the armed forces, whilst on active service in Iraq, enjoy the protection of rights under the European Convention, specifically Article 2 (the right to life), granted by the Human Rights Act 1998? Was a blanket increase in the minimum age for the admission of spouses wishing to reside in the UK proportionate to the threat posed by the perceived increase in forced marriages? Was the Director of Public Prosecutions entitled to take over, and discontinue, a private prosecution, on the ground that in his view it was more likely than not that the prosecution would be unsuccessful? Should legal advice privilege apply to legal advice provided by a chartered accountant just as it would do if the advice were provided by a barrister, solicitor or other form of recognised professional advocate? Was the restriction by the Treasury of Bank Mellat's access to the UK's financial markets a disproportionate measure, and one which was unfairly imposed?

Quite often the distinctly *personal* nature of the response to the issue at hand can be seen from the robustness and force with which it has been expressed. Many instances of this spring to mind, but for present purposes the judgments of Lord Brown serve to underline the point. Thus he made it plain that he thought it absurd a court should not take into account events subsequent to a repudiatory breach of contract when assessing the loss suffered by an innocent party. "Must", he asked, "the judge really shut his eyes to the known facts and speculate how matters might have looked at some earlier date?" In the party donations case he made it perfectly clear that he thought that what the majority had chosen to do was to disregard the plain and unambiguous language of the relevant statute, and therefore to disregard the clear intention of Parliament. His contempt for the suggestion that the court had a discretion to order the forfeiture of a lesser sum than the full amount of the "impermissible donation" was unmistakable: "Where the draftsman had explicitly chosen the words 'an amount equal to the amount of the donation' it could hardly be thought he intended them to mean an 'up to' that value or 'an amount not exceeding that value'." He thought the dispute which gave rise to the race discrimination issue in the case of the Jewish free school was not one which should concern the courts. Given that the criteria for admission reflected orthodox Jewish religious doctrine, and those treated more favourably and those less favourably were within the same ethnic group, it was wholly unrealistic to regard the admission policy as discriminatory on racial, and not on religious, grounds. In the miscarriage of justice case he thought the expression straightforwardly meant the wrongful conviction of an innocent person, and that it was perfectly reasonable for the State to compensate generously the comparatively few who could demonstrate their innocence "rather than the larger number who may or may not be innocent." He thought it absurd (as proposed by the majority) that a foreign national should receive compensation for false imprisonment because he was detained after completion of his prison sentence and pending deportation under wrongly applied rules, when he would have been lawfully detained anyway had the correct rules been applied.[5] And in regard to the change in the immigration rules affecting the increase in the minimum age for foreign spouses seeking permission to reside in the UK, he thought it was no business of the courts to second guess the judgment of the Secretary of State and to interfere so blatantly with a policy decision. (It may seem that we have here something akin to the judicial equivalent to "Disgruntled, Tunbridge Wells." However, that would be an unfair impression when judged in the context of the whole of Lord Brown's record as a Law Lord and Justice of the Supreme Court.)

Another conclusion to be drawn from the disagreements which have formed the backbone of this study is the perhaps rather obvious the one, that the sheer variety and range of issues which the Law Lords and Justices have been required to determine militate against the emergence of any recognisable "ideological" division within the ranks at any particular time. Whilst some of the issues around which these disagreements have revolved

---

5 The case referred to above in footnote 2 on pp. 85–86.

could well have been the kind of issues which might have been litigated in the US Supreme Court, the majority would not; and this at once serves to underline the essential difference between the US Court and our own Court and its predecessor, the House of Lords. Unlike the US Supreme Court, the UK Court does not aspire to be a constitutional court, and does not have the power to strike down legislation.[6] Whereas the political stance of members of the US Court has proved to be very much a reality in its judicial decision-making over the years, the political complexion of the members of our own court of last resort has remained well below the radar. And, as has already been emphasised, in the US Court judgments in the more politically or socially sensitive cases have largely, though by no means exclusively, to be seen in terms of a philosophical divide.

The question does arise, however, whether the cases selected for inclusion in this study provide at least just a hint of a Law Lord or Supreme Court Justice being influenced in his decision-making by his own over-arching ideological position or "mindset", and whether in the light of his position or particular perspective, his response to a specific issue could be confidently predicted. Although the sample of cases may not be large enough to convince entirely, the answer would appear on the whole to be, "no". The example of Lord Templeman might at first blush suggest otherwise. It is certainly true that on the evidence of his judgments in the three cases discussed in this book – one involving breach of confidence for personal profit, one involving sadomasochistic practices, and one concerning issues associated with consensual underage sex – he could be relied upon to take the high moral ground and to react accordingly. Thus, the wretched author of *Spycatcher* and those members of the security services who harboured thoughts of following his example, needed to be taught a lesson; those who engaged in sadomasochistic practices involving violence and bodily injury should not find themselves beyond the reach of the criminal law; and under no circumstances should doctors play any part in facilitating opportunities for girl under 16 to engage in consensual sex. All that one can conclude from this is that Lord Templeman was prone to adopt a distinctly conservative and uncompromising approach to what he clearly recognised as moral and ethical issues. It does not provide any real indication as to how Lord Templeman would have responded to the many and varied issues

6 The most it can do, provided the engagement of Convention rights happens to be in issue, is to declare legislation "incompatible" with the Convention, a rather limited power derived from section 4 of the Human Rights Act 1998, and one which is also exercisable by the High Court.

which confronted him during his 12 years as a Law Lord, in which a clear moral or ethical dimension would have been absent.[7]

Lord Bingham is an interesting case in point. In regard to the neurosurgeon who failed to warn his patient that a proposed operation carried a 2 per cent risk of partial paralysis, he was not prepared to depart from the conventional rule governing causation in negligence claims. In the case of the disabled mother who sought damages arising from the birth of an unwanted child, he adhered to the established policy of denying the mother damages if the child was healthy. And in regard to the compensating of the innocent party for the loss arising from a wrongful repudiation of a contract, he saw no reason to depart from the traditional rule that the innocent party was entitled to recover such loss that it was likely he would have incurred when the contract was wrongfully repudiated, and not in the light of subsequent events. All this points very much to a distinctly conservative cast of mind in terms of the direction the law should take. However, this is the same Lord Bingham who thought that it was indefensible that an elderly lady placed by a local authority in a residential care home should be denied the protection of Article 8 of the European Convention; who regarded it as an abuse of power by the Government to remove the residents of a British colony to make way for an American base in the Pacific Ocean, and subsequently to resile from a promise to let them return; and who clearly regarded it as a moral imperative to interpret the new constitution of Trinidad and Tobago in such a way as to ensure that it could not be read as countenancing the mandatory death sentence for murder. The picture which emerges from the stance which Lord Bingham took in these six cases is simply that in some areas of law (for example, commercial contracts and negligence) he was inclined to take a "conventional" or traditional line, partly grounded – certainly in the cases of the disabled mother and the repudiated contract – on moral principle; whereas in cases involving constitutional and human rights, he was inclined to take what can fairly be described as the firm and uncompromising position that such rights had to be taken seriously, and

---

7 Much the same could be said about Lord Templeman's contemporary, Lord Keith. He had a distinctly "restrictionist", or conservative, view on the scope of the duty of care in negligence cases, as indeed was apparent from his judgment in the case of the disappointed beneficiaries. In only five out of the 20 appeals which he heard between 1987 and 1995, and in which the scope of the duty of care was in issue, was he disposed to decide an appeal in favour of the claimant: D. Robertson, (1998) *Judicial Discretion in the House of Lords*, Clarendon Press. But this "restrictionist" stance could not be said to have been a feature of his judgments in other areas of law.

should be upheld and enforced, however unpalatable and inconvenient this may be from the authorities' point of view.[8]

Much the same, for example, can be said of Lord Mance. It is of course a fact, and one which has been previously noted, that Lord Mance found himself in the minority in three cases involving constitutional and human rights. He saw no reason why a decision of the European Court of Human rights (the Belgrade bombing case) and a decision of the House of Lords (the Iraqi civilians case) should be treated as an obstacle to holding that the Convention had extra-territorial effect in relation to members of the armed forces on active service in Iraq, and saw every reason for holding that the Convention *did* apply in such circumstances. He regarded the treatment by successive Governments of the Chagos Islanders as an abuse of power, and the right of abode as a historical constitutional right. He thought that the right to pursue a private prosecution was likewise a constitutional right, and one which was not to be frustrated by the *diktat* of the Director of Public Prosecutions unless the prosecution was virtually bound to fail. And he thought that it could not be right that a political party should be penalised under the Political Parties, Elections and Referendum Act 2000 for failing to appreciate that a donor to party funds was not on an electoral register, although he was resident in the UK. In all this one can discern a common theme.

Yet on other hand Lord Mance was unwilling to hold that an elderly lady placed by a local authority in a private residential care was protected by the European Convention, and specifically Article 8. He took the view that the Jewish free school operated a racially discriminatory admissions policy despite recognising that the school's motive for operating their criteria was a non-racial one, and did so because he thought that this is what the policy of the legislation required. He was a party to the decision that time ran under the Limitation Act 1980 in a personal injury claim against the claimant once that claimant reasonably believed he or she may have a "cause of action", and *not* when the claimant definitely knew this to be the case. And along with the majority of his colleagues, he took the view that the issue of

---

8 In fact it is generally acknowledged that the influence which Lord Bingham has exercised on the direction of the law of human rights in this country is a profound one. Of particular importance was his leading judgment (as the senior Law Lord) in the case concerning the legality of the detention without charge of foreign nationals under the Prevention of Terrorism Act 2005, in which he cautioned against the courts showing an excessive degree of deference to the political judgment of ministers.

whether legal advice privilege should cover legal advice provided by accountants was essentially a policy matter which could only properly be resolved by Parliament. All that one can glean from this is that in some cases a moral imperative (or, in other words, a sensitivity to what he saw as a moral dimension to the particular case) seems to have been the driving force behind Lord Mance's response, and that in other cases his response would appear unsurprisingly to have been governed by his assessment of the competing arguments, and by wholly different considerations. His attitude to the proposed extension of legal advice privilege to accountants, for example, was one which was determined by purely pragmatic considerations.

The case of Lord Hoffmann is perhaps less straightforward. It will be recalled that he was resistant to awarding damages to a patient who had not been warned of a slight risk of partial paralysis when undergoing an operation: in his view the conventional rules of causation should have applied. He agreed with the majority that a council was entitled to withdraw support services for an elderly disabled man because of lack of financial resources. He adopted an uncompromising position as to the interpretation of the new constitution of Trinidad and Tobago, a position which permitted the retention of the mandatory death penalty for murder. And he rejected in equally robust terms the claim by the Chagos Islanders that their treatment at the hands of successive governments amounted to abuse of power and was a violation of their right of abode. It could be argued that what this all suggests is a conservative (as opposed to an "expansionist") mindset and a somewhat purist approach to points of law. But this is far from amounting to evidence of Lord Hoffmann's espousal of some distinctive and over-arching philosophy in the course of his 14 years as a Law Lord, either aligning him with, or distinguishing him from, any of his colleagues. Like Lord Bingham, for example, he delivered a strong judgment concurring in the rejection of the detention of foreign nationals without charge under the Prevention of Terrorism Act 2005 as unlawful.[9]

In terms of a consistent point of view and, arguably, a certain predictability, the judgments of Baroness Hale provide a much more telling illustration. The following is a fair summary. She thought there was a compelling case for concluding that a resident of a private care home, placed there by a local council, had the protection of Article 8 of the European Convention:

[9] See above, footnote 8.

crucially, the home was carrying out a "public function" within the meaning of the Human Rights Act 1998. She thought the Jewish free school operated a racially discriminating admissions policy by not accepting the son of an Italian Catholic mother who had subsequently converted to a Jewish sect. She thought that the threshold for obtaining compensation for a wrongful conviction should be less onerous than proof of innocence. She thought it wrong that time should run under the Limitation Act 1980 against a claimant seeking damages for personal injury when that claimant was still unsure whether the injury was caused by the negligent act or omission alleged. Like Lord Mance, she thought the European Convention, through the mechanism of the Human Rights Act 1998, should have extra-territorial effect in relation to the armed forces on active service in Iraq; and that the Director of Prosecutions had no business to stop a private prosecution in its tracks because he could not be confident of the outcome. And she thought that the Home Secretary was wrong to introduce a blanket age restriction of 21 on foreign spouses seeking to settle in the UK as a means of reducing the risk of forced marriages. Simply put, the theme common to all these judgments is the assertion of the rights of the individual and of those who may be in an otherwise vulnerable position. However, it would be a mistake to elevate this to some kind of over-arching ideological or philosophical position. It shows simply a strong moral perspective which Baroness Hale happens to share with Lord Bingham and Lord Mance.

(3) CONCERNS ABOUT ACCOUNTABILITY

Some of the disagreements which have been discussed serve to highlight what for a long time has been a controversial aspect of judicial decision-making both formerly in the House of Lords and now in the Supreme Court: namely, the fact that the outcome has hinged on what was essentially a choice-of-policy decision, and often openly acknowledged to be such. In the case of the partially disabled mother, the Law Lords acknowledged that the principle that damages for the cost of bringing up an unwanted but healthy child was a policy choice reflecting the personal views of those who were parties to the decision, and the specific issue in the case – namely, whether there should be an exception in the case of a disabled mother – depended on a policy decision as to whether any distinction ought properly to be made between disability and any other kind of significant disadvantage. The sadomasochism case is also an obvious example. As the Law Lords were agreed that the precedents relating to consensual violence were neither directly in point nor particularly helpful, they were unanimous in treating the issue as one of public policy, although they disagreed as to what that policy should be. Again, in the case concerning contraceptive advice for underage girls, all the Law Lords treated the issue essentially as one of public policy rather than one of pure law, although again they disagreed as to what the policy should be. And in the most recent of the cases discussed in this study, the majority recognised the "compelling" nature of the case for extending the privilege to accountants, but made what was expressly acknowledged to be a policy decision to treat the issue as being one for Parliament to address if it so wished.

Should this trouble us in any way? Stern warnings have been administered from time to time against the danger of judges succumbing to the temptation of allowing their own views on ethical and social issues to encroach on their decision-making, and in particular when engaged in the exercise of determining what solution is best in the public interest. In the 1930s one eminent Law Lord famously observed that "public policy should only be invoked in clear cases in which the harm to the public is ... incontestable, and does not depend upon the idiosyncratic inferences of a few judicial minds."[10] In 1944 the then Master of the Rolls wrote that it was not the function of the judiciary to concern itself with policy or to decide what was in the public interest. In the late 1970s and early 1980s there were repeated calls from then senior Law Lord, Lord Diplock, for judicial "restraint" when interpreting legislation, in the sense of avoiding the temptation to inject a personal preference as to the meaning of the relevant words;[11] and since then there have been periodic expressions of unease by both politicians and the media about what is perceived to be the power of the Law Lords – now the Supreme Court Justices – effectively to "legislate" on our behalf.

The fact is that policy choices have continued to be a feature of judicial decision-making both in the House of Lords and now in the Supreme Court, a feature which is inherent in our common law/case law system. Indeed the development of much of the law of negligence over the last 40 years, for example, has been almost entirely shaped by policy decisions: decisions concerning the scope of the liability for negligence of public authorities, when exercising their statutory functions, have been determined almost exclusively by policy considerations. For practical purposes, in this context

---

10 Lord Atkin in *Fender v St John Mildmay* [1938] AC 1, at 12.

11 In fact those calls were largely directed at Lord Denning, presiding as Master of the Rolls in the Court of Appeal, who allowed his strong views on the power of trade unions to influence his interpretation of industrial relations legislation.

there is no real distinction between decisions taken on a principled basis and those taken on a choice-of-policy basis, and perhaps more to the point there would appear to be no real distinction between legal policy and public policy. In fact so far as the cases which have been analysed in this study are concerned, only in one instance – the legal privilege case – can it be said there was any recognition of any distinction between legal policy (conventionally acknowledged to be a legitimate concern of the judiciary) on the one hand, and public policy (regarded as the domain of Parliament and Government) on the other.

The reality is that the "court of last resort" is considerably less constrained than the courts below it by precedent and the weight of authority, which means that the role of moral judgments, instinctive responses and policy choices is an inescapable fact of judicial life at that level. Furthermore, on the evidence of the cases which have been discussed, and which have social or political ramifications, what has tended to divide opinion is no more and no less than what would have divided opinion among non-lawyers over the dinner table: arguably, therefore, the Supreme Court is as good a forum as any in which to thrash these issues out. In that sense, as has been said of its US counterpart, the Supreme Court can be said to represent "democracy in action".

Another concern, and one which may have marginally more substance, is that the relative freedom which Supreme Court Justices enjoy, and the Law Lords formerly enjoyed, to give expression and effect to their personal views on social issues, may lead to the Supreme Court heading in the same direction as its US counterpart, and evolve into something of a polarising institution, operating as a buffer or brake on Government policy. This has to some extent been fuelled by periodic complaints that in their handling of applications for judicial review, the courts are increasingly entering into the political arena. Once upon a time such complaints were the preserve of politicians, and successive Home Secretaries in particular, but this is no longer the case. As has already been seen, Lord Brown, in the foreign spouses case, warned of dire consequences if what he saw as this trend towards active intervention by the courts continued. A similar warning was issued by another Supreme Court Justice, Lord Sumption. In a lecture delivered shortly prior to taking up his appointment in January 2012, he argued that it was apparent that on occasions what the court was actually doing was reviewing the policy and the merits of the relevant legislation, and not the actions and decisions of the executive, which was its proper function.[12]

It is undoubtedly the case that an ever-increasing number of appeals involving human rights and related issues are finding their way to the Supreme Court (typically concerning immigration, asylum, deportation and anti-terrorism legislation), with concepts such as proportionality playing a key role;[13] and it is inevitable that policy will come more and more under judicial scrutiny whenever Convention rights have to be thrown into the scales: this is what human rights law actually requires. Over a period of just over two years there were some 13 appeals in cases of judicial review heard by the Supreme Court to which the Home Secretary was a party, and in which she was unsuccessful; but in none of them could it be said that the Court (or, when split, the majority) had adopted a confrontational stance. Indeed sometimes quite the reverse. Take, for example, the opening words of a judgment of Baroness Hale:

> Mr Shepherd Kambadzi may not be a very nice person. He is certainly not a very good person. He has overstayed his welcome in this country for many years. He has abused our hospitality by committing assaults and sexual assaults. It is not surprising that the Home Secretary wishes to deport him.[14]

In fact the Supreme Court has made it clear that, in line with decisions of the European Court of Human Rights, in the case of challenges to Government regulations and rules on the basis they involve discriminatory treatment in breach of Article 14 of the Convention, the courts should only intervene if the treatment in question was "manifestly without reasonable foundation": a difficult test for a claimant to satisfy.[15] There is no reason to suppose that

---

12 The F.A. Mann Lecture, 2011. There was a swift response from the distinguished former Court of Appeal Judge, Sir Stephen Sedley, who pointed out that none of the examples cited by Lord Sumption actually supported his argument: "Judicial Politics", *London Review of Books*, 23 February 2012.

13 In addition to the foreign spouses and Bank Mellat cases, a perfect illustration of how proportionality and the exercise of personal value judgments can be central to a human rights related issue can be seen in a case involving a successful appeal to the Supreme Court against the strictness of the conditions attached to a control order imposed under the Prevention of Terrorism Act 2005. (The claimant complained of being isolated from his family: *Secretary of State for the Home Department v AP* [2010] UKSC 24, [2011] AC 1.)

14 *SK (Zimbabwe) v Secretary of State for the Home Department* [2011] UKSC 23, [2011] 1 WLR 1299, at [61].

15 *Humphreys v Revenue and Customs* [2012] UKSC 18, [2012] 1 WLR 1545.

this approach will be confined to policy choices by the Government where the immigration rules and specifically discriminatory treatment are in issue.

Much of what has just been discussed has fed into some very specific concerns about accountability: or to be more precise, the accountability of our most senior judges – the way they are appointed, and *who* exactly should be responsible for their appointment. After all, there was no change in the "job specification" when the old Appellate Committee was supplanted by the Supreme Court in 2009. (Until recently Justices of the Supreme Court were selected by a commission which included the President and Deputy President of the Court and one lay member.) The question seems to have troubled a lot of people, and was recently tackled by the House of Lords Select Committee on the Constitution.[16]

The Committee heard evidence and received written submissions to the effect that since so many decisions of our most senior judges impact on policy and determine how legislation enacted by Parliament should be interpreted or applied, politicians, and specifically members of Parliament, had a legitimate interest in their appointment, and should have some kind of input in the selection process analogous to the confirmation hearings in the US. The Committee firmly rejected the suggestion that there should be some form of "pre-appointment" hearing at which the prospective appointee could be questioned. In the Committee's view, this would undermine the independence of those subsequently appointed and would appear to pre-judge their future decisions. "In the United Kingdom", the Committee observed, "judges' legitimacy depends on their independent status and appointment on merit, not on any democratic mandate."

The Committee did, however, accept there were strong arguments to support the conclusion that the lay representation on the selection commission should be significantly increased, and made a recommendation to that effect. (The Committee also recommended that the commission should be chaired by a lay person.) These recommendations have since been implemented. On the face of it, the case for strengthening the lay element is a strong one: the evidence of the disagreements which have been discussed in this study demonstrate, if nothing else, the importance of the individual judge's own perspective on social and other strictly non-legal (in the technical sense) matters. A well-rounded personality is obviously more likely to turn out to

16 25th Report of Session 2010–2012, published 28 March 2012.

be a successful appointment. But one does wonder what an increased lay representation would really achieve in practice. Would an enhanced lay presence really help in flushing out views which might provide a significant clue as to how the particular applicant is likely to perform as a Supreme Court Justice, or for that matter help in providing any other valuable insights? Perhaps it is for this reason that it has become customary for an applicant to be asked to submit what is in effect a "mission statement" outlining his or her views as to what the purpose and role of the Supreme Court should be, and how it should function. However, one would think that the temptation for a 60-something-year-old applicant, with 10 years of experience of the Court of Appeal and countless published judgments in the Law Reports, to respond facetiously, must be quite irresistible.

Finally, what of the composition of the Court? Leaving aside the vexed question of gender, is talk of ensuring a balance – other than the fulfilling of a statutory requirement to have representation from Scotland and Northern Ireland – simply, as P.G. Wodehouse's Bertie Wooster would say, "babble from the sickbed"? As there are no factions in terms of ideology or legal philosophy, the only sense in which the concept of balance is relevant is the need to ensure that there is adequate expertise in all the main areas of law likely to be the subject of serious litigation. (On this point there was a consensus in the evidence before the Select Committee.) There continues to be a reassuring unpredictability as to outcome prior to the hearing of an appeal, irrespective of the Court's composition. Many years ago a Law Lord more than once thought it appropriate to characterise the view he and his colleagues felt they should take on what was essentially a matter requiring a value judgment on a social issue as an "educated response", presumably on the touchingly naïve assumption that that there could be only one such response. This was not the case then, and it certainly is not the case now. The truth of Lord Steyn's comment that "it is unrealistic to say there is only one right answer" is constantly being borne out, which is why legal philosophers have written reams on the subject.

APPENDIX ONE

List of Law Lords and Supreme Court Justices whose judgments are discussed or referred to in the text, and date of their appointment

Lord Ackner	1986–1992	Part Two (2)
Lord Bingham of Cornhill (Formerly Master of the Rolls, and Lord Chief Justice)	2000–2008	Part One (2), (3), (4) Part Two (4) Part Three (1)
Lord Brandon of Oakbrook	1981–1991	Part Two (2), (3)
Lord Bridge of Harwich	1982–1992	Part Two (2), (3)
Lord Brown of Eaton-under-Heywood	2004–2012	Part One (4) Part Two (5) Part Three (2), (3), (4) Part Four (2), (3)
Lord Browne-Wilkinson	1991–2000	Part One (1)
Lord Carswell (Formerly Lord Chief Justice of Northern Ireland)	2004–2012	Part One (4) Part Four (1)
Lord Clarke of Stone-cum-Ebony	2008–	Part Three (2) Part Four (5)
Lord Clyde (Formerly a Scottish judge)	1996–2001	Part Three (1)
Lord Collins of Mapesbury	2009–2012	Part Four (2)
Lord Fraser of Tullybelton	1975–1985	Part Two (3)
Lord Goff of Chieveley	1986–1994	Part One (1) Part Three (2)
Lord Griffiths	1985–1993	Part Three (2)

Baroness Hale of Richmond	2004–	Part Three (1), (2), (3), (4) Part Four (2), (3), (4)
Lord Hoffmann	1995–2001	Part One (3) Part Two (4) Part Four (1)
Lord Hope of Craigshead (Formerly a Scottish judge)	1996–2013	Part One (2), (3) Part Two (4) Part Three (2), (3) Part Four (2), (3), (5)
Lord Hutton (Formerly Lord Chief Justice of Northern Ireland)	1997–2004	Part One (2)
Lord Jauncey of Tulichettle (Formerly a Scottish judge)	1988–1996	Part Two (1)
Lord Keith of Kinkel (Formerly a Scottish judge)	1977–1996	Part One (1)
Lord Kerr of Tonaghmore (Formerly an Appeal judge from Northern Ireland)	2009–	Part Three (2), (3), (4) Part Four (2), (4)
Lord Lloyd of Berwick	1993–1998	Part Three (1)
Lord Lowry (Formerly Lord Chief Justice of Northern Ireland)	1998–1994	Part Two (1) Part Three (2)
Lord Mance	2005–	Part Two (5) Part Three (1), (2), (3) Part Four (1), (2), (4), (5)
Lord Millett	1998–2004	Part One (2)
Lord Mustill	1992–1997	Part One (1) Part Two (1)
Lord Neuberger of Abbotsbury	2007–	Part Three (1) Part Four (4), (5)
Lord Nicholls of Birkenhead	1998–2007	Part One (2) Part Three (1)
Lord Nolan	1994–1998	Part One (1)
Lord Oliver of Aylmerton	1986–1991	Part Two (2)

Lord Phillips of Worth Matravers (Formerly Master of the Rolls, then Lord Chief Justice)	1998–2012	Part Two (5) Part Three (3), (4), (5) Part Four (2), (3)
Lord Reed (Formerly a Scottish judge)	2012–	Part Four (5), (6)
Lord Rodger of Earlsferry (Formerly a Scottish Judge)	2001–2012	Part Two (5) Part Three (2), (3) Part Four (1)
Lord Scarman	1977–1986	Part Two (3)
Lord Scott of Fostcote	2000–2009	Part One (2), (4) Part Three (1)
Lord Slynn of Hadley	1992–2002	Part Two (1)
Lord Steyn	1995–2005	Part One (2), (3) Part Three (1)
Lord Sumption	2012–	Part Four (5), (6)
Lord Templeman	1982–1994	Part Two (1), (2), (3)
Lord Walker of Gestingthorpe	2002–2013	Part One (2), (3) Part Three (1), (5)
Lord Wilson	2011–	Part Three (5) Part Four (3)

APPENDIX TWO

A SELECTION OF SAMPLE JUDGMENTS

Reproduced below are six full judgments taken from three of the cases discussed in this book. Two represent the House of Lords era, and the third, the new Supreme Court era.

The judgments of Lord Templeman and Lord Bridge in the *Spycatcher* case[1] tell riveting stories from opposing points of view, and were delivered in unusual circumstances: the majority decision to continue the injunction had already been announced before the reasons set out in the judgments were published, and to a uniformly hostile reception from the media. Neither can be characterised as bland or excessively urbane.

The judgments of Lord Lloyd and Lord Nicholls in the "lack of resources" case[2] are economical and clear in the treatment of the central issue, and neatly encapsulate the competing arguments. (Common to all four judgments of the House of Lords is what may strike any readers unaccustomed to scanning the law reports as a curious feature: because judgments delivered in the House of Lords were technically speeches, it was the invariable custom to prefix them with the expression "My Lords, …".)

Lastly, the judgments of Lord Phillips and Lord Rodger in the "political donations" case[3] illustrate the present trend in the Supreme Court to engage with arguments and specific points advanced or raised in the draft judgments of one's colleagues. In the case of the leading majority judgment of Lord Phillips, the use of sub-headings does a lot to enhance its clarity.

---

1 *Attorney General v Guardian Newspapers Ltd (No. 1)* [1987] UKHL 13.

2 *R v Gloucestershire CC and Another ex p Barry (Conjoined Appeals)* [1997] UKHL 58.

3 *R (on the application of the Electoral Commission) (Respondent) v City of Westminster Magistrates Court (Respondent) and The United Kingdom Independence Party (Appellant)* [2010] UKSC 40.

ATTORNEY GENERAL v GUARDIAN NEWSPAPERS LTD (NO. 1) [1987] UKHL 13

House of Lords

LORD TEMPLEMAN

My Lords,

On the 30 July this year your Lordships by a majority decided to continue injunctions restraining the appellant newspapers from disclosing or publishing any information obtained by Peter Maurice Wright in his capacity as a member of the British Security Service. The principle affirmed by that decision was that the law will prevent the mass circulation in this country of confidential information which prejudices the public interest in the maintenance of an efficient and effective secret Security Service. Three defences were put forward by the appellant newspapers, first, that Mr. Wright intended his treachery to be helpful to the British public, secondly, that damage to the Security Service arising from Mr. Wright's treachery had already been fully inflicted, and thirdly, that the public interest in receiving information entitled the press to publish treachery at home provided it had been published abroad. A majority of your Lordships rejected these defences.

The Secretary to the Cabinet, Sir Robert Armstrong, in an affidavit sworn in these proceedings, deposed as follows:

> "The main function of the British Security Service is the defence of the realm as a whole, from external and internal dangers arising from attempts at espionage and sabotage, or from actions from persons and organisations whether directed from within or without the United Kingdom, which may be judged to be subversive at this date."

Mr. Wright was employed by the British Security Service. On 1 September 1955 he signed a declaration that he understood the effect of section 2 of the Official Secrets Act 1911 which was set out in the declaration and renders liable to prosecution any person in possession of information:

> "... which he has obtained or to which he has had access owing to his position as a person who holds or who has held office under His Majesty . . . and

> communicates the information to any person, other than a person to whom he is authorised to communicate it, or a person to whom it is in the interests of the State his duty to communicate it."

When Mr. Wright left the Security Service he signed a further declaration, dated 30 January 1976, acknowledging, inter alia, that the provisions of the Official Secrets Acts applied to him after his appointment had ceased, that he was fully aware that serious consequences might follow any breach of the provisions of those Acts, and that he understood:

> "that I am liable to be prosecuted if either in the United Kingdom or abroad I communicate, either orally or in writing, including publication in a speech, lecture, radio or television broadcast, or in the press or in book form or otherwise, to any unauthorised person any information acquired by me as a result of my appointment (save such as has already officially been made public) unless I have previously obtained the official sanction in writing of the department by which I was appointed."

In addition to the obligations of secrecy expressly acknowledged by Mr. Wright, he was also under an obligation arising out of his employment by the Security Service and enforceable in equity not to divulge any information which he obtained in the course of his employment. The obligation arises because of:

> "the broad principle of equity that he who has received information in confidence shall not take unfair advantage of it. He must not use it to the prejudice of he who gave it:" per Lord Denning M.R. in *Seager v. Copydex* [1967] 1 W.L.R. 923 at 931.

The same obligation attaches to the press and anyone else who receives confidential information knowing that it is confidential. It is unlawful to make further disclosure.

The Cabinet Secretary further deposed that the work of Mr. Wright for the Security Service:

> "Involved him in frequent and close liaison with the Intelligence and Security Services of friendly foreign countries and the exchange of information with those Services. It was, and continues to be, essential to the effectiveness of all such liaison and exchanges that they are conducted upon a basis of mutual trust and confidence."

The Cabinet Secretary also said that the effective functioning of the British Security Service requires that its affairs be kept secret. The Attorney General who represents the public and who has brought these proceedings in their interest, could not, in the view of the Cabinet Secretary:

> "particularise the damage that would be caused by specific disclosures of fact by Mr. Wright without, himself, making further disclosures of material which is confidential, and undermining the efficacy of the duty of confidentiality which is also sought to be in force."

He continued:

> "It is likely that any disclosures of facts relating to the Security Service by Mr. Wright would not only be a breach of his contract and of his duty of confidence owed to the Service but would be likely to endanger the effective discharge by the Service of its current and future responsibilities, and as a consequence be of value for a foreign power and highly detrimental to the public interest of the United Kingdom as well as causing harm to individual officers, former officers, their families and other persons who might be identified by or as a consequence of such disclosures. The dangers could arise notwithstanding that the information disclosed was unclassified and is on its face and in isolation apparently innocuous. Such information may take on a wider significance if put together with other information in possession of other persons and thereby, for example, enable them to check the veracity of their sources of information. Furthermore, information which appears to be innocuous at a particular date or to a particular officer may at a later date become significant."

It follows that Mr. Wright could not publish his memoirs as an employee of the Security Service without committing flagrant breaches of the duty of secrecy and confidentiality which he owed to the public in the national interest. No publisher or newspaper in this country may lawfully publish Mr. Wright's memoirs or disclose information obtained by Mr. Wright in the course of his service concerning any aspect of the work of the Security Service. Mr. Wright, apart from making money out of his memoirs, protests that his memoirs will be helpful to the British public. The press and others consider that his memoirs will be helpful in achieving the objects of an enquiry into the working of the Security Service, an amendment of the Official Secrets Acts, and the enactment of freedom of information legislation. But these objects are unlikely to be attained so long as the British press is prepared to publish confidential information relating to the British Security Service without investigation or corroboration and in disregard of orders of the court designed to preserve the Security Service from harm.

Mr. Wright could not, of course, hope to be allowed to publish his memoirs in England. He accordingly entered into arrangements with an Australian company in New South Wales, Heinemann Publishers Australia Pty. Ltd., which is a subsidiary of the English Heinemann Publishers. In September 1985 the Crown began proceedings in New South Wales to restrain such publication. Interim relief obtained in New South Wales apparently did not prevent Mr. Wright and the Australian Heinemanns from publishing outside Australia. Seizing upon this loophole the Australian Heinemann company granted the American rights in Mr. Wright's memoirs to Viking Penguin Incorporated. This is an American subsidiary of the English Pearson Group. In the United States of America an injunction might have been obtained against Mr. Wright if he had been within the jurisdiction but under the law of the United States could not be obtained against Viking Penguin Incorporated or anyone else in the United States. Mr. Wright's memoirs were written by him or written for him either in Australia or in the United States and were given the name *Spycatcher*. On 22 June 1986 and 23 June 1986 respectively, *The Observer* and *The Guardian* published in their newspapers in this country, an outline of Mr. Wright's allegations. *The Observer* stated that it:

> "... has obtained details of what is disclosed in the manuscript written by retired senior MI5 officer, Peter Wright, who lives in Tasmania."

The Observer subsequently explained that *The Observer* had not seen the manuscript or extracts from it.

Thc publication of *The Observer* and *The Guardian* articles was unlawful and on 11 July 1986 Millett J. granted injunctions ("the Millett injunctions") against *The Observer* and *The Guardian* restraining them from disclosing or publishing any information obtained by Mr. Wright in his capacity as a member of the British Security Service and which they know or have reasonable grounds to believe to have come or been obtained directly or indirectly from Mr. Wright. The order had two provisos. The first proviso allowed the newspapers to reproduce attributions to Mr. Wright already made by Mr. Chapman Pincher's published works or in a television programme or programmes broadcast by Granada Television. The second proviso allowed disclosure of any material disclosed in open court in the Supreme Court of New South Wales unless prohibited by the judge there sitting or which, after the trial there in action No. 4382 of 1985 is not prohibited from publication. Millett J. delivered a lucid and convincing judgment explaining his reasons for coming to the conclusion that it would be against the public interest for newspapers in this country to publish information derived from Mr. Wright. On the 25 July 1986 the Court of Appeal dismissed an appeal from the judgment of Millett J. subject to certain minor modifications.

Between 27 April 1987 and 14 July 1987 the following events took place:

1. On 27 April 1987 *The Independent* stated that a copy of the manuscript of *Spycatcher* had been "passed unsolicited" to *The Independent.* The newspaper quoted extracts from the book but added that "*The Independent* has destroyed all copies of the manuscript in its possession." On the same day the London *Evening Standard* and the London *Daily News* followed suit and published information which could only have been derived from Mr. Wright in the final analysis. The Attorney General applied to commit the three newspapers for contempt since they were clearly acting in breach of the object of the Millett injunctions.

2. Shortly after 27 April 1987 *The Guardian* and *The Observer* applied to the court to discharge the Millett injunctions on the grounds of changed circumstances including the articles in *The Independent* and the other two London evening papers on 27 April.

3. On 28 April 1987 Australian newspapers published articles about *Spycatcher.*

4. On 3 May 1987 the *Washington Post* announced that it had "obtained" a manuscript copy of *Spycatcher* and published extracts and comments.

5. On 12 July 1987 *The Sunday Times* published "major extracts from the book *Spycatcher* by Peter Wright the former MI5 officer. Its serialisation has been timed to coincide with the publication of the book in the United States."

6. On 14 July 1987 the Court of Appeal which heard argument before and after 12 July, declared that *The Independent*, the London *Daily News* and the London *Evening Standard* "could indeed have been in contempt of court and so could *The Sunday Times* and any other newspaper which published information attributed to Mr. Wright. It could not be said that

they were in contempt of court because none had yet had an opportunity of putting forward a defence." Contempt proceedings had been or were then instituted against *The Sunday Times.*

All the newspaper articles were bound to put pressure on the court to allow publication of *Spycatcher* in this country regardless of any damage to the Security Service and despite the reasoned judgment of Millett J. that the disclosure of any relevant information derived from Mr. Wright would be contrary to the public interest and ought to be restrained. On 22 July 1987 the Vice-Chancellor discharged the orders made by Millett J. but his decision was reversed by the Court of Appeal on 24 July 1987, hence the appeal to this House.

My Lords, this appeal involves a conflict between the right of the public to be protected by the Security Service and the right of the public to be supplied with full information by the press. This appeal therefore involves consideration of the Convention for the Protection of Human Rights and Fundamental Freedoms ("the Convention") to which the British Government adheres. Article 10 of the Convention is in these terms:

> "1. Everyone has the right to freedom of expression. This right shall include freedom to hold opinions and to receive and impart information and ideas without interference by public authority and regardless of frontiers . . . .
>
> 2. The exercise of these freedoms, since it carries with it duties and responsibilities, may be subject to such formalities, conditions, restrictions or penalties as are prescribed by law and are necessary in a democratic society, in the interests of national security, territorial integrity or public safety, for the prevention of disorder or crime, for the protection of health or morals, for the protection of the reputation or rights of others, for preventing the disclosure of information received in confidence, or for maintaining the authority and impartiality of the judiciary."

In *The Sunday Times'* case (Eur. Court H.R. *The Sunday Times* case, decision of 27 October 1978, series A 30), the European Court of Human Rights decided by a majority of 11 to 9 that there had been a violation of the Convention by reason of the judgment of this House which restrained *The Sunday Times* from publishing:

> "Any article which prejudges the issues of negligence, breach of contract or breach of duty or deals with the evidence relating to any of the said issues arising in any actions pending or imminent against Distillers ... in respect of the development, distribution or use of the drug Thalidomide."

The European Court pointed out that this House applying domestic law had balanced the public interest in freedom of expression and the public interest in the due of administration of justice. But the European Court:

> " ... is faced not with the choice between two conflicting principles but with a principle of freedom of expression which is subject to a number of exceptions which must be narrowly interpreted .... It is not sufficient that the interference involved belongs to that class of exceptions listed in Article 10 which has been invoked; neither is it sufficient that the interference was imposed because its subject-matter fell within a particular category or was caught by a legal rule formulated in general or absolute terms; the Court has to be satisfied that the interference was necessary having regard to the facts and circumstances prevailing in the specific case before it."

The question is therefore whether the interference with freedom of expression constituted by the Millett injunctions was, on 30 July 1987 when they were continued by this House, necessary in a democratic society in the interests of national security, for protecting the reputation or rights of others, for preventing the disclosure of information received in confidence or for maintaining the authority and impartiality of the judiciary having regard to the facts and circumstances prevailing on the 30 July 1987 and in the light of the events which had happened. The continuance of the Millett injunctions appears to me to be necessary for all these purposes.

My Lords, in my opinion a democracy is entitled to take the view that a public servant who is employed in the Security Service must be restrained from making any disclosures concerning the Security Service and that similar restraints must be imposed on anybody who receives those disclosures knowing that they are confidential.

There are safeguards. No member of the Secret Service is immune from criminal prosecution or civil suit in respect of his actions. Instructions from superior officers are no defence. In addition, anyone, whether public servant, newspaper editor or journalist who is aware that a crime has been committed or is dissatisfied with the activities of the Secret Service is free to report to the police in relation to crime and in other matters is free to report to the Prime Minister who is charged with the responsibility of the security services and to the Security Commission which advises the Prime Minister. The Security Services are not above the law. In the present case there is not the slightest evidence that these safeguards have failed. Furthermore there is nothing to prevent the press investigating all the allegations made by Mr. Wright and reporting the results of their investigations to the public. It is only unlawful for the press to publish information unlawfully disclosed by Mr. Wright and which may or may not be true.

In terms of the Convention there are three reasons why in the present case restraints are necessary to prevent the press publishing information disclosed by Mr. Wright.

Any person who joins the Security Service accepts that he cannot defend himself or the Security Service against false accusations and cannot give any explanation for his actions or for the activities of the Security Service without himself thereby endangering the secrecy of the Security Service which is of paramount importance. Any person who joins the Security Service knows that no official defence or explanation can be given. He accepts that accusations may be made and circulated abroad and that rumours may reach individuals in this country. But he relies on the Attorney General, acting in the public interest, to seek to prevent the mass circulation of accusations and attributions and insinuations in this country and to prevent so far as possible the revelation of Security Service activities. And he relies on the courts acting within their jurisdiction to prevent mass circulation of secret and confidential information in this country if the courts consider that such protection is necessary. The hundreds of pages of *Spycatcher* which embellish but cannot improve the general allegations already known to have been made by Mr. Wright may include accusations, purported conversations, and unfair criticisms which no individual member of the Secret Service can wish to be made the subject of sensational newspaper headlines or delivered up to the newspaper reading public. So long as there are in this country only odd copies of *Spycatcher*, members of the Security Service are substantially free from harrassment. But once mass circulation takes place in newspapers and particularly once *The Sunday Times* publishes *Spycatcher* in serial form, then members of the Security Service will be liable to be harrassed with accusations to which they cannot respond. The publication in this country of *Spycatcher* will thus cause grievous harm to individuals and deal a blow to the morale of the Security Service. The British public will lose confidence in the Security Service. Our friends will be dismayed and our enemies will rejoice at the failure of the British to protect the Security Service from calumny reported in the British press. Whatever may happen abroad it must be harmful to the Security Service and contrary to the public interest for Mr. Wright to be allowed to attack the Security Service in this country by revealing or pretending to reveal information which he is forbidden to reveal by law and loyalty. There is a great difference between the power of the press operating through mass circulation and the power of Mr. Wright confined to the export to this country of individual copies of *Spycatcher*.

I reject the argument that the law will appear ridiculous if it imposes a restriction on mass circulation when any individual member of the public may obtain a copy of *Spycatcher* from abroad. The court cannot exceed its territorial jurisdiction but the court can prevent the harm which will result from mass circulation within its own jurisdiction and can prevent Mr. Wright and British newspapers from profiting from the unlawful conduct of Mr. Wright. It is said that the same result could be achieved by an order on Mr. Wright and the newspapers to account to the Attorney General for any profits they will make from *Spycatcher*. The public interest does not lie in making profits but in preventing profits being made in this country from treachery to this country.

In my opinion, therefore, the injunctions are necessary in terms of the Convention because harm will be caused to the Security Service if the press insist on disclosing to their readers not the general nature of Mr. Wright's uncorroborated allegations but the mass circumstantial hearsay contained in *Spycatcher* relating to the Security Service and its activities.

The second reason which makes it necessary to continue restrictions on the press lies in the fact that if the injunctions are discharged in the present case an immutable precedent will have been created. If the injunctions are discharged it must follow that any disgruntled public servant or holder of secret or confidential information relating to the Security Service can achieve mass circulation in this country of damaging truths and falsehoods by the device of prior publication anywhere else abroad. Nothing will ever again be confidential save the identity of a source whom a newspaper wishes to conceal. If the Millett injunctions were discharged, Mr. Wright could write to the *Washington Post* making a serious new allegation or bolstering up old allegations citing names and actions and purporting to give chapter and verse. Once the *Washington Post* had entertained an American audience with these revelations, then the products of Mr. Wright's recollections and imaginations could be plastered across the British press. I reject the allegation that the press are being gagged or censored or submitted to Soviet discipline. The Millett injunctions were not imposed by the Government, the injunctions were imposed and are being continued by independent and impartial judges because they consider that despite the importance of the right of freedom of expression it is necessary in the national interest to prevent the Security Service being harmed now and in the future. The imposition of restraints on the press in the exercise of a judicial discretion in conformity with the Convention is an expression and not a negation of democracy in action.

There is a third and final reason why the restraints imposed in the present case satisfy the tests of the Convention. All the newspaper reports between the 27 April and 14 July 1987 were contrary to the object and purpose of the Millett injunctions. Those reports originated with Mr. Wright and his publishers abroad and were intended to bring pressure on the English courts to allow *Spycatcher* to be published here. The Millett injunctions cannot now be discharged without surrendering to the press an untrammelled, arbitrary and irresponsible power to evade an order of the court designed for the safety of the realm to protect the confidentiality of information obtained by a member of the Secret Service.

Finally, I must refer to one proviso to the Millett injunctions which was deleted by the order of your Lordships' House on 30 July. The proviso was in these terms:

> "(2) No breach of this order shall be constituted by the disclosure or publication of any material disclosed in open court in the Supreme Court of New South Wales unless prohibited by the judge there sitting or which after the trial in action No. 4382 of 1985 is not prohibited from publication."

When Millett J. made that proviso in the interests of *The Guardian* and *The Observer* it would not have occurred to him that other newspapers would subsequently publish extracts from *Spycatcher.* It is very likely that in the course of the proceedings in New South Wales long extracts from *Spycatcher* have been read in open court. *The Sunday Times* has demonstrated that it is prepared to go to any lengths to publish extracts from *Spycatcher.* The order of this House prohibiting inter alia the publication of extracts from *Spycatcher* in this country was made on Thursday, 30 July. It was quite possible that if the proviso had not been deleted then on Sunday, 2 August, *The Sunday Times* would have published long extracts from *Spycatcher* explaining that these had been read in open court in New South Wales. Indeed, when deletion of the proviso was discussed, counsel for *The Sunday Times* very properly and prudently asked whether, if the proviso were deleted, *The Sunday Times* would be forbidden from publishing extracts from *Spycatcher* which had been read out in open court, and he was informed that such was the object and intent of the order proposed and made by this House.

At the conclusion of the hearing of this appeal I was satisfied that it was the duty of this House in its judicial capacity to stand firm in order to prevent harm to the Security Service, to preserve the right and duty of the court to uphold within the jurisdiction the secrecy of the Security Service when necessary and to ensure that the object and intent of orders made by the court are not flouted.

Since writing this speech I have read in draft the speeches to be delivered by my colleagues. I agree with the observations of Lord Brandon of Oakbrook and Lord Ackner. I agree with Lord Oliver of Aylmerton that this is a uniquely difficult case but for the reasons I have set out I am unable to agree with the conclusions reached by my noble and learned friends, Lord Bridge of Harwich and Lord Oliver of Aylmerton.

LORD BRIDGE OF HARWICH

My Lords,

I write this opinion in wholly exceptional circumstances. On 30 July your Lordships announced in the House your decision by a majority of three to two to maintain in full force the injunctions granted by Millett J. and affirmed by the Court of Appeal last year ("the Millett injunctions") against publication of what I shall refer to for brevity as Mr. Wright's *Spycatcher* allegations and to extend the scope of the injunctions to cover reports on the proceedings now current in Australia against Mr. Wright and his publishers there. Because I am about to leave the country and shall not be back until September I thought it would not be possible to publish the reasons for the decision before September and I so indicated to the House. I had in mind that, in the usual way, each member of the House participating in the decision would wish to have the opportunity, before publication, of reading the considered opinions of the others. I have since been persuaded that the urgency of informing the public of the reasons which underlie the conclusions reached by the majority and the minority alike is such that delay until September would be unacceptable. I understand that your Lordships all share this view. This means, however, that I must accept the disadvantage of expressing my dissent before I have had a chance of reading and at least trying to understand the reasons which your Lordships in the majority are going to give in support of your decision.

The proceedings arise from an application to discharge the Millett injunctions. I have no doubt that the Millett injunctions were properly granted in the first place. As the law now stands, under a decision of the

Court of Appeal in contempt proceedings which for present purposes I assume to be correct, the Millett injunctions operate as a universal ban on any publication within the jurisdiction of anything which would contravene the injunctions. I attach little importance, as relevant changes of circumstance, to the partial disclosures of the *Spycatcher* allegations which some newspapers have succeeded in making. The watershed, to my mind, came with the publication of *Spycatcher* in the United States of America. Her Majesty's Government did not attempt to stop this, because they knew they would fail. They have also announced that they will not attempt to prevent the importation of *Spycatcher* into this country. These two vital facts set the scene for the present controversy.

I shall excuse myself from giving any extended account of the proceedings in the courts below. I note however that no judge considering the matter so far has thought it appropriate to maintain the Millett injunctions without qualification. The Vice-Chancellor favoured their total discharge for the reasons which he gave. The Court of Appeal favoured a variation of the injunctions with the introduction of a new proviso to permit publication of "a summary in very general terms" of the *Spycatcher* allegations. Sir John Donaldson M.R. thought that the existing injunctions were "clearly much too wide" to achieve the strictly limited purpose which he believed still to be capable of achievement and that was why he added the new proviso. Ralph Gibson L.J. said:

> "If the choice were between discharging the injunctions entirely and maintaining the injunctions in the form in which they were made, notwithstanding the alterations in the circumstances already described by my Lord and in the judgment of the learned Vice-Chancellor, I would, I think, with regret at the impotence of the law as the Vice-Chancellor expressed it, but having had the benefit of the Vice-Chancellor's judgment without the hesitation which he experienced, have upheld his conclusion that the injunctions must be discharged. ... I accept that it is not reasonable to try to maintain the injunctions in their original form because so to do causes public inconvenience and impairment of public discussion and information for no sufficient benefit in maintenance of the rights which the Attorney General is seeking to enforce."

Russell L.J. said:

> "In the amended form of injunctions proposed by my Lord the Master of the Rolls there is built in a measure of protection for the legitimate interests of the press, which it is no part of the function of this court to stultify."

Before your Lordships all parties accepted that the compromise solution favoured by the Court of Appeal could not be supported in law and would be unworkable in practice. There was and is no escape by way of any compromise from the need to resolve the issue. The injunctions must either be maintained or discharged.

I appreciate that the decision of your Lordships' House is in form merely interlocutory. But it was quite rightly accepted by Mr. Mummery, for the Attorney General, that the case in favour of maintaining the injunctions cannot be any stronger at the trial than it is today. It must follow from this, in my view, that the real question raised by the newspapers' appeals and the cross-appeal of the Attorney General is whether the Attorney General, on the relevant and undisputed facts, can sustain a claim for permanent injunctions. If no case for permanent injunctions can be made out, it must be absurd to keep the interim injunctions in force. Conversely, although a trial of the action would, at least theoretically, leave the door open for the newspapers to canvass afresh every issue canvassed before your Lordships in these appeals and, of course, to adduce fresh evidence and argument on issues not already canvassed, I fear that, in practice, your Lordships' decision of the present appeals will effectively foreclose the options open to the trial judge.

The basis of the claim for the Millett injunctions was to prevent disclosure of the *Spycatcher* allegations in breach of the life-long obligation of confidence which Mr. Wright, as a former officer of the Security Service, owed to Her Majesty's Government. So long as any of the *Spycatcher* allegations remained undisclosed, I should have been wholeheartedly in favour of maintaining the injunctions in the interests of national security for all the reasons so cogently deployed in the affidavit of Sir Robert Armstrong. But it is perfectly obvious and elementary that, once information is freely available to the general public, it is nonsensical to talk about preventing its "disclosure." Whether the *Spycatcher* allegations are true or false is beside the point. What is to the point is that they are now freely available to the public or, perhaps more accurately, to any member of the public who wants to read them. I deliberately refrain from using expressions such as "the public domain" which may have technical overtones. The fact is that the intelligence and security services of any country in the world can buy the book *Spycatcher* and read what is in it. The fact is that any citizen of this country can buy the book in America and bring it home with him or order the book from America and receive a copy by post. Some enterprising small traders have apparently found it worth their while to import copies of the book and sell them by the roadside. It remains to be seen whether the

Attorney General will institute proceedings for contempt of court against any public library which imports copies of *Spycatcher* and makes it available to borrowers. Mr. Mummery had no instructions which enabled him to answer the question I asked about that.

If, as I have always thought, the interest of national security in protecting sensitive and classified information is to conceal it from those who might make improper use of it, it is manifestly now too late for the Millett injunctions to serve that interest. If the confidence of friendly countries in the ability of this country to protect its secrets has been undermined by the publication in the United States of America of *Spycatcher*, the maintenance of the Millett injunctions can do nothing to restore that confidence. So much, I believe, is obvious and incontrovertible.

I well understand the sense of indignation which all of us must feel that Mr. Wright, to use the colloquialism, should have got away with it, worse still that he should make a profit from his breach of confidence. Perhaps his publishers come under the same condemnation. But the remedy for that wrong lies not in a futile injunction but in an action for an account of profits.

The legal basis for the Attorney General's claim to enjoin the newspapers is that any third party who comes into possession of information knowing that it originated from a breach of confidence owes the same duty to the original confider as that owed by the original confidant. If this proposition is held to be of universal application, no matter how widely the original confidential information has been disseminated before reaching the third party, it would seem to me to lead to absurd and unacceptable consequences. But I am prepared to assume for present purposes that the Attorney General is still in a position to assert a bare duty binding on the conscience of newspaper editors which is capable of surviving the publication of *Spycatcher* in America.

The key question in the case, to my mind, is whether there is any remaining interest of national security which the Millett injunctions are capable of protecting and, if so, whether it is of sufficient weight to justify the massive encroachment on freedom of speech which the continuance of the Millett injunctions in present circumstances necessarily involves.

There is no fresh evidence from Sir Robert Armstrong or anyone else who can speak for the Security Service about the security implications following the American publication of *Spycatcher*. Sir Robert's original affidavit was made in the radically different circumstances obtaining before that publication. So, in effect, the hapless Mr. Mummery was left to make bricks without straw (which of course he did with his usual skill) in seeking to persuade your Lordships that, despite the free availability of the book *Spycatcher* itself and despite the citations from it and discussion of its contents which have been and will continue to be available in foreign newspapers freely circulating in this country, a blanket ban on any repetition, citation or discussion of its contents in the British press was necessary in the interests of national security. If I have understood the argument, stripped of rhetorical embellishment, it amounts to this. First, unless enjoined Mr. Wright may make yet further disclosures about the Security Service not already contained in *Spycatcher.* This may be true, but is entirely beside the point. If the Attorney General were prepared to modify the Millett injunctions so as to exclude from their ambit the *Spycatcher* allegations, in the same way that anything in Mr. Chapman Pincher's book *Their Trade is Treachery* is excluded, there would be nothing left to argue about. What the newspapers seek is liberty to repeat and discuss the *Spycatcher* allegations – no more, no less. Secondly, Mr. Mummery takes material from Sir Robert's affidavit out of the context in which it was made and seeks to rely on it for the proposition that the Millett injunctions should be maintained in their full rigour to deter other officers of the intelligence or security services from following Mr. Wright's deplorable example. The suggestion must be, I take it, that a future Mr. Wright contemplating going into exile and publishing his memoirs in the United States and who would not be deterred by the prospect of having to account to Her Majesty's Government for his profits, would nevertheless be deterred by the knowledge he would be denied by injunction any more than a limited access for his story to the general reading public in this country. This seems to me a rather fanciful suggestion, but if there is anything in it, now that the original aim of preventing disclosure of secret material can no longer be attained, the deterrent argument can only carry minimal weight.

What of the other side of the coin and the encroachment on freedom of speech? Having no written constitution, we have no equivalent in our law to the First Amendment to the Constitution of the United States of America. Some think that puts freedom of speech on too lofty a pedestal. Perhaps they are right. We have not adopted as part of our law the European Convention on Human Rights to which this country is a signatory. Many think that we should. I have hitherto not been of that persuasion, in large part because I have had confidence in the capacity of the common law to safeguard the fundamental freedoms essential to a free society including the right to freedom of speech which is specifically safeguarded by Article 10 of the

Convention. My confidence is seriously undermined by your Lordships' decision. All the judges in the courts below in this case have been concerned not to impose any unnecessary fetter on freedom of speech. I suspect that what the Court of Appeal would have liked to achieve, and perhaps set out to achieve by their compromise solution, was to inhibit *The Sunday Times* from continuing the serialisation of *Spycatcher*, but to leave the press at large at liberty to discuss and comment on the *Spycatcher* allegations. If there were a method of achieving these results which could be sustained in law, I can see much to be said for it on the merits. But I can see nothing whatever, either in law or on the merits, to be said for the maintenance of a total ban on discussion in the press of this country of matters of undoubted public interest and concern which the rest of the world now knows all about and can discuss freely. Still less can I approve your Lordships' decision to throw in for good measure a restriction on reporting court proceedings in Australia which the Attorney General had never even asked for.

Freedom of speech is always the first casualty under a totalitarian regime. Such a regime cannot afford to allow the free circulation of information and ideas among its citizens. Censorship is the indispensable tool to regulate what the public may and what they may not know. The present attempt to insulate the public in this country from information which is freely available elsewhere is a significant step down that very dangerous road. The maintenance of the ban, as more and more copies of the book *Spycatcher* enter this country and circulate here, will seem more and more ridiculous. If the Government are determined to fight to maintain the ban to the end, they will face inevitable condemnation and humiliation by the European Court of Human Rights in Strasbourg. Long before that they will have been condemned at the bar of public opinion in the free world.

But there is another alternative, the Government will surely want to reappraise the whole *Spycatcher* situation in the light of the views expressed in the courts below and in this House. I dare to hope that they will bring to that reappraisal qualities of vision and of statesmanship sufficient to recognise that their wafer thin victory in this litigation has been gained at a price which no Government committed to upholding the values of a free society can afford to pay.

I add a postscript to record that I have now had the opportunity to read first drafts of the opinions of my noble and learned friends, Lord Templeman and Lord Ackner. I remain in profound disagreement with them.

R v GLOUCESTERSHIRE CC AND ANOTHER EX PARTE BARRY (CONJOINED APPEALS) [1997] UKHL 58

House of Lords

LORD LLOYD OF BERWICK

My Lords,

Under section 29 of the National Assistance Act 1948 as originally enacted local authorities had the *power* to make arrangements for promoting the welfare of disabled persons. Under section 1 of the Chronically Sick and Disabled Persons Act 1970 local authorities were, for the first time, placed under a *duty* to inform themselves of the need for making arrangements for disabled persons within their area. Section 2 of the Act of 1970, on which the present appeal turns, provides that where a local authority is satisfied in the case of a disabled person within their area that it is necessary to make arrangements in order to meet the needs of that person, then the local authority is under a further *duty* to make those arrangements. It was common ground that the duty imposed on the local authority under section 2 of the Act of 1970 is a duty owed to the disabled person individually. In that respect section 2 is almost unique in the field of community care, the only other example of such a duty (so it was said) being section 117 of the Mental Health Act 1983.

Mr. Michael Barry lives in Gloucestershire. He was born in 1915, so he is coming up for his 82nd birthday. In the summer of 1992 he spent a short spell in Gloucestershire Royal Hospital suffering from dizzy spells and nausea. He was told that he had suffered a slight stroke. He has also had several heart attacks, and cannot see well. After discharge from hospital, he returned home, where he lives alone. He gets around by using a zimmer frame, as a result of having fractured his hip several years ago. He has no contact with any of his family. But two friends call from time to time to do things for him. On 8 September 1992 he was referred to the Social Services Department of Gloucestershire County Council ("the Council"). On 15 September his needs were assessed as follows:

> "Home care to call twice a week for shopping, pension, laundry, cleaning. Meals-on-wheels four days a week."

The Council arranged to provide these services. Nearly a year later, on 3 August 1993 Mr. Barry received a routine visit from the Social Services Department. His needs were assessed as being the same.

Then on 29 September 1994 Mr. Barry received a letter from the Council regretting that they would no longer be able to provide Mr. Barry with his full needs as assessed. Cleaning and laundry services would be withdrawn. The reason given was that the money allocated to the Council by central Government had been reduced by £2.5 million and there was "no-where near enough to meet demand." It is only fair to add that the letter was sympathetic in tone.

Mr. Barry, and other residents, commenced proceedings for judicial review. His case is that his needs are the same as they always were. Parliament has imposed a duty on the Council to do what is necessary to meet those needs, and it is no answer that they are short of money, as no doubt they are. The Council's case is that in assessing Mr. Barry's *needs* they are entitled to have regard to their overall financial resources.

The case came before the Divisional Court on 6 June 1994. In the meantime the Council had, very properly, continued to provide Mr. Barry with the same services as before, pending the outcome of the proceedings. Mr. Gordon Q.C., who appeared for Mr. Barry, did not press his claim for an order of mandamus to compel the Council to perform their statutory duty. But he was granted a declaration in the following terms:

> "That the respondent has acted unlawfully in that it has, on the sole basis of having exhausted available resources, withdrawn services previously provided or offered to the applicant pursuant to section 2 of the Chronically Sick and Disabled Persons Act 1970, without a lawful reassessment of the applicant."

On the broader question of whether the Council is entitled to take resources into account in assessing an individual's needs, McCowan L.J. said that a local authority would face an impossible task unless it could have regard to the size of the cake before deciding how to cut it.

> "For these reasons I for my part have concluded that a local authority is right to take account of resources both when assessing needs and when deciding when it is necessary to make arrangements to meet those needs."

The test proposed by the Divisional Court was as follows:

> "A balancing exercise must be carried out assessing the particular needs of that person in the context of the needs of others and the resources available, but if no reasonable authority could conclude other than that *some* practical help was necessary, that would have to be its decision."

This seems to reduce the minimum obligation under section 2 of the Act of 1970 to the level of *Wednesbury* unreasonableness.

Following the decision of the Divisional Court on the narrow question, the Council reassessed some 1,500 people in receipt of services under section 2 of the Act of 1970. As a result of the reassessment the number was reduced to 1,060. But meanwhile Mr. Barry had launched an appeal on the broader question. On 27 June 1996 the Court of Appeal [1996] 4 All E.R. 421 allowed his appeal by a majority, with Hirst L.J. dissenting. The Court of Appeal granted declarations as follows:

> "1) By withdrawing the said services without the Council being satisfied that the applicant's previously assessed needs had diminished, the respondent is in breach of its continuing duty under section 2 of the Chronically Sick and Disabled Persons Act 1970;
>
> 2) That in assessing or re-assessing whether it is necessary to make arrangements to meet them, a local authority is not entitled to take account of the resources available to such local authority."

The first of these declarations is no longer of practical effect, since the re-assessment has been carried out, and the services reduced as a consequence. But if the second of the declarations is correct, the Council would be obliged to revert to their former practice, and if necessary carry out a further re-assessment *without* taking their resources into account. The Council now appeals to the House. The Secretary of State for Health is joined in the appeal. It is as well that he should be for it is the failure of central Government to supply the funds necessary to enable the Council to carry out what I regard as their statutory duty which, departing from the fine words contained in the Government White Paper "*Caring for People: Community Care in the Next Decade and Beyond*" (1989) (Cm. 849), has put the Council into what the Divisional Court called an impossible position; truly impossible, because even if the Council wished to raise the money themselves to meet the need by increasing council tax, they would be unable to do so by reason of the government-imposed rate capping.

The construction of section 2 of the Act of 1970 does not seem to me to present any real problems. I set out the relevant part of the section verbatim:

> "***Provision of welfare services***
>
> (1) Where a local authority having functions under section 29 of the National Assistance Act 1948 are satisfied in the case of any person to whom that section applies who is ordinarily resident in their area that it is necessary in order to meet the needs of that person for that authority to make arrangements for all or any of the following matters, namely -
>
> (a) . . . (h) . . .
>
> then, . . . subject . . . [. . . to the provisions of section 7(1) of the Local Authority Social Services Act 1970 (which requires local authorities in the exercise of certain functions, including functions under the said section 29, to act under the general guidance of the Secretary of State)] [and to the provisions of section 7A of that Act (which requires local authorities to exercise their social services functions in accordance with directions given by the Secretary of State)], it shall be the duty of that authority to make those arrangements in exercise of their functions under the said section 29."

The section contemplates three separate stages. The Council must first assess the individual needs of each person to whom section 29 of the Act of 1948 applies. Having identified those needs, the Council must then decide whether it is necessary to make arrangements to meet those needs. There might be any number of reasons why, in the circumstances of a particular case, it might not be necessary for the local authority to make arrangements, for example, if the person's needs were being adequately met by a friend or relation. Or he might be wealthy enough to meet his needs out of his own pocket. But if there is no other way of meeting the individual's needs, as assessed, and the Council is therefore satisfied that it is necessary for them to make arrangements to meet those needs, then the Council is under a duty to make those arrangements. It is essential to a proper understanding of section 2 of the Act of 1970 to keep the three stages separate. Confusion arises if the stages are telescoped.

There is not much dispute about the second and third stages. Mr. Pleming on behalf of the Secretary of State conceded that at the third stage the duty is absolute. In other words, the Council cannot escape their duty to make arrangements to meet the need by saying that they do not have the money. Mr. Gordon, for his part, accepts that the Council must obviously be allowed a good deal of flexibility as to the arrangements which they make, provided always that the need is met. So the second and third stages do not require elaboration. It is over the first stage that the battle was joined.

It was as I have said common ground that the duty under section 2 is owed to the disabled person individually. It is not surprising, therefore, that the starting point of the whole exercise is the assessment of his individual needs. The assessment is, to adopt the departmental jargon, "needs-led." The word "need" like most English words has different shades of meaning. You can say to an overworked Q.C. at the end of a busy term "You look as though you need a holiday." The word "need" in section 2 is not used in that sense; which is not to say that there may not be disabled people living in very restricted circumstances who may not *need* a holiday in the sense which Parliament intended. To need is not the same as to want. "Need" is the lack of what is essential for the ordinary business of living.

Who then is to decide what it is that the disabled person needs, and by what yardstick does he make his decision? I do not find the answer difficult. In the simplest case it is the individual social worker who decides. In more complicated cases there may have to be what is called a comprehensive assessment. But in every case, simple or complex, the need of the individual will be assessed against the standards of civilised society as we know them in the United Kingdom, or, in the more homely phraseology of the law, by the standards of the man on the Clapham omnibus. Those standards may vary over time. What was acceptable in Victorian England might not be acceptable today. Expectations have risen. But this does not pose any difficulty. The assessment of the needs of the disabled individual against contempoary standards is left to the professional judgment of the social worker concerned, just as the need for a by-pass operation is left to the professional judgment of the heart specialist.

Who then decides what are the contemporary standards against which the social worker assesses the individual's needs? Again the answer seems straightforward. The standard is that set by the social services committee of the local authority in question. No doubt this was one of the reasons why social services committees were set up in the first place by section 2 of the Local Authority Social Services Act 1970, so as to represent the views of ordinary members of the public. Standards may vary from one local authority to another. But since the United Kingdom is relatively homogeneous, the standards may be expected to approximate to each other over time.

It is said that the standards of civilised society as interpreted by the social services committee of a particular local authority is too imprecise a concept to be of any practical value. I do not agree. But even if it were so, I do not see how it becomes less imprecise by bringing into consideration the availability of resources. Resources can, of course, operate to impose a cash limit on what is provided. But how can resources help to measure the need? This, as it seems to me, is the fallacy which lies at the heart of the Council's argument.

The point can be illustrated by a simple example. Suppose there are two people with identical disabilities, living in identical circumstances, but in different parts of the country. Local authority A provides for his needs by arranging for meals-on-wheels four days a week. Local authority B might also be expected to provide meals-on-wheels four days a week, or its equivalent. It cannot, however, have been Parliament's intention that local authority B should be able to say "because we do not have enough resources, we are going to reduce your needs." His needs remain exactly the same. They cannot be affected by the local authority's inability to meet those needs. Every child needs a new pair of shoes from time to time. The need is not the less because his parents cannot afford them.

There was much discussion in the course of the hearing of the appeal about "eligibility criteria." This is the departmental way of describing the standard against which an individual's needs are judged. Local authorities are encouraged to publish their own eligibility criteria. The Council has not fallen behind in this respect. There are elaborate tables included among our papers in which different degrees of disability are set against varying degrees of isolation from the community and other relevant factors. There are recommendations about the level of services which are appropriate for different combinations of disability and individual circumstances. Thus for a given degree of disability and a given degree of isolation (to take two of the relevant factors) the recommended home care might be for meals-on-wheels three times a week (or equivalent), cleaning twice a week and laundry once a fortnight. What is interesting about all this for present purposes is that nowhere in the tables is there any reference to resources. Nor is there any reason why there should be. The eligibility criteria can work perfectly well without taking resources into account, as Mr. Pleming was prepared to concede. With respect to those who take a different view, I can see no necessity on grounds of logic, and no advantage on grounds of practical convenience, in bringing resources into account as a relevant factor when assessing needs.

Is it then open to a local authority to raise the threshold artificially if it does not have sufficient resources to meet the previously assessed need? This is just what Parliament did *not* intend when enacting section 2 of the Chronically Sick and Disabled Persons Act of 1970. If a local authority could arbitrarily reduce the assessed need by raising the eligibility criteria, the duty imposed by Parliament would, in Mr. Gordon's graphic phrase, be collapsed into a power. The language of section 2 admits of no half-way house.

In the course of the argument it was suggested that "needs" in section 2 might mean "reasonable needs." Mr. Eccles, on behalf of the Council, did not accept this suggestion. But I have no difficulty in reading "needs" as meaning reasonable needs, in the sense that the social worker, in the exercise of his or her judgment, must act reasonably. In any event, if the needs are not reasonable it would not be necessary to make arrangements to meet the needs under the second of the three stages of the exercise. What I cannot accept is that the reasonable needs of the individual require consideration of the local authority's ability to meet those needs.

Mr. Pleming put the same point a different way. He argued that all the relevant circumstances have to be taken into account in assessing an individual's needs, and that among the relevant circumstances are the resources of the local authority. I agree that all the circumstances relating to the individual are to be taken into account. But the local authority's resources are external to the individual. There is nothing in the language of the section which permits, let alone suggests, that external resources are to be taken into account when assessing the individual's needs.

Then it is said that section 2 must be construed in the light of section 29 of the National Assistance Act 1948, to which it refers. I agree. But a consideration of section 29, and the other provisions of Part III of the Act of 1948, which have been analysed in the very recent decision of the Court of Appeal in *Reg. v. Hammersmith and Fulham London Borough Council, Ex parte M., The Times, 19 February 1997* leads me in the exact opposite direction to that in which Mr. Eccles would have me go.

Sections 21 to 28 of Part III as originally enacted cover the provision of accommodation. Under section 21 it was the *duty* of every local authority to provide residential accommodation for those in need of care and attention not otherwise available to them by reason of age, infirmity or any other circumstances. Sections 29 to 31 are concerned with welfare services. They conferred a *power* on local authorities to promote the welfare of the blind, deaf or dumb and other persons who are substantially and permanently handicapped by illness, injury, congenital deformities or other disabilities. By section 195(6) of and Schedule 23 to the Local Government Act 1972 section 21(1) of the Act of 1948 was amended. It now provides that the local authorities *may* provide residential accommodation and *shall* do so if directed by the Secretary of State. The Act of 1972 also made a similar amendment to section 29(1) of the Act of 1948. Thus there are now the same powers under both sections and the same duties if directed by the Secretary of State. But in the meantime Parliament had passed the Act of 1970. Like section 29 of the Act of 1948, sections 1 and 2 of the Act of 1970 are concerned with welfare services. It seems plain enough that the legislative purpose behind sections 1 and 2 was to impose a duty towards the disabled where hitherto there had been no more than a power. That duty was *not* made dependent on directions having been given by the Secretary of State. So far, therefore, from the inference being that the availability of resources was to remain a proper consideration, the inference is the other way.

It was pointed out that the Act of 1970 started life as a Private Member's Bill. So indeed it did. But it received strong all-party support. In any event the fact that the Act of 1970 owed its origin to the initiative of a private Member – Mr. Alf Morris – hardly throws light on its interpretation.

Simply looking at the language of section 2 of the Act of 1970, against the background of Part III of the Act of 1948, it is clear enough that Parliament did not intend that provision for the needs of the disabled should depend on the availability of resources. The intention was to treat disability as a special case. That is why the Act of 1970 has always been regarded as such an important landmark in the care of the disabled.

The point becomes all the clearer when one looks at the subsequent legislation, following on the Griffiths Report and the Government White Paper "*Caring for People*" published in November 1989 (Cm. 849). The disabled might at that stage have been brought back into line with others in need of community care services. But that was not the course which Parliament took when enacting the National Health Service and Community Care Act 1990. Section 47 provides:

> "*Assessment of needs for community care services:*
>
> "(1) Subject to subsections (5) and (6) below, where it appears to a local authority that any person for whom they may provide or arrange for the provision of community care services may be in need of any such services, the authority (*a*) shall carry out an assessment of his needs for

those services; and (*b*) having regard to the results of that assessment, shall then decide whether his needs call for the provision by them of any such services.

"(2) If at any time during the assessment of the needs of any person under subsection (1)(*a*) above it appears to a local authority that he is a disabled person, the authority:

(*a*) shall proceed to make such a decision as to the services he requires as is mentioned in section 4 of the Disabled Persons (Services, Consultation and Representation) Act 1986 without his requesting them to do so under that section; and

(*b*) shall inform him that they will be doing so and of his rights under that Act."

It was common ground, as is indeed obvious from the language of section 47(1)(*b*), that a local authority has a discretion whether to meet a person's needs under section 47(1). In exercising that discretion the local authority is entitled to take its available resources into account. But in sharp distinction, section 47(2) gives the local authority no such discretion. Once it appears that the person in question is disabled, the local authority is bound to decide whether his needs call for the provision of services under section 2 of the Act of 1970. By preserving and reinforcing the beneficial provisions of the Act of 1970, Parliament has underlined its intention to treat the needs of the disabled as a special case in the consideration of which resources play no part. Otherwise, why was it thought necessary to make separate provision for the disabled under section 47(2)?

There is another point. Section 47(1) contemplates a two-stage process. There is to be an assessment of needs followed by a decision whether to meet those needs. Since resources come in at the second stage, it is difficult to see why resources should also come in when assessing needs at the first stage. But if resources do not come in when assessing needs under section 47(1), how can it be argued that they come in when assessing the needs of the disabled under section 47(2)?

I return to section 2 to consider a further argument to which Hirst L.J. in his dissenting judgment attached importance. It is necessary to refer in this connection to the list of services set out in section 2 which are as follows:

"2(1)(*a*) the provision of practical assistance for that person in his home;

(*b*) the provision for that person of, or assistance to that person in obtaining, wireless, television, library or similar recreational facilities;

(*c*) the provision for that person of lectures, games, outings or other recreational facilities outside his home or assistance to that person in taking advantage of educational facilities available to him;

(*d*) the provision for that person of facilities for, or assistance in, travelling to and from his home for the purpose of participating in any services provided under arrangements made by the authority under the said section 29 or, with the approval of the authority, in any services provided otherwise than as aforesaid which are similar to services which could be provided under such arrangements;

(*e*) the provision of assistance for that person in arranging for the carrying out of any works of adaptation in his home or the provision of any additional facilities designed to secure his greater safety, comfort or convenience;

(*f*) facilitating the taking of holidays by that person, whether at holiday homes or otherwise and whether provided under arrangements made by the authority or otherwise;

(*g*) the provision of meals for that person whether in his home or elsewhere;

(*h*) the provision for that person of, or assistance to that person in obtaining, a telephone and any special equipment necessary to enable him to use a telephone,"

It is argued that the very width of these services indicates that resources must be a relevant consideration. Hirst L.J. [1996] 4 All E.R. 421, 433 put the point as follows:

> "Nor do I consider that the safety-net concept fits several of the individual items in the service list, in particular items (*b*) to (*f*) inclusive, which hardly rate as basic requirements, and whose selection would seem to involve choices in which cost would be an inevitable consideration. Despite Mr. Gordon's plea to the contrary, I do not think it proper to ignore the service list when construing the opening words of the section . . ."

I agree with Hirst L.J. that it would not be right to exclude the service list from consideration when construing the opening words of the section. But I do not myself find that they throw much light on the meaning of "need" or on the question whether resources are to be taken into account in assessing an individual's needs. Disabled persons may not need recreational facilities, or a holiday, as often as they will need practical assistance in the home, or the provision of meals. But this does not lead to the conclusion that the assessment of need is dependent on sufficient resources being available. It is not what the section says.

Like my Lords, I do not find it necessary to refer to the non-statutory guidance issued by the Department. It is conveniently set out in Hirst L.J.'s judgment, at pp. 427–430. I note only that the guidance relates to the provision of community services generally, where resources are admittedly relevant. Where there is specific reference to section 2 of the Act of 1970, the guidance is, from the Council's point of view, at best ambivalent as to whether resources are to be taken into account or not.

For the above reasons I find myself in full agreement with the judgment of Swinton Thomas L.J. I also agree with the judgment of Sir John Balcombe. His reasoning is criticised in the Council's printed case, because of his acceptance that need is a relative concept, which may vary according to outside circumstances. It would follow that on this view (so it is argued) *all* outside circumstances should be taken into account, including the local authority's available resources. But when Sir John Balcombe refers, at p. 441, to "outside circumstances" and to need being "a relative concept", it is plain from the very next sentence what he had in mind:

> "Thus, the needs of a disabled person may be assessed differently now than they would have been in years gone by, because standards rise and expectations change."

I agree. But it does not follow that needs *today* should be assessed differently in different parts of the United Kingdom; and still less does it follow that needs may be assessed differently on the ground that some local authorities (including Gloucestershire) have suffered more than others as a result of central Government's abrupt decision to distribute a special transitional grant for 1994–95 on the basis of standard spending assessments alone, instead of partly on that basis and partly on the basis of historic spending on income support.

The error in the Council's criticism of Sir John Balcombe's judgment can be illustrated by a single quotation from paragraph 24 of their case:

> "If increased national wealth is relevant in raising standards and expectations, so too should pressure on local resources be admissible in determining whether it is necessary to meet expectations."

The non-sequitur is evident. Parliament cannot have intended that the standards and expectations for measuring the needs of the disabled in Bermondsey should differ from those in Belgrave Square.

This brings me, last of all, to the wretched position in which the Council now find themselves, through no fault of their own. I have read the affidavits of Mr. Deryk Mead, the Director of Social Services, and Mr. Honey, Chief Executive, with something approaching despair. Equally depressing is the evidence of Margaret Newland, Chair of Age Concern, Gloucestershire, and the numerous letters written by the Council to the Secretary of State. Most depressing of all are the minutes of the Community Care Sub-Committee of the Social Services Committee, especially the meeting held on 14 October 1994, in which members expressed their abhorrence at the choices which the Social Services Department was being required to make. The Chairman commented:

> "It was deplorable that there was no other way forward apart from the exclusion of certain people from access to community care through the device of rationing services."

By your Lordships' decision today the Council has escaped from the impossible position in which they, and other local authorities have been placed. Nevertheless, I cannot help wondering whether they will not be regretting today's decision as much as Mr. Barry. The solution lies with the government. The passing of the Chronically Sick and Disabled Persons Act 1970 was a noble aspiration. Having willed the end, Parliament must be asked to provide the means.

I would dismiss the appeal.

LORD NICHOLLS OF BIRKENHEAD

My Lords,

This appeal raises an important point of interpretation of section 2(1) of the Chronically Sick and Disabled Persons Act 1970. Can a local authority properly take into account its own financial resources when assessing the needs of a disabled person under section 2(1)? The appellants, the

Gloucestershire County Council and the Secretary of State for Health say yes, the respondent Mr. Barry says no. The question has given rise to a considerable difference of judicial opinion, so I shall give my conclusion in my own words.

At first sight the contentions advanced on behalf of Mr. Barry are compelling. A person's needs, it was submitted, depend upon the nature and extent of his disability. They cannot be affected by, or depend upon, the local authority's ability to meet them. They cannot vary according to whether the authority has more or less money currently available. Take the case of an authority which assesses a person's needs as twice weekly help at home with laundry and cleaning. In the following year nothing changes except that the authority has less money available. If the authority's financial resources can be properly be taken into account, it would be open to the authority to re-assess that person's needs in the later year as nil. That cannot be right: the person's needs have not changed.

This is an alluring argument but I am unable to accept it. It is flawed by a failure to recognise that needs for services cannot sensibly be assessed without having some regard to the cost of providing them. A person's need for a particular type or level of service cannot be decided in a vacuum from which all considerations of cost have been expelled.

I turn to the statute. Under section 2(1) "needs" are to be assessed in the context of, and by reference to, the provision of certain types of assistance for promoting the welfare of disabled persons: home help, meals on wheels, holidays, home adaptation, and so forth. In deciding whether the disability of a particular person dictates a need for assistance and, if so, at what level, a social worker or anyone else must use some criteria. This is inevitably so. He will judge the needs for assistance against some standard, some criteria, whether spoken or unspoken. One important factor he will take into account will be what constitutes an acceptable standard of living today.

Standards of living, however, vary widely. So do different people's ideas on the requirements of an acceptable standard of living. Thus something more concrete, capable of being applied uniformly, is called for assessing the needs of a given disabled person under the statute. Some more precisely defined standard is required, a more readily identifiable yardstick, than individual notions of current standards of living.

Who is to set the standard? To this there can be only one answer: the relevant local authority, acting by its social services committee. The local authority sets the standards to be applied within its area. In setting the standards, or "eligibility criteria" as they have been called, the local authority must take into account current standards of living, with all the latitude inherent in this concept. The authority must also take into account the nature and extent of the disability. The authority will further take into account the manner in which, and the extent to which, quality of life would be improved by the provision of this or that service or assistance, at this or that level: for example, by home care, once a week or more frequently. The authority should also have regard to the cost of providing this or that service, at this or that level. The cost of daily home care, or of installing a ground floor lavatory for a disabled person in his home and widening the doors to take a wheelchair, may be substantial. The relative cost will be balanced against the relative benefit and the relative need for that benefit.

Thus far the position is straightforward. The next step is the crucial step. In the same way as the importance to be attached to cost varies according to the benefit to be derived from the suggested expenditure, so also must the importance of cost vary according to the means of the person called upon to pay. An amount of money may be a large sum to one person, or to one person at a particular time, but of less consequence to another person, or to the same person at a different time. Once it is accepted, as surely must be right, that cost is a relevant factor in assessing a person's needs for the services listed in section 2(1), then in deciding how much weight is to be attached to cost some evaluation or assumption has to be made about the impact which the cost will have upon the authority. Cost is of more or less significance depending upon whether the authority currently has more or less money. Thus, depending upon the authority's financial position, so the eligibility criteria, setting out the degree of disability which must exist before help will be provided with laundry or cleaning or whatever, may properly be more or less stringent.

I have considered whether, instead of taking into account the actual resources of the paying authority, the significance of cost could be evaluated by some more general criterion, for instance, that there should be attached to cost the weight which would be attributed to the amount in question by any reasonable authority. This could not work. This would be meaningless as a yardstick. What are the resources to be attributed to the hypothetical reasonable authority at any particular time?

In the course of the argument some emphasis was placed upon a submission that if a local authority may properly take its resources into account in the way I have described, the section 2(1) duty would in effect be limited to making arrangements to the extent only that the authority should decide to allocate money for this purpose. The duty, it was said, would collapse into a power. I do not agree. A local authority must carry out its functions under section 2(1) in a responsible fashion. In the event of a local authority acting with *Wednesbury* unreasonableness, a disabled person would have a remedy.

This interpretation does not emasculate section 2(1). The section was intended to confer rights upon disabled persons. It does so by giving them a valuable personal right to see that the authority acts reasonably in assessing their needs for certain types of assistance, and a right to have their assessed needs met so far as it is necessary for the authority (as distinct from others) to do so. I can see no basis for reading into the section an implication that in assessing the needs of disabled persons for the prescribed services, cost is to be ignored. I do not believe Parliament intended that to be the position.

For these reasons, which are substantially to the same effect as those of my noble and learned friend Lord Clyde, I would allow this appeal and declare that when assessing needs under section 2(1) a local authority may take its resources into account.

R (ON THE APPLICATION OF THE ELECTORAL COMMISSION) (RESPONDENT) v CITY OF WESTMINSTER MAGISTRATES COURT (RESPONDENT) AND THE UNITED KINGDOM INDEPENDENCE PARTY (APPELLANT) [2010] UKSC 40

Supreme Court

LORD PHILLIPS (with whom Lord Clarke agrees)

Introduction

1. The Political Parties, Elections and Referendums Act 2000 ("the Act") introduced, for the first time in this country, restrictions on the donations that can be made to registered political parties. All statutory references in this judgment are to the Act.

2. Part IV of the Act specifies those from whom it is permissible for political parties to accept donations. Donations from an individual may only be accepted if the donor is on an electoral register. The Act confers on a magistrates' court the power, at the instigation of the Electoral Commission ("the Commission"), to forfeit from party funds a sum equal to a donation that has been accepted from an impermissible source. This appeal raises the question of the criteria that should properly be applied by a magistrates' court when exercising this power.

3. This question is of particular interest to the United Kingdom Independence Party ("UKIP"), a small registered political party which has yet to succeed in returning a member to Westminster. UKIP has relied for the majority of its funding on a single supporter, Mr Alan Bown. Since 2003 Mr Bown has made donations to the party, in one form or another, amounting to over £1 million. By inadvertence, between 1 December 2004 and 2 February 2006, he ceased to be on any electoral register. During this period his donations to UKIP amounted to £349,216. On 16 March 2007 the Commission made an application to the Senior District Judge in the City of Westminster Magistrates' Court for an order forfeiting the whole of this sum. The Senior District Judge ordered the forfeiture of only a small proportion of this sum. The Act gives a political party a right to appeal to the Crown Court against a forfeiture order but no right of appeal is given to

the Commission. UKIP did not appeal against the order of the Senior District Judge, but the Commission challenged his decision by an application for judicial review.

4. In a judgment delivered on 22 January 2009 [2009] EWHC 78 (Admin) Walker J identified a wide range of matters to which the Senior District Judge should have had regard when considering the forfeiture application. He held that the Senior District Judge had failed to give adequate reasons for his decision and ordered that the case should be remitted to the magistrates' court for further consideration.

5. The Commission appealed to the Court of Appeal, and was successful [2009] EWCA Civ 1078. On 19 October 2009, giving the only reasoned judgment, Sir Paul Kennedy held that, on a true construction of the relevant provisions of the Act, the discretion of the Senior District Judge was very tightly circumscribed. There was a strong presumption in favour of forfeiture. Where a donation was received by a political party from an impermissible source a forfeiture order should follow as a matter of course in the absence of exceptional circumstances. The magistrates' court should, on remission, reconsider the matter in accordance with this approach.

6. Before this Court Mr Patrick Lawrence QC for UKIP has sought to uphold the approach of Walker J, whereas Mr Michael Beloff QC for the Commission has urged that the analysis of the Court of Appeal was correct. The difference between the two has been described as "the presumption issue".

The relevant provisions of the Act

7. Part I of the Act establishes the Commission which is given a wide range of regulatory powers and duties in relation to elections and political parties, including keeping under review "the registration of political parties and the regulation of their income and expenditure" (section 6(1)(e)).

8. Part IV deals with "Control of Donations to Registered Parties and their Members etc". Chapter II imposes restrictions on the receipt of donations. Section 54(1) provides that a donation must not be accepted if the person seeking to make it is not, at the time of its receipt, a

permissible donor, or if his identity cannot be ascertained. Section 54(2) identifies those who are permissible donors. These include an individual registered in an electoral register and a company registered under the Companies Act 2006, incorporated within the United Kingdom or another member state, and carrying on business in the United Kingdom. Section 54(3) provides that a donation made in the form of a bequest will have been made by a permissible donor provided that he was registered in an electoral register at any time within the five year period that terminated with his death.

9. Section 56 imposes duties in relation to the acceptance or return of donations and imposes criminal sanctions for breach of those duties. Where section 54 prohibits acceptance of a donation it must be returned within 30 days of receipt. If it is not, both the party and the treasurer of the party are guilty of an offence, albeit that it is a defence to prove that all reasonable steps were taken to verify or ascertain whether the donor was a permissible donor and that, as a result, the treasurer believed that he was a permissible donor. The effect of section 56(5) is that a donation will be deemed to have been accepted, even if it is returned within 30 days, unless a record can be produced of its receipt and its return.

10. Section 58 contains the provision that has given rise to this appeal. It deals with forfeiture of donations that have been made by impermissible or unidentifiable donors. Where these have been accepted, notwithstanding that their acceptance was prohibited, section 58(2) provides:

> "The court may, on an application made by the Commission, order the forfeiture by the party of an amount equal to the value of the donation."

Section 58(4) makes it plain that such an order may be made whether or not proceedings are brought against any person for an offence connected with the donation. Section 58(5) provides that in England and Wales the "court" is a magistrates' court.

11. Section 60 provides that proceedings under section 58 shall be brought against the party in its own name and not in the name of any of its members and that any amount forfeited is to be paid out of the funds of the party.

12. It is notable that section 58 does not provide for the automatic forfeiture of any donation that is accepted from an impermissible source. The provision that the court *may* order its forfeiture confers a discretion on the court. Furthermore it has been common ground, rightly in my view, that the Commission also enjoys a discretion whether or not to make an application for forfeiture to the court. The Act itself gives no indication of the criteria that should govern the exercise of either discretion. It is the former discretion that is critical, but it would be strange if the court's discretion was narrower than that of the Commission.

The second issue of interpretation

13. The primary issue is the presumption issue. Does section 58(2) confer a broad discretion on the court whether or not to make a forfeiture order, or is there a strong presumption in favour of forfeiture? But section 58(2) raises a secondary issue of interpretation. It confers on the court a power to order forfeiture of "an amount equal to the value of the donation". Where the court exercises this power, does it have to order forfeiture of an amount equal to the total value of the donation, or is it implicit that the court has a discretion to order forfeiture of a lesser sum if it considers this appropriate? This has been described as the "all or nothing" issue.

14. There is a potential interrelationship between the presumption issue and the all or nothing issue. The Commission argues that Parliament has deliberately chosen a stringent regime in order to ensure that political donations come from acceptable sources. There is no half-way house. Similar policy considerations support both a strong presumption in favour of forfeiture and a requirement that forfeiture should be total. Conversely a wide discretion whether to forfeit or not sits better with a power to order partial forfeiture, so that the court has the flexibility to tailor its order to the particular facts.

The approach to interpretation

15. The answer to the all or nothing issue will not, however, determine the presumption issue. This is demonstrated by the fact that both Walker J and the Court of Appeal held that the power conferred on the magistrates' court by section 58(2) was an "all or nothing" power. In these circumstances I have not found it helpful to try to answer the all

or nothing issue first. The more helpful approach is to consider the interpretation of section 58(2) having regard to the mischief at which it is aimed. The parties are agreed that the discretion conferred by section 58(2) should be used to promote the policy and objects of the statute. This proposition is supported by high authority – see *Padfield v Minister of Agriculture, Fisheries and Food* [1968] AC 997 at 1030 per Lord Reid. This principle led Lord Bridge to observe in *R v Tower Hamlets London Borough Council, Ex p Chetnik Developments Ltd* [1988] AC 858, at p 873:

> "Thus, before deciding whether a discretion has been exercised for good or bad reasons, the court must first construe the enactment by which the discretion is conferred. Some statutory discretions may be so wide that they can, for practical purposes, only be challenged if shown to have been exercised irrationally or in bad faith. But if the purpose for which the discretion is intended to serve is clear, the discretion can only be validly exercised for reasons relevant to the achievement of that purpose."

16. In applying the *Padfield* principle in this case there are two questions to be asked. The first is: what are the objects of the forfeiture permitted by section 58(2)? The second is: why has Parliament chosen to give the court a discretion whether or not to order forfeiture of a donation that has come from an impermissible source rather than to make such forfeiture automatic? To answer these questions it is necessary to look at the legislative history, which I believe provides the answer to each question.

The legislative history

17. The Labour Party's 1997 *Election Manifesto* announced the following intention:

> "We will oblige parties to declare the source of all donations above a minimum figure … Foreign funding will be banned."

On 12 November 1997, shortly after taking up office, the Prime Minister extended the terms of reference of the Committee on Standards in Public Life to add:

> "To review issues in relation to the funding of political parties, and to make recommendations as to any changes in present arrangements."

This led to the Fifth Report of the Committee, under the chair of Lord Neill of Bladen QC, on "the Funding of Political Parties in the United Kingdom" ("the Neill Report"), which was published in October 1998.

18. Chapter 4 of the Neill Report dealt with "Donations: Transparency and Reporting". It recommended the imposition on political parties of a duty to report the sources of donations, backed by criminal sanctions:

> "4.61 The reporting obligations of the political parties should be backed by criminal sanctions. These should be so drafted as to distinguish between inadvertent and deliberate failure to report a disclosable donation. In the latter case those responsible could be fined or imprisoned. In both cases the court would have power to order the defaulting political party to forfeit a sum not exceeding the unreported donation. Knowingly to make a false return should also be an offence. Prosecutions would be put in the hands of the Director of Public Prosecutions and should not be the concern of the Election Commission. Private prosecutions should be allowable."

19. Chapter 5 of the Neill Report dealt with "Foreign Donations". After setting out the arguments for and against a ban on foreign donations, the Committee reached the following conclusion:

> "5.16 … We have, therefore, concluded that, at a time when the whole question of the funding of political parties is being re-examined, it is right to take the opportunity to lay down the principle that those who live, work and carry on business in the United Kingdom should be the persons exclusively entitled to support financially the operation of the political process here."

20. The Report explained that the Committee had found it difficult to produce a definition of foreign donations for the purpose of banning these. Accordingly they decided to approach the problem from the opposite direction by defining "permissible sources" from which alone donations could be received. The Report explained:

> "5.20 We begin by considering those individuals from whom the political parties should be able to receive donations. We believe that they come under two headings:
>
> (1) those who are registered voters in the United Kingdom; and
>
> (2) those who are eligible to be put on an electoral register in the United Kingdom.

5.21 As to the distinction between (1) and (2) above, we think that a donation could be properly received from a person who was eligible to be put on the electoral register because such a person already has, under existing legislation, the right to participate in the electoral process subject to taking the additional step of securing registration.

5.22 Categories (1) and (2) cover not only British subjects resident here, but extend to Commonwealth citizens resident here, citizens of the Republic of Ireland resident here, and citizens of the European Union resident here. The categories also include persons known as 'overseas voters'."

21. The test of entitlement to be entered on an electoral register was a rational basis for discriminating between donors with adequate connections with the United Kingdom and "foreign" donors. British, Republic of Ireland, Commonwealth and European Union citizens are entitled to register on an electoral register in the electoral area in which they reside – section 4 of the Representation of the People Act 1983. If a donor is not qualified to be entered on an electoral register in the United Kingdom it is not unrealistic to treat that donor as lacking sufficient connection with the United Kingdom to be a desirable source of party funding.

22. The following paragraph of the Report dealt with "enforcement and penalties" in relation to the ban on foreign donations:

"5.42 In essence, what we said in Chapter 4 at paras 4.60 and 4.61 should apply here too with necessary modifications. Thus, the Election Commission will have statutory powers to call for information and to institute an investigation into any donation which it suspects has not come from a permissible source. If a party were to be guilty of a deliberate acceptance of a donation from a source outside the definition of a permissible source, criminal sanctions should attach to all responsible, and a sum not less than the donation should be liable to forfeiture from the party's funds; in significant cases of attempted evasion of the rules a penalty of up to ten times the overspend might be levied. A forfeiture power should also apply even if the receipt were innocent or inadvertent, although the courts would clearly take into account the degree of culpability in setting the level of forfeiture.

R30 The Election Commission should have wide powers to call for information and to institute investigations into any suspect foreign donations received by a political party or a sub-unit.

R31 Criminal sanctions should attach to a deliberate acceptance of a donation from a source falling outside the definition of a permissible source. There should be a power for the court to order a defaulting political party to forfeit a sum of up to ten times the donation wrongfully accepted."

23. There is a contrast between the power of forfeiture recommended in para 4.61, "a sum *not exceeding* the unreported donation", and that in para 5.42, "a sum *not less than* the donation". The reason for this contrast seems likely to be the following. Para 4.61 was providing for a sanction for failure to report a donation from a permissible source. Para 5.42 was dealing with the receipt of a donation from an impermissible and, under the Neill Committee's scheme, a foreign source. In the latter case the forfeiture of the entire donation was likely to be desirable, regardless of whether or not the breach of the regulations had been deliberate. It is noteworthy that the Committee recommended that, where acceptance of an impermissible donation was innocent or inadvertent, there should still be a power of forfeiture but that the courts would take into account the degree of culpability when setting the level of forfeiture.

24. The Government published a White Paper (Cm 4413) to which was annexed a draft Bill dealing with the funding of political parties. Clause 51 of the Bill does not differ significantly from section 58 of the Act. At the beginning of Chapter 4, which dealt with the sources of funding, the Government welcomed the Neill Committee's endorsement of the manifesto commitment to ban the foreign funding of political parties. Dealing with permissible sources of funding the White Paper commented as follows:

"*Individuals*

4.5 The Neill Committee recommended (R26) that political parties should be able to receive donations both from those who are registered voters in the United Kingdom and from those who are entitled to register to vote in the United Kingdom. Clause 50(2)(a) departs from this recommendation by providing that registered political parties may accept donations only from those individuals whose names appear on the electoral register. Entitlement to register, whether as a resident or overseas elector, will not qualify an individual as a permissible source.

4.6 Checking that a particular donor appears on the electoral register offers a test that is both conclusive and simple to administer. It would be far less straightforward for political parties to verify that a donor not appearing on the register was nevertheless entitled to do so. It is in the interests of the parties to have available a test which offers certainty as to the eligibility of a donor. With the introduction of rolling registration it would be open to anyone who was entitled to be registered as an elector, but was not on the register for whatever reason, to take the necessary steps at any time to secure his or her registration. Once registered, it would then be open to a political party to accept a donation from such a person. In practice, therefore, little is lost by the proposed departure from the Neill Committee's recommendation."

The objects of the legislation

25. The legislative history provides a particularly clear picture of the objects of Chapter II of Part IV of the Act. The primary object is to prevent donations to political parties from foreign sources. From the Labour Party manifesto in 1997 the concern in relation to the source of funds has focussed exclusively on foreign donors. The Neill Committee recommended that the exclusion of foreign funding should, in the case of individual donors, be achieved by prohibiting donations from anyone who was not a registered voter in the United Kingdom or eligible to be put on an electoral register in the United Kingdom. As I have observed this test drew a realistic line between domestic and foreign donors. Eligibility to be placed on an electoral register demonstrated a sufficient connection with the United Kingdom. Ineligibility demonstrated a lack of such connection.

26. Parliament made a significant change in restricting permissible donors to those on an electoral register, excluding those eligible to be put on one. This change was made not because there is anything intrinsically undesirable about parties being funded by those who are not on an electoral register, provided that they are eligible to be placed on one. So far as connection with the United Kingdom is concerned there is no distinction between a person who is on an electoral register and one who is entitled to be placed on an electoral register. The change was made for purely pragmatic reasons. It is much easier to demonstrate that a person is not on an electoral register than it is to demonstrate that he is not entitled to be placed on an electoral register.

27. Two facts demonstrate that Parliament did not consider that entitlement to vote was, of itself, an essential quality in a donor, rather than a convenient test of the donor's connection with the United Kingdom. The first is that section 54 permits donations from corporations, trade unions, building societies, limited liability partnerships, friendly

societies and unincorporated associations, provided that they have sufficient presence in the United Kingdom, notwithstanding that none of them can vote. The second is that donations by bequest are permissible from anyone who was on an electoral register at any time during the period of five years before his death. Such a person cannot, of course, cast a vote posthumously, but it is significant that it is permissible for his bequest to have been made at a time when he was not on the register, provided that he was registered to vote at some point during the five years before his death. Had Mr Bown bequeathed, rather than bestowed, his donations during the period that he was off the electoral register, and then died, there would have been no objection to UKIP receiving the bequests.

28. The White Paper's comments that I have quoted at para 24 above underline the fact that entry on an electoral register is not *per se* an essential attribute of a donor. The comment that "little is lost" by the proposed departure from the Neill recommendations appears to recognise that depriving parties of donations from those entitled to be on an electoral register, but not actually registered, involves a degree of sacrifice, albeit one that is justified on grounds of practicality.

29. The secondary object of Chapter II of Part IV of the Act is to provide a scheme for achieving the primary object that is easy to apply, easy to police and that contains adequate sanctions for non-compliance.

The purposes of the power to forfeit

30. Mr Beloff submitted in his written case that there were three purposes of the power to forfeit. The first was to deprive a political party of the "wrongful gain" acquired by accepting a donation from an impermissible source. The second was to deter breaches of the Act. The third was to provide simple and effective sanctions in the form of a rigorous civil enforcement scheme to enforce the prohibition on acceptance of impermissible donations. The third object is, in fact, no more than a more detailed way of describing the second object.

31. I agree that there are two distinct objects of the power to forfeit. As to the first, I do not find the description "wrongful gain" helpful. The primary object of forfeiture is the direct prevention of the mischief that the legislation is designed to prevent – the receipt by a political party of foreign funding. This would normally dictate the forfeiture of the acceptance of any donation received by a party from a foreign source,

regardless of whether or not that acceptance had come about as a result of a culpable fault on the part of the party. As I have said, that is probably why the Neill Committee recommended that where a donation was received from a person who was not entitled to be placed on an electoral register, forfeiture from the party funds should be of *not less than* the amount of the donation. The fact that the donor was not entitled to be placed on the register demonstrated that he had insufficient connection to the United Kingdom to be an acceptable source of funding.

32. The Act has radically changed the Neill Committee's scheme. A donor whose connection with the United Kingdom would entitle him to be placed on the electoral register and thus to vote is rendered an impermissible donor by reason of the simple fact that he is not on the register. Under this scheme an unregistered donor may or may not be "foreign". If he is "foreign", or if he is unable to prove that he is not "foreign", then his donation is intrinsically undesirable. It is the type of funding that the Act was designed to prevent. His donation should, barring exceptional circumstances, be automatically subject to forfeiture in its entirety. If it is not forfeited, the very mischief that the Act was designed to prevent will have occurred. Whether or not the party accepting the donation exercised due care should not normally be relevant. This may well be why the Act expressly provides that a forfeiture order may be made, whether or not proceedings have been brought against any person for an offence in connection with the donation.

33. I agree with Mr Beloff that the second object of the power to forfeit is to provide a deterrent or sanction against failure to comply with the requirements of the Act that are designed to make sure that donations are not received from an impermissible donor. Thus the power to forfeit is intended to further both the primary and the secondary object of the legislation.

The nature and purpose of the discretion

34. I now come to the interrelated questions of whether the power to forfeit is "all or nothing" and how the discretion whether or not to exercise that power should be exercised.

35. If Parliament had enacted the Neill Committee scheme there would have been a strong presumption in favour of forfeiting the whole of a

donation from an impermissible source. It would, or would be likely to, be a foreign donation and objectionable as such. Indeed there would have been a case for making forfeiture of such donations automatic. But Parliament adopted a scheme under which impermissible donations may or may not be foreign. Under this scheme the significance of an individual impermissible donation may vary widely. At one extreme it may be a donation from a foreign source, accepted by a political party with full knowledge of its provenance. At the other extreme it may be a donation from an individual who is entitled to be on an electoral register and has in the past been on an electoral register, been believed to be on an electoral register, but who, because of some administrative error for which he is not responsible, has been removed from the register at the time when he made his donation.

36. Parliament plainly made the power to forfeit discretionary with the intention that the magistrates' court should discriminate between cases where forfeiture was warranted and cases where it was not. It seems to me natural to assume that Parliament intended the court to consider whether forfeiture was a proportionate response to the facts of the particular case. This involves considering whether forfeiture is necessary to achieve either the primary or the secondary object of the Act. The most relevant consideration is whether forfeiture is necessary to prevent the retention of a foreign donation in the individual case. Proof of acceptance of a donation from an impermissible source should raise a presumption that the donation is foreign. If the party cannot rebut that presumption, forfeiture should follow. If the party succeeds in demonstrating that the donor was entitled to be placed on an electoral register, forfeiture should then depend on whether it is an appropriate sanction for such shortcomings as led to the acceptance of the donation. This will require consideration of culpability, the size of the donation and the effect that forfeiture will be likely to have on the political party. Partial forfeiture, if permitted (as to which see below), will enable the court to impose an appropriate sanction where total forfeiture would be disproportionate.

37. The Court of Appeal held that the power to forfeit was all or nothing and that there was a presumption that it should be exercised in the absence of exceptional circumstances. The Court's reasons for holding that there was a strong presumption that the power to forfeit should be exercised were as follows:

i) Unless forfeiture was the normal consequence of the acceptance of an impermissible donation, parties would be free to disregard with impunity the obligations not to accept or to return impermissible donations.

ii) Forfeiture would never be disproportionate if it was limited to a donation which should never have been accepted.

iii) It was irrelevant whether or not the impermissible donor was a foreign donor, because Parliament had not made that the test. Parliament had made being on an electoral register the test. The Court should not re-introduce the Neill Committee test by the back door.

iv) The fact that a party might not know that the donation was impermissible was irrelevant. Parliament had not made that a bar to forfeiture.

v) The fact that the state of the party's finances might make forfeiture particularly onerous was irrelevant. The receipt of the donation was illegal and the full extent of the donation was an advantage that the party should not have had.

vi) Furthermore, if it was necessary to investigate a party's finances before making a forfeiture order, the sanction would be unwieldy. Mr Beloff expanded this to a more general point. If there was a wide discretion, this would give rise to complex factual inquiries that the simple scheme of the Act was designed to avoid.

I will deal with each of these points in turn.

38. I do not accept that almost automatic forfeiture of the totality of an impermissible donation is necessary to provide a realistic sanction against non-compliance with the requirements of the Act. In the first place there are criminal sanctions for non-compliance. In the second place, the mere risk of forfeiture of the entirety of a donation might be thought a sufficient incentive to carry out the relatively simple check that a donor is on an electoral register. A party should not need much incentive to check that the position of anyone who wishes to make a donation is regularised.

39. The suggestion that forfeiture of a sum limited to the impermissible donation can never be disproportionate is founded on the premise that the party should never have received the donation in the first place. But where a person within the United Kingdom wishes to make a donation to a party, there is nothing intrinsically wrong about the party receiving that donation. Of course the party and the donor should make sure that the donor complies with the statutory requirement of being placed on an electoral register. But if, by inadvertence, or even negligence, they fail to do so, it does not follow that it cannot be disproportionate for the donation to be forfeited. Proportionality will depend on the degree of culpability, the size of the donation and its importance to the party.

40. I disagree that it is irrelevant whether or not the donor is a foreign donor. If he is, then forfeiture is clearly appropriate. Parliament has made electoral registration the test, but Parliament has also made forfeiture discretionary. To allow the party to show that the donor could have been registered to vote is not to introduce the Neill test by the back door. Parliament's scheme usefully transfers the burden of showing that the donation is not a foreign donation onto the donor and the party. If this burden can be discharged, the primary object of the legislation has not been defeated, and this fact is highly relevant to the issue of whether the power to forfeit should be exercised.

41. The fact that Parliament has not made ignorance of the impermissibility of the donation a defence is no reason why it should not be a relevant extenuating circumstance when considering whether or not to forfeit the donation. Once again the Court of Appeal has ignored the fact that Parliament has chosen to make forfeiture of the donation discretionary.

42. The argument that the effect of forfeiture on a party is irrelevant turns on the proposition that the party should never have had the donation in the first place. This ignores the fact that where the impermissibility of the donation results simply from an inadvertent, or even negligent, failure to register there is nothing intrinsically undesirable about the source of the funding.

43. Finally I must deal with the point that, if there is a general discretion whether or not to forfeit, forfeiture proceedings will involve a lengthy investigation of all the material circumstances. In the first place, this will not normally be true where the donor is, in fact a foreign donor. The party will not be in a position to show that the donor was entitled to be placed on an electoral register. If, where this is the case, forfeiture

is virtually automatic, forfeiture proceedings are unlikely to be protracted in those cases where forfeiture is most readily justified. Where, however, the donor is not a foreign donor, the fact that forfeiture is discretionary is likely to involve a significant investigation of the facts, whether the discretion is broad or narrow. However narrow the discretion it will surely be necessary for the party or the donor to show that the donor was not a foreign donor and to demonstrate, insofar as steps were taken to comply with the statutory requirements, what was in fact done.

44. None of these arguments persuades me that where the donor is not foreign, but has for some reason failed to exercise his right to be placed on an electoral register, Parliament intended that forfeiture of the entire donation should be virtually automatic. On the contrary, where the donor is shown not to be foreign, I consider that Parliament would have intended, by conferring a discretion whether or not to forfeit, that there would be a careful evaluation of all the circumstances in order to decide whether the draconian step of forfeiture was justified.

The Commission's approach to its discretion

45. My conclusions receive some, if modest, support from the Commission's own approach to the exercise of its discretion. If Parliament had intended that a donation from an impermissible source should be forfeited unless there were exceptional circumstances, the Commission might have been expected automatically to make an application for forfeiture once satisfied that a donation was from an impermissible source. There would seem to be no basis upon which the Commission could properly decide not to make an application in circumstances where Parliament intended that forfeiture should occur.

46. In the course of the hearing the Commission provided the Court with internal guidelines drawn up by the Commission in February 2007 in relation to the forfeiture of impermissible donations. These included the following:

> "3.1 . . . In all cases where the Commission is clear that section 58 applies the Commission will apply for a forfeiture order, unless there are reasons to conclude that on balance, the public interest is such that would lead us to exercise our discretion in favour of not seeking forfeiture.
>
> 3.2 The Commission will have regard to all relevant considerations, which may include:

> Steps taken by the regulated organisation or individual for the verification of permissibility
>
> Steps taken by the regulated organisation or individual in relation to acceptance or return of donations
>
> Any other extenuating circumstances that may be relevant."

These guidelines do not suggest that the Commission itself applies a strong presumption in favour of forfeiture where a party has accepted a donation from an impermissible source.

Conclusions

47. Where it is shown that a political party has accepted a donation from an impermissible source, there should be an initial presumption in favour of forfeiting the donation. In order to prevent parties receiving funding from individuals who have insufficient connection with the United Kingdom, Parliament has chosen to lay down a simple test. Donations must only be accepted from those who are on an electoral register. The onus should be on the party concerned to show why a donation that has been received from an impermissible source should not be forfeited.

48. A first step in discharging this onus will normally be to show that the mischief against which the relevant part of the Act is directed did not occur – that the donation in question was not, in fact, a foreign donation. Where an individual is concerned this should require demonstration that the individual was entitled to be entered on an electoral register. If this cannot be demonstrated, forfeiture should normally follow. In such circumstances it can properly be assumed that retention of the funding would defeat the policy underlying the legislation.

49. If it is shown that the donor was in a position to qualify as a permissible donor by registering on an electoral register, the initial presumption in favour of forfeiture will have been rebutted. The question will then be whether there have been failures to comply with those requirements of the Act that are designed to ensure that such donations are not accepted, and the nature of those failures. Once again the onus will be on the party to explain how it was that the donation came to be accepted. If the donation is large, and if the power to forfeit is an all or nothing power, significant shortcomings are likely to be required to make forfeiture of the donation a proportionate response. It

is in the light of that conclusion that I turn to consider whether the power to forfeit is all or nothing.

Is the power to forfeit "all or nothing"?

50. Both Walker J and the Court of Appeal concluded that the power to forfeit was an all or nothing power. Walker J concluded that this was the only meaning that could properly be given to a power to forfeit "an amount equal to the value of the donation" (para 117). This finding was not challenged in the Court of Appeal and was accepted by Sir Paul Kennedy as correct (para 49). My initial inclination was to agree. The language of section 58(2) suggests that there is only one amount that can be forfeited. Furthermore, forfeiture normally relates to a specific fund, or right, not part of one. But in this case, "forfeit" is used in an unusual way. It was the Neill Committee that first used the word, in recommending that a sum "not less than the donation should be liable to forfeiture from the party's funds". It has been common ground that a forfeiture order will create a debt to be met from UKIP's funds, as and when monies are paid into them. So the forfeiture in this case is more akin to a fine. Furthermore, the Neill Committee contemplated that the amount to be forfeited would be variable when commenting that where the receipt was innocent or inadvertent "the courts would clearly take into account the degree of culpability in setting the level of forfeiture".

51. Having regard to these considerations I have reached the conclusion that the better interpretation is to treat the power to order forfeiture of an amount equal to the value of an impermissible donation as implicitly including the power to order forfeiture of a lesser sum. Such an interpretation is desirable to cope with the situation where the magistrates' court is persuaded that the donor is not foreign. In those circumstances, total forfeiture of the donation may be disproportionate. If so, it should not be ordered, both under the ordinary principles that apply to the imposition of sanctions and having regard to the requirements of article 1 of the First Protocol to the European Convention on Human Rights. The magistrates' court should have the power to make a partial forfeiture order that reflects the facts of the particular case. I would interpret section 58(2) as conferring that power.

Disposal

52. Walker J rightly held that the reasons given by the Senior District Judge were too brief. He reached, however, decisions on the issues of

principle which this Court has endorsed. He concluded that, in circumstances where the donor was entitled to be on the electoral register, no presumption of total forfeiture should be applied, but forfeiture should reflect fault on the part of the party accepting the donation or donations.

53. As to the application of that principle to the facts of this case, he applied a very broad brush that effaced most of the detail of communications between the Commission and UKIP. He allowed UKIP to retain all donations up to the point at which they learned that Mr Bown was not on the electoral register, and ordered forfeiture of all donations from that moment until Mr Bown was again on the register. He erred however in stating that it was on 19 June 2005 that UKIP learned that Mr Bown was not on the register. In fact they did not learn this until 13 December 2005. On this erroneous basis he ordered forfeiture of donations totalling £14,481.

54. The parties were anxious, if possible, to avoid a further hearing before the Senior District Judge. I have reached the conclusion that the amount of the forfeiture that was ordered adequately reflected the facts of this case and, accordingly, I would restore the order of the Senior District Judge.

LORD RODGER

55. In the 1990s there was considerable public unease about the funding of political parties. The Committee on Standards in Public Life under the chairmanship of Lord Neill of Bladen QC looked into the matter and in 1998 they produced a report (Cm 4057) which contained many recommendations. In particular, they formulated a principle to the effect that those who live, work and carry on business in the United Kingdom should be the persons exclusively entitled to give financial support to the operation of the political process here (para 5.16). In order to create a workable system, they recommended that political parties should be able to receive donations from (1) people who are registered voters in the United Kingdom and (2) those who are eligible to be put on an electoral register in the United Kingdom (para 5.20).

56. In due course the government issued a White Paper giving their considered response to the Neill Committee's recommendations (Cm 4413). The government accepted the thrust of the committee's recommendation on foreign donors, but they introduced a significant

modification: only individuals who were registered voters should be permitted to make donations to political parties. As the White Paper explained in para 4.6, in a very real sense this was in the parties' interest: checking whether a particular donor appeared on the electoral register would offer a test of acceptability that was both conclusive and simple for the parties to operate. It would be much less straightforward for parties to verify that a donor who did not appear on the register was nevertheless entitled to be registered. Of course, the downside was that the new test excluded more potential donors than the Neill Committee test: those who were eligible to be registered, but who were not registered. The White Paper pointed out, however, that, with the introduction of rolling registration, people in that position could readily apply to be registered and it would then be open to a political party to accept a donation from them. "In practice, therefore, little is lost by the proposed departure from the Neill Committee's recommendation."

57. This was the scheme which was encapsulated in clause 50 of the draft Bill and was given effect in section 54 of the Political Parties, Elections and Referendums Act 2000 ("the Act"). So far as relevant, that section provides:

> "(1) A donation received by a registered party must not be accepted by the party if—
>
> > (a) the person by whom the donation would be made is not, at the time of its receipt by the party, a permissible donor….
>
> (2) For the purposes of this Part the following are permissible donors—
>
> > (a) an individual registered in an electoral register…".

58. Nothing could be clearer than the language used by Parliament and nothing could be clearer than the intention behind the language: political parties were not to accept donations from any individual who was not registered in an electoral register. In particular, parties were not to accept donations from individuals who were entitled to be registered, but who were not on the register. That situation would be adequately catered for by the simple expedient of the individual concerned getting himself registered: the party could then accept a donation from him.

59. Obviously, the Act envisages that, when they receive a donation, a political party must check the electoral register to ensure that the

individual is registered. If, as a result of that check, it appears that he is not on the register, then he is not a permissible donor and the party must return the donation, or a payment of an equivalent amount, within thirty days: section 56(2)(a). The party must keep a record of the receipt of the donation and of its return within the thirty-day period. In addition, the party must include a report of the receipt and return of the impermissible donation in their donation report to the Electoral Commission for the relevant period: section 62(9). If they fail to do so, section 65(6) comes into play:

> "Where the court is satisfied, on an application made by the Commission, that any failure to comply with any such requirements in relation to any donation to a registered party was attributable to an intention on the part of any person to conceal the existence or true amount of the donation, the court may order the forfeiture by the party of an amount equal to the value of the donation."

60. The present case concerns exactly the situation of a donor who was entitled to be registered but was not actually on the register. Although he had previously been registered, Mr Alan Bown was not registered in any electoral register between 1 December 2004 and 2 February 2006. During that period he made a number of donations to UKIP which amounted in total to almost £350,000. Since Mr Bown was not registered to vote, by virtue of section 54(1)(a), UKIP were bound not to accept the donations. In terms of section 56(2)(a), the party should therefore have returned them to Mr Bown within thirty days – and pointed out to him that they could not accept the donations until he was on the register again. When the party duly reported the donations to the Electoral Commission, the Commission drew their attention to the fact that Mr Bown did not appear to be on the register. The party none the less retained the donations. So they have made a gain of roughly £350,000 by accepting donations which they were prohibited from accepting under section 54(1)(a).

61. Lord Phillips deprecates the use of the phrase "wrongful gain" to describe this type of gain. He would apparently confine any such description to gains made from donations by foreign donors who are not entitled to be on the electoral register in this country – because the true object of section 54(1)(a) is to prevent parties receiving donations from such persons. But that is to substitute the ultimate aim of the legislation for the means by which the legislation seeks to achieve that aim. The ultimate aim is indeed to catch foreign donors. But the

legislature has chosen to pursue that aim by prohibiting parties from accepting donations from all except a narrowly defined class of permissible donors. That class excludes foreign donors who are not entitled to be registered, but – quite deliberately – it also excludes donors, like Mr Bown, who are entitled to be, but are not, registered. As the White Paper explained, there were good practical reasons for adopting that legislative approach. In these circumstances it is not open to the courts to second-guess Parliament and to proceed on the footing that some impermissible donors are less impermissible than others.

62. Since UKIP kept the donations from Mr Bown which they were prohibited from accepting, the Electoral Commission eventually applied to the City of Westminster Magistrates' Court in terms of section 58(1) and (2):

> "(1) This section applies to any donation received by a registered party—
>
> (a) which, by virtue of section 54(1)(a) or (b), the party are prohibited from accepting, but
>
> (b) which has been accepted by the party.
>
> (2) The court may, on an application made by the Commission, order the forfeiture by the party of an amount equal to the value of the donation."

In the case of England and Wales the court in question is a magistrates' court.

63. Where a party have accepted a donation which they are prohibited from accepting and they show no sign of being willing to return it, the starting point must surely be that the court will take steps to ensure that the party are deprived of the gain which they are determined to keep in defiance of the law. In other words, an order will be made for the forfeiture of the whole value of the unlawful donation. And that is exactly what section 58(2) says: the court may order the forfeiture of "an amount equal to the value of the donation". Had parliamentary counsel intended to give the court power to order the forfeiture of a lesser sum, as Lord Brown points out, there is a variety of other phrases which could have been used to embody that intention.

64. The same words are to be found in section 65(6) (quoted at para 59 above) and in para 12(4) of Schedule 7 to the Act. Both of these

provisions deal with a situation where there has been a deliberate failure to comply with the relevant reporting requirements in order to conceal the existence, or true amount, of a donation. In such a situation, also, it is hard to see why forfeiture of a sum which is less than the donation would be appropriate. So these provisions tend to confirm the straightforward interpretation of the equivalent words in section 58(2). Like Lord Brown, I have no hesitation in agreeing with Walker J's conclusion on this issue.

65. Lord Phillips takes a different view. He goes back to the report of the Neill Committee who first suggested the idea of forfeiture, but described the sum to be forfeited in various ways ("a sum not exceeding the unreported donation" and "a sum not less than the donation"). The committee may well have envisaged the court selecting what it regarded as the appropriate sum to be forfeited in the particular circumstances. On this basis, Lord Phillips considers that "the better interpretation" is to treat the words in section 58(2) as implicitly including the power to order forfeiture of a lesser sum. The Neill Committee report stands, however, at two removes from the text of section 58(2) which embodies the law enacted by Parliament. Moreover, as Lord Phillips himself points out, the Act radically changed the scheme envisaged by the committee. In these circumstances their report cannot displace the plain meaning of Parliament's words. The system is all or nothing: either the court orders the forfeiture of the value of the donation or it makes no order.

66. Having armed the court with a discretion to award a lesser sum, Lord Phillips proceeds to construct an elaborate scheme for the exercise of this discretion. If the donation is not from a permissible donor, the onus will be on the party to show why it should not be forfeited. If the donation is from a foreign donor, then the party will not normally be able to show this, since it can properly be assumed that retention of the funding would defeat the policy underlying the legislation. But if the party can show that the donor was in a position to qualify as a permissible donor by registering on an electoral register, the initial presumption in favour of forfeiture will have been rebutted. In that situation the court will have to see whether there have been failures to comply with the requirements of the Act that are designed to ensure that impermissible donations are not accepted and, if so, the nature of those failures. If the donation is large, significant shortcomings are likely to be required to make forfeiture of the donation a proportionate

response. In other words – apparently – the larger the impermissible donation, the less likely it is that the party will have to give it up.

67. It seems to me unlikely – to say the least – that Parliament would have intended that a provision, which is designed to ensure compliance with the statutory scheme, should operate so as to make large impermissible donations harder to forfeit than small impermissible donations. That apart, many may admire the scheme outlined by Lord Phillips – which might have commended itself to the Neill Committee. Indeed, had it been proposed to Parliament, it might well have been enacted. But there is not the slightest hint of such a scheme in the wording of the provision which Parliament did enact – and, in fact, as I have already explained, the wording of section 58(2) is inconsistent with a scheme of that kind. Moreover, it would have been surprising if such a nuanced decision had been left to the magistrates' court. For these reasons I would respectfully reject Lord Phillips' construction of the subsection.

68. If a party return an impermissible donation after the end of the thirty-day period, under section 56(5) they are treated as having accepted it for the purposes of section 58(2). It might well be, however, that the Electoral Commission would often not make an application to the court in such a case. And if it did, the context for the exercise of the court's discretion would be significantly different from the situation where the party had kept a donation. Similarly, the rationale of any forfeiture order would be to mark some blameworthy failure to comply with the regulations – and pour encourager les autres. I would therefore reserve my opinion on whether there is room for the court to exercise its discretion differently in such cases.

69. In a case, like the present, however, where the party have held on to the donations, the real difficulty, as Lord Brown points out, is to see how the court could properly do other than make an order for forfeiture, since forfeiture so clearly promotes the statutory object of preventing parties from accepting donations from individuals who are not permissible donors. Moreover, since the party had no right to the donations in the first place, there is no room for an argument that taking them away infringes article 1 of the First Protocol to the European Convention on Human Rights.

70. Consideration of the exact scope of the court's discretion is not made any easier by the lack of any real indication in the Act of how the forfeiture order takes effect. As Lord Phillips points out, the discussion

at the hearing proceeded on the (unexamined) premise that it would create a debt to be met out of the party's funds, as and when monies are paid into them. Although it is tempting to think of the Act as concerned with the major parties, it actually applies to a large number of political parties, many of them very small. Some may well have shaky finances. It is therefore quite conceivable that a forfeiture order would tip a party into insolvency and so cause at least as much prejudice to the party's unsecured creditors as to the party. So the creditors might argue that, for this reason, the court should exercise its discretion not to make an order. In that connexion it may be worth noting that section 60(1)(b) and (c) envisage that rules of court may allow persons affected by any possible forfeiture order to be joined as parties to the proceedings in the magistrates' court. Since, however, the point does not arise for decision and was not argued in this case, I merely raise the possibility that such circumstances might have a bearing on the way that the court exercised its discretion under section 58(2).

71. For these reasons, and for those given by Lord Brown, with which I agree, I would dismiss the appeal.

Index